The Trade Game

PUBLISHED BY
ACADEMIC FOUNDATION
IN ASSOCIATION WITH

LIBERTY

Liberty Institute
New Delhi

Read more about Liberty Institute
on the last page of this book

Rajiv Gandhi Institute for Contemporary Studies
New Delhi

Read more about RGICS
on the last page of this book

The Trade Game

Negotiation Trends at WTO and Concerns of Developing Countries

Editors

Bibek Debroy

Debashis Chakraborty

Academic Foundation

NEW DELHI

First published in 2006
by :

ACADEMIC FOUNDATION
4772-73 / 23 Bharat Ram Road, (23 Ansari Road),
Darya Ganj, New Delhi - 110 002 (India).
Phones : 23245001 / 02 / 03 / 04.
Fax : +91-11-23245005.
E-mail : academic@vsnl.com
www : academicfoundation.com

in association with :

Liberty Institute, New Delhi
www.libertyindia.org

and :

Rajiv Gandhi Institute for
Contemporary Studies,
New Delhi

The Trade Game:
Negotiation Trends at WTO and Concerns of Developing Countries
Editors: Bibek Debroy and Debashis Chakraborty

ISBN 81-7188-538-1

Typeset by Italics India, New Delhi.
Printed and bound in India.

Contents

List of Tables, Figures and Boxes

TABLES

FIGURES

BOXES

Acronyms

ACP	Africa, Caribbean and Pacific Group
ADB	Asian Development Bank
AEC	ASEAN Economic Community
AFAS	ASEAN Framework Agreement on Services
AFTA	ASEAN Free Trade Area
AIA	ASEAN Investment Area
AI-TNC	ASEAN-India Trade Negotiations Committee
AIDS	Acquired Immune Deficiency Syndrome
AMS	Aggregate Measure of Support
ANC	African National Congress
AoA	Agreement on Agriculture
APMC	Agricultural Produce Marketing Committee
APMC Act	Agricultural Produce Marketing Committee Act
ASEAN	Association of Southeast Asian Nations
BIMST-EC	Bangladesh India Myanmar Sri Lanka Thailand Economic Cooperation initially. Later changed to Bay of Bengal Initiative for Multisectoral Technical and Economic Cooperation
BLNS	Botswana, Lesotho, Namibia, Swaziland
BPO	Business Process Outsourcing
CAIRNS Group	Group of Countries Interested in Agricultural Trade Liberalisation
CAP	Common Agricultural Policy
CBD	Convention on Biological Diversity
CECA	Comprehensive Economic Cooperation Agreement
CEPT	Common Effective Preferential Tariff
CER	Closer Economic Relations
CLMV	Cambodia, Laos, Myanmar & Vietnam

COMESA	Community of Southern and Eastern African States
CPC	Central Product Classification (UN)
CPs	Contracting Parties
CSIS	Centre for Strategic and International Studies
CTE	Committee for Trade and Environment
CTS	Council for Trade in Services
DCs	Developing Countries
DDA	Doha Development Agenda
DMT	Draft Ministerial Text
DNA	Designated National Authority
DR	Doha Round
DSB	Dispute Settlement Body
DSU	Dispute Settlement Understanding
EC	European Commission
EEC	European Economic Commission
EFTA	European Free Trade Association
EGS	Environmental Goods and Services
ESCAP	Economic and Social Commission for Asia and the Pacific
EU	European Union
EUROSTAT	Statistical Office of the European Communities
FDI	Foreign Direct Investment
FIPB	Foreign Investment Promotion Board
FIPs	Five Interested Parties
FTA	Free-Trade-Agreement
FTAA	Free Trade Area of the Americas
G10	Group of 10 Developed and Developing WTO Member Countries
G15	Group of 17 Developing Countries from Asia, Africa and Latin America
G20	The Negotiating Group of Developing Countries formed in 2003
G33	The Negotiating Group of 42 Developing Countries at WTO
G77	Developing Country Grouping at UNCTAD Forums

G90	A Grouping of the WTO's 90 Poorest Member Countries
GATS	General Agreement on Trade in Services
GATT	General Agreement on Tariffs and Trade
GCC	Gulf Cooperation Council
GDP	Gross Domestic Product
GFTA	Global Free Trade Alliance
HIV	Human Immunodeficiency Virus
HS	Harmonised System of Trade Classification
IC	Integrated Circuit
ICTs	Information and Communications Technologies
IDBI	Industrial Development Bank of India
IMF	International Monetary Fund
IPIC	Treaty on Intellectual Poverty in Respect of Integrated Circuits
IPR	Intellectual Property Rights
IT	Information Technology
ISI	Import Substituting Industrialisation
LDCs	Least Developed Countries
LMG	Like-Minded Group
MAI	Multilateral Agreement on Investment
MERCOSUR	The Southern Common Market (Created by Argentina, Brazil, Paraguay and Uruguay in March 1991.)
MFA	Multi Fiber Arrangement
MFN	Most Favored Nation
MNCs	Multi National Corporations
MSP	Minimum Support Price
NAFTA	North American Free Trade Agreement
NAMA	Non-Agricultural Market Access
NGO	Non Governmental Organisation
NPC	Nominal Protection Coefficient
NTBs	Non-Tariff Barriers
ODA	Official Development Assistance
OECD	Organisation of Economic Cooperation and Development

OEEC	Organisation for European Economic Cooperation (predecessor of OECD)
PECC	Pacific Economic Cooperation Council
PPP	Purchasing Power Parity
PRC	Peoples Republic of China
PSE	Producer Support Estimate
PTAs	Preferential Trade Agreements
R&D	Research and Development
RCA	Revealed Comparative Advantage
ROO	Rules of Origin
RTAs	Regional Trade Agreements
SA	South Africa
S&D/SDT	Special and Differential Treatment
SACU	Southern African Customs Union
SADC	Southern African Development Community
SAFTA	South Asian Free Trade Agreement
SEBs	State Electricity Boards
SP	Special Products
SPS	Sanitary and Phyto-sanitary Measures
SSI	Small Scale Industries
SSM	Special Safeguard Mechanism
TBT	Technical Barriers to Trade
TNC	Trade Negotiations Committee
TRIMS	Trade Related Investment Measures
TRIPS	Trade Related Intellectual Property Rights
UN	United Nations
UNCTAD	United Nations Conference of Trade and Development
UPOV	Union for the International Protection of New Plant Varieties
UR	Uruguay Round
VER	Voluntary Export Restraints
WHO	World Health Organisation
WIPO	World Intellectual Property Organisation
WTO	World Trade Organisation

Editors/Contributors

Editors:

Bibek Debroy is Secretary General, PHD Chamber of Commerce and Industry, New Delhi. He is a professional economist and was educated in Presidency College (Calcutta), Delhi School of Economics and Trinity College (Cambridge). He has worked at Presidency College (Calcutta), Gokhale Institute of Politics and Economics (Pune), Indian Institute of Foreign Trade (Delhi), National Council of Applied Economic Research (Delhi) and as Consultant, Department of Economic Affairs, Ministry of Finance, Government of India. He has been the Director of the Rajiv Gandhi Institute for Contemporary Studies (RGICS), Rajiv Gandhi Foundation, New Delhi. He was also the Director for a project known as LARGE, set up by the Ministry of Finance and UNDP to examine legal reforms. He is the author and editor of several books, papers and popular articles and is also Consulting Editor with Business Standard. Bibek Debroy's special interests are international trade (in particular the WTO), law reform and the political economy of liberalisation in India. He has been listed in many bibliographies and has been a member of several government committees.

Debashis Chakraborty is Assistant Professor at the Indian Institute of Foreign Trade, New Delhi. Debashis has been educated at University of Calcutta and Centre for International Trade and Development, JNU. He has worked on issues pertaining to international trade policy, WTO issues and Indian economic development, and presented and published his research at various academic and policy forums in India and abroad. He has earlier worked in Rajiv Gandhi Institute for Contemporary Studies (RGICS), New Delhi as a researcher. Debashis has recently edited two titles on WTO and is currently working on a manuscript relating to Contract Farming in India.

Contributors:

Anthony B. Kim Research Associate in the Centre for International Trade and Economics (CITE) at the Heritage Foundation, Washington DC.

Brett D. Schaefer Jay Kingham Fellow in the International Regulatory Affairs in the Margaret Thatcher Center for Freedom at the Heritage Foundation, Washington DC.

Jean-Pierre Lehmann Professor of International Political Economy, International Institute for Management Development (IMD), Lausanne, Switzerland and Founding Director of The Evian Group.

John C. Hulsman Senior Research Fellow for European affairs in the Margaret Thatcher Center for Freedom at the Heritage Foundation, Washington DC., and a contributing editor to *The National Interest*.

Oindrila De Research Associate, Centre for Global Agreements Legislation and Trade, The Energy and Resources Institute (TERI), New Delhi.

P.D. Kaushik Director, Rajiv Gandhi Institute for Contemporary Studies, New Delhi.

Pavel Chakraborty Research Associate, Centre for Global Agreements Legislation and Trade, The Energy and Resources Institute (TERI), New Delhi.

Peter Draper Research Fellow, The South African Institute of International Affairs, Johannesburg.

Rahul Sen Fellow, Regional Economic Studies, Institute of Southeast Asian Studies (ISEAS), Singapore.

Razeen Sally Senior Lecturer, International Political Economy, London School of Economics, London and visiting Senior Research Fellow, ISEAS, Singapore.

Stephen Woolcock Lecturer, Department of International Relations, The London School of Economics, London.

Introduction

BIBEK DEBROY and
DEBASHIS CHAKRABORTY

Ongoing Negotiations under the WTO

The negotiating table at the GATT/WTO forums has never been so broad-based. While during the sixties and the seventies only a handful of countries participated in the multilateral discussions, the Uruguay Round suffered from the scepticism of the developing countries. Even after the inception of WTO in 1995, till the Doha Ministerial (2001), the developing countries were not very active at the negotiating table. It is indeed ironic, as free trade is much more favourable for a developing country than its developed counterparts. However, a new trend emerged from Cancun (2003) onwards, and since then the former group has become much more vocal at the multilateral trade forums on the protectionist policies of the latter.

Nevertheless, participation alone cannot guarantee success, and WTO negotiations are perhaps the best proof of this age-old adage. While the developing countries prided themselves on the rejection of the EU-US joint proposal at Cancun, the alternate solution reached in Geneva (2004) through the negotiation between five interested countries did not ensure great achievements in practical terms. The recently concluded sixth Ministerial Conference at Hong Kong (2005) was thought to be a key event in multilateral negotiations on two counts. First, for enabling the Doha Development Agenda negotiations to move forward sufficiently to conclude the Round and secondly, for initiating discussions on new areas of reform.

Despite nearly 100 hours being spent at the negotiating table in Hong Kong, the 'success' or rather the lack of it, at the Ministerial deserves closer attention. While the discussions held at Hong Kong resulted in a much more acceptable Ministerial Declaration as compared to the "Derbez Draft" circulated at Cancun, the developing countries are yet to reach their goal (especially over the last two years)—reduction in agricultural subsidisation level in developed countries. Similarly, there exists enough scope for expanding market access in other areas in the developed country markets (e.g. Mode 4 of services trade for India). At best, it could be argued that some deal is probably better than a Cancun-type no-deal, thereby portraying the result of the ministerial as a second-best outcome.

Rather than blaming the negotiators at Hong Kong for the moderate outcome, the focus should be on the determinants of the negotiating position of a country at a multilateral level. It is a well-known fact that free trade ensures market access. However, from an independent perspective, tapping market access opportunities requires supply-side adjustments and improved governance. That cannot be ensured in ministerial meetings, be it Hong Kong, Geneva or Cancun. Furthermore, the selection of right partners in negotiating groups for pursuing a goal, given the national interest of a particular member, is of extreme importance. Stated alternatively, whenever surrounded by partners with a diverse interest pattern, a country might need to downplay some of its focus areas to keep everyone in the group happy.

Now developing countries are in no way homogeneous; nor are their developed counterparts, for that matter. But disparities are visibly greater in the former group, which consists of advanced developing economies, small and vulnerable economies, landlocked countries and least developed countries (LDCs) thrown in together. As a matter of fact, only 31 out of the 49 LDCs are members of the WHO. The developing countries and LDCs are scattered in various groups. There are the 77 ACP (African, Caribbean and Pacific) countries, beneficiaries of preferential trade with EU, whose interest revolves around preference erosion in items like sugar and bananas. The 41-member strong African Group, APEC (Asia-Pacific Economic Cooperation) and ASEAN could also be mentioned in this regard. The Cancun Ministerial witnessed the evolution of G-20, with Brazil, China, India and South Africa constituting the core. There is also the G-33 with a defensive interest in agriculture through special products and the special safeguard mechanism (SSM). There is the G-90, a coalition of the African Group, the ACP countries and member LDCs. In addition, the Hong Kong Ministerial witnessed the emergence of the NAMA-11, focusing on non-agricultural market access. Some developing countries are also members of the agro-exporting Cairns Group; though what Pakistan (joined during the Hong Kong Ministerial) is doing there is anyone's guess. Nevertheless, linking the presence of all these groups with negotiating capacity of the LDCs as a whole could be misleading, as the Central African Republic didn't even have a delegation in Hong Kong.

Despite the lack of homogeneity within the South, the fourth day of the Hong Kong Ministerial witnessed a North-South divide, with G-20 and G-90 coming together as G-110. This was partly to push the development agenda of the Doha Work Programme, sometimes interpreted as additional aid. ODA (official development assistance) is outside WTO's purview. Hence, beyond pious sentiments about aid for trade and a task force with a recommended deadline of July 2006, there was little one could have expected about ODA from the ministerial declaration. Incidentally, had the developed countries not dithered over the LDC package, the G-110 solidarity might not have materialised. There was a special problem for the C-4 cotton producers: Burkina Faso, Benin, Chad and Mali. The difference in opinion between EU-US over this issue has been discussed in the last chapter of this volume. As regards the solidarity among G-20 members, China generally kept quiet throughout the Hong Kong Ministerial, although the implicit preference for a dealmaking meeting in Hong Kong was manifest.

The developing-country solidarity was fuelled primarily by the US opposition towards 'duty-free', 'quota-free' export coverage to all LDCs, with three per cent of tariff lines being exempt. Bangladesh and garments export would have been the major victim in this case. Apart from pointing to the protectionist mindset of the developed countries for the umpteenth time, this incident clearly brought to the surface the fact that there is no incentive for countries to graduate out of LDC status. On the contrary, there is a perverse incentive for some to move to LDC status, as Pakistan attempted to, in Hong Kong. While the material achievements from the G-110 solidarity are doubtful, thanks to it, India will now have to work out a duty-free, quota-free package for LDCs.

The Hong Kong Ministerial is being described as a great victory—the elimination of agro export subsidies by 2013, for instance is being quoted extensively. However, all the available facts, taken together, do not lead to such conclusion. Measured against the July 2004 (package) framework agreement the incremental changes on various heads—be it agriculture, NAMA or the services sector, are actually minor. There is no great victory unless it is presumed that the July 2004 contract would be reneged. India should have more market access flexibility (the defensive intent) in NAMA and agriculture, and there is now a link between the two. But thanks to G-110 solidarity, the negotiating stance has ultimately contributed to weakening service sector liberalisation (the offensive intent). A total of 149 trade ministers (with Tonga soon to be added) will need to meet again between April and July 2006 to resolve what has temporarily been brushed under the carpet, so as to adhere to the time-line of December 2006 for completion of the round. It is quite prudent to understand that hidden from public glare, both the battle and the war will now continue in Geneva, which is less of a free trade bastion than Hong Kong. Given the experience of Cancun and Hong Kong, instead of organising ministerial conferences every two years, it might be better to have continuous official-level meetings, which would enhance the efficiency of the process.

It is by now a time-honoured fact that the intensity of liberalisation undertaken at home makes handling the WTO-induced reforms easier, and the priorities for Indian policymakers are therefore, obvious. Furthermore, G-110 solidarity is a double-edged weapon. What one gain on the swings, might well be lost on the roundabouts. G-110 is a good shield against developed countries but not an effective sword. All said and done, multilaterially and bilaterially, India needs close economic ties with the US, China and Brazil. If that could be managed, the rest of the world (including the EU) will not matter.

Given this scenario, there is a need to look at the ongoing negotiation trends, the stances adopted by India and other developing country partners, and to analyse the future direction. While understandably India, so far, has not been able to gain a lot from the negotiations, it came out of seclusion during the Doha Ministerial (2001) and is currently leading the developing country coalitions at WTO. Furthermore, expansion of the negotiating agenda (e.g. environmental services) in recent years depicts an evolving learning curve, which is no less important. A similar 'learning through trading' is observed in the case of several other developing countries as well. The chapters in this volume look at these issues in particular and comment on the negotiating options available to the developing countries and the challenges faced by them. On the other hand, the aversion of several developed countries towards ensuring free trade is becoming quite obvious in recent years. To highlight this concern, the last chapter critically analyses the negotiating strategy of France, the key EU member state, at the Hong Kong Ministerial.

The Structure of the Volume

During the last couple of years, especially since Doha (2001) and subsequently from Cancun Ministerial onwards (2003), the trade negotiations have witnessed a bitter tussle among the developed and developing countries ranging over a number of issues, namely—subsidisation in agriculture, TRIPS and public health concerns, liberalisation of service sectors, etc. The first four chapters of the current volume look into the negotiation trends and their potential outcomes in the global context. While the first chapter highlights the benefits of free trade; the second and the third chapter talks about the evolving patterns in the negotiation trends over the years, from a global perspective and a developing country coalition outlook respectively. The fourth chapter looks into the negotiating trends from a regional standpoint; focusing on the trade policies of the Southeast Asian countries.

The optimality of free trade is well known in international trade literature, and the *Index of Economic Freedom* supports the theory that trade liberalisation is indeed a factor in generating greater economic growth. Yet in the real world scenario, countries often find it more beneficial to adopt protectionist policies. Hulsman *et al.* note that the struggle during the Doha round negotiations clearly demonstrates that many governments continue to see trade as a zero-sum game in which their goal is to lower barriers in other countries while seeking to keep their own barriers as high as possible. The consequent slow pace of WTO negotiations hurt all the members. The authors propose an innovative Global Free Trade Alliance (GFTA) formed on the basis of existing policies, rather than negotiated concessions, for the willing members to take advantage of free trade. Rather than having a standing secretariat, the GFTA would merely be a formalised meeting of the memberships' trade ministers, where specific technical working groups would exist only as long as their specific tasks (e.g., agreeing on common accounting standards) were being addressed. It would secure the benefits of increased trade and investment without forcing members to undergo any new major policy reforms. The authors argue that the GFTA offers an intriguing alternative means for advancing global free trade that does not force unwilling countries to liberalise more quickly than they desire.

The progressive increment in the coverage of trade policy (both widening and deepening) to include new issues has been a major feature of WTO. On the other hand, the number of countries actively participating in the negotiations has also significantly increased, causing more rigorous negotiation exercise owing to the conflicts in interest. Furthermore, civil society groups, sometimes organised at a 'global' level are challenging the existing decision making processes, the legitimacy of 'the WTO' and the assumption of progressive liberalisation of trade and investment in a rules based international order. Consequently trade policymakers now need to deal with a wider range of 'domestic' actors as well. As a result of all these issues, the complexity of trade policy has increased substantially. In this scenario, the high growth of regional trade diplomacy is probably reflecting scepticism of the members towards the multilateral trade regime. Taking note of the negotiation trends and these concerns, Stephen Woolcock concludes that there is an urgent need for re-establishing a clear set of criteria for determining the scope of the trade regime, enhancing transparency and inclusiveness in policy making and undertaking institutional reform of the WTO.

Before the Uruguay Round, most developing countries followed import-substitution and other trade-restrictive policies, and consequently were not very active at the GATT forums. The chapter by Peter Draper and Razeen Sally focuses on the coalition building by developing countries in recent years, which is a key indicator of their overall capacity and effectiveness in the WTO. In the recent period, smaller, defensive coalitions among developing countries have become more prominent. However, one-sided pan-developing-country alliances are wrong in principle and likely to cause only the 'UN-isation' of the WTO, and the negotiations need to be forward-looking, i.e., 'system-maintaining' rather than 'system-wrecking' by nature. After analysing evolution of the developing-country coalitions of past and the present, the chapter focuses on the trade policies of prominent members of these alliances, namely—China, India, Brazil and South Africa. The chapter observes that despite playing a significant role in developing-country coalitions, India is most protectionist in this group. The authors conclude that the constructive leadership by the 30-plus countries (including developed and key developing countries and counting the EU as one) that account for around 90 per cent of international trade and foreign direct investment, is vital for the key liberalising and rule-making deals in the WTO. The chapter argues that remaining 100-or-so developing countries, with limited-to-very-limited trade policy capacity, even in coalition-formation, should be accorded generous S&D treatment.

The chapter by Razeen Sally and Rahul Sen analyses trade policies in Southeast Asian countries in their wider Asian and global contexts. In essence, it not only compares and contrasts trade policies of individual Southeast Asian countries, but also analyses them in the context of regional and global economic integration, as well as the economic emergence of two other major Asian economies, China and India. The chapter first looks at recent trends in trade and FDI patterns in ASEAN. Then it summarises key trade-policy features in ASEAN countries, especially to get a sense of policy variety within the region and to see how policies have changed since the Asian crisis. Then follows an assessment of the performance of ASEAN countries in international trade negotiations and agreements: first within ASEAN; second on cross-regional FTAs; and third at the WTO, especially in the Doha Round. The chapter concludes that ASEAN countries cannot rely on external tracks 'from above' for meaningful trade policy reform. Rather they have to rely on themselves—'from below' as it were. The engine of liberalisation and regulatory reform has to be home-driven, with governments taking unilateral measures in response to internal and external conditions.

The next four chapters of the volume focus on the Indian participation in the negotiating process. While the fifth chapter highlights the changing pattern of India's negotiations on trade in goods and services and the evolution in the outlook towards regional trade agreements, the other three chapters focus on sectoral concerns. Textile and agriculture jointly account for a sizable proportion of the total employment as well as the merchandise export basket in India and the sixth chapter explores whether there is any lesson to learn from the multilateral reform experience of the former for the latter. Focusing on India's negotiating approach on TRIPS over the years, the seventh chapter looks into the available options for the country on that front. Finally, the recent focus of India's negotiations under trade in services has been on environmental services. The eighth chapter focuses on the pertinent issues and India's concerns in this area.

Despite being a founder member of GATT, India never actively participated at the multilateral negotiations before the Uruguay Round. Even during the post-WTO period it adopted a non pro-active role upto the Seattle ministerial, which however changed in the subsequent period. In particular, India's voice became audible at the multilateral forums from Doha ministerial onwards. Since the Cancun ministerial, India has started actively coordinating with other developing countries at multilateral negotiations on various issues, with a focus on enhancement of market access in agriculture. Furthermore, there has been a distinct shift in attitude of India towards Regional Trade Agreements (RTAs). The chapter by Debashis Chakraborty intends to focus on the major determinants of the shift in India's attitude and certain features of its negotiating pattern over the last decade, apart from exploring some concern areas.

During the Uruguay Round of discussions, it was decided that the MFA system would be phased-out over a period of 10 years. It was implicit that the developing countries need to enhance their competitiveness during this period. India during the last few years of the phase-out attempted to remove various restrictions historically imposed on the industry and introduced a set of packages to facilitate its growth. Partly as a result of these policies, the Indian textile firms could withstand the competition from their Chinese counterparts to an appreciable extent during the last eight months. Debashis Chakraborty and Pavel Chakraborty try to explore a parallel of this experience with the negotiating stance and domestic policies adopted by India on agriculture. While India's stance at the multilateral forum is broadly defensive and focused on the availability of special and differential treatment, special products and special safeguard mechanism for developing countries to a major extent; at home the sector has been traditionally subject to various restrictive polices, which hurt its competitiveness. Interestingly, far from being heavily subsidised like the EU or the US, the sector is actually a net taxed one. It is very much likely that the developed countries in future would link further reform in other interest areas (e.g. Mode 4 in services for India) with opening of agricultural sector in developing countries and India need to be prepared for that. Therefore, the authors argue that India should attempt to enhance competitiveness of this sector by removing various restrictions still present, and focus more on WTO-compatible supports that could be provided to this sector rather than input subsidies.

The introduction of the product patent regime in India in 2005 has been a much-debated issue, with various arguments floated in support of the two opposing views. After focusing on the TRIPS provisions and the Doha Development Agenda, P. D. Kaushik identifies India's stance on various related concerns. The negotiating stance of the country so far has been a combination of defensive and offensive measures. On one hand, it in association with other developing countries has tried to extend Geographical Indications treatment to products other than wines and spirits as a means of protecting products such as *basmati* rice; while asking for special and differential treatment on some issues on the other. The chapter notes that despite the growing consensus on issues like harmonisation of CBD and TRIPS, concerns on disclosures and patentability remains a major impediment in striking out a deal with developed countries. The recent moves by developing countries focuses on an amendment to the TRIPS agreement which require patent applications to include a disclosure of the origin of biological materials and traditional knowledge, strongly opposed by the United States and Japan. No wonder that there has not been any major breakthrough in the TRIPS-Public Health debate in the Hong Kong Ministerial. However, the December 6 decision taken earlier to amend the TRIPS provision is a welcome move. Nevertheless, attempts of linking agricultural negotiations with harmonisation of CBD and TRIPS, further makes the negotiating agenda more complicated for India. The chapter concludes that the option of trying to negotiate, loosen and modify TRIPS to suit Indian interests has limited potential, which nonetheless gets further complicated by the growing pressures and continued opposition of developed countries on certain issues.

India has been involved in the negotiations on trade in services for some time and submitted its request and offer list to a number of trade partners, ranging over a wide number of service categories. Although India has so far negotiated for opening up of all the four modes under trade in services, the priority area has always been liberalisation of mode 4 (movement of natural persons). Among the various service categories, the recent focus of India's negotiations has been on environmental service. Oindrila De and Pavel Chakraborty focus on the environment service industry in India in general, and note that there exists no major export potential even if the commitments are made in WTO. The industry is suffering from a plethora of problems including inadequate funds, R&D and data unavailability, which leaves little hope for its expansion in foreign markets in coming future. This fact, coupled with the ongoing debates over the definition and classification of environmental goods and services, caused India to move cautiously in international forums, and the project approach adopted by the country is quite different from the list approach proposed by its developed counterparts. Although several developed countries have questioned the effectiveness of India's proposed modality in fulfilling the Doha mandate, the authors note that India has adopted this careful approach owing to the domestic constraints, and likely to keep moving along this line in coming future, too.

The Doha Agenda is potentially highly beneficial to Europe. However, the continuation of agricultural subsidy in the EU is a major roadblock for the successful completion of DDA. France, the leading EU member state, despite being quite open to trade and investment otherwise, has been vocal over the issue of agricultural subsidy for some time. The last chapter by Jean-Pierre Lehmann focuses on the role of France at the Hong Kong Ministerial and tries to figure out the future negotiating position of the EU in this light. France made it quite clear at Hong Kong that regarding agriculture there would be no compromise on the position that had been tabled in July earlier. The inflexible negotiating attitude over domestic interest was coupled with unrealistic activeness over cotton subsidy, which is indeed peculiar. On the other hand, the offered concession for extending duty-free market access to 97 per cent of the exports of the poorest developing countries favours the failures at the expense of the successful and amounts to almost nothing in volume terms, given the current trade scenario. The French government decision in 2004 to block the proposed liberalisation of services in the EU further shows the increasing hostility of French policies to both foreign trade and foreign investment. The author argues that by putting a brake on global trade, France is responsible for lower growth, less welfare, less poverty reduction and less employment generation, not only across the planet, but also at home. However, the scenario is unlikely to change very soon, as the domestic political scenario is most likely to generate more rigidity than flexibility in the French negotiating position. Taking note of the protectionist mindset gathering steam in other EU member states, the chapter cautions against the possibility of the French position being likely to capture the EU agenda—favouring a very modest package to offer or an indefinite postponement of negotiations during 2006.

1

The Benefits of a Global Free Trade Alliance[1]

JOHN C. HULSMAN, BRETT D. SCHAEFER and ANTHONY B. KIM

Economic theory, dating back at least to Adam Smith and David Ricardo, has concluded that free markets are the cornerstone of economic growth and prosperity. Exhaustive analyses and evidence have consistently pointed toward adoption of liberal economic policies and a strong, fair rule of law as the optimal means for increasing economic growth.

This conclusion has been corroborated by the *Index of Economic Freedom* over its 11 years of research and analysis of economic policies across over 160 counties around the world. The *Index* clearly demonstrates that countries that embrace economic freedom—including freedom of trade, labour, and capital—experience stronger economic growth than those that seek to thwart the market through regulatory hurdles and policy restrictions. Moreover, average GDP growth rates increase as a country's *Index* score improves.[2]

Liberal trade policy is a key component of economic freedom and contributes to long-term, stable economic growth by increasing efficiency and reducing costs for producers and consumers. Yet resistance to trade liberalisation remains strong in both developed and developing countries. The struggle in the World Trade Organisation during the current Doha Round of trade negotiations clearly demonstrates that many governments continue to see trade as a zero-sum game in which their goal is to lower barriers in other countries while seeking to keep their own barriers as high as possible. The slow

---

1. The chapter has been reprinted from the *2005 Index of Economic Freedom: The Link Between Economic Opportunity and Prosperity*, Marc A. Miles, Ph.D., Edwin J. Feulner, Ph.D., and Mary Anastasia O'Grady, with Ana Isabel Eiras, and Aaron Schavey, Ph.D. (eds.), published by the Heritage Foundation, and The *Wall Street Journal*, USA, Heritage Foundation, Washington, D.C., Chapter 3, pp. 37-48. We thank The Heritage Foundation for granting us the necessary permissions for re-printing this paper.
2. Marc A. Miles, Edwin J. Feulner, and Mary Anastasia O'Grady, *2004 Index of Economic Freedom* (Washington, D.C.: The Heritage Foundation and Dow Jones & Company, Inc., 2004), p. 21.

pace of WTO negotiations does not mean that they are without merit, but countries that grasp the value of free trade should not hold themselves hostage to glacial progress in that body.

Instead, countries eager to take advantage of free trade should consider forming a Global Free Trade Alliance (GFTA). Because the GFTA would be a free trade coalition of the willing, membership would be based on existing policies, not negotiated concessions. It would secure the benefits of increased trade and investment without forcing members to undergo any new major policy reforms. With the potential to encompass every nation—provided only that they meet the criteria and wish to open their markets to goods and services from other GFTA members—the GFTA offers an intriguing alternative means for advancing global free trade that does not force unwilling countries to liberalise more quickly than they desire.

Do Low Trade Barriers Increase Economic Growth?

Economic theory argues that freer trade should contribute to economic growth in all countries over the long term. The outcome was proposed in 1776 by Adam Smith in his seminal *Wealth of Nations*. Smith argued that lower barriers would lead to increased efficiency and reduced costs through specialisation.

In other words, an individual could make all the goods he needs for survival, but only at an enormous cost in time, resources, and effort. Moreover, that effort would most likely result in goods inferior to those produced by individuals with more experience, talent, knowledge, or skill in making specific goods. It would be far more sensible for an individual to specialise in one activity in which he excels and then use the proceeds from that activity to buy goods that he cannot produce as cheaply or skillfully from those who can do so.

Smith extended this idea to trade between nations; i.e., trade allowed nations to produce goods more efficiently than another country and trade those goods for items that other nations could produce more efficiently:

> It is the maxim of every prudent master of a family, never to attempt to make at home what it will cost him more to make than to buy.... What is prudence in the conduct of every private family, can scarce be folly in that of a great kingdom. If a foreign country can supply us with a commodity cheaper than we ourselves can make it, better buy it of them with some part of the produce of our own industry, employed in a way in which we have some advantage.[3]

3. Smith, Adam, *The Wealth of Nations*, Book IV, Chapter II, at *www.adamsmith.org/smith/quotes.htm*.

In this way, trade increased wealth in both trade partners. David Ricardo made a critical addition to the theory by demonstrating that countries benefit from trade even if they do not have absolute advantage in producing a good.[4] Producing goods 'relatively' more cheaply (comparative advantage) is sufficient for countries to benefit from trade.

More modern economic studies support Smith's and Ricardo's theses by demonstrating that free trade should increase economic growth by pressuring producers to increase efficiency and reduce costs in several ways:

- *Through comparative advantage:* Trade permits a nation to use existing resources more efficiently by specialising in activities that it creates relatively well and more cheaply and by trading for goods or services that it could produce only at a relatively higher cost than in other nations. Trade thereby permits each trade partner to achieve a higher living standard by increasing the available quantity (and quality) of goods or services more than is likely with no trade.
- *By permitting consumers and businesses access to a greater variety of goods at a lower cost than would be possible without trade:* Moreover, with access to cheaper elements of production on a larger pool of consumers, producers can provide goods that would not be profitable if the market were limited to domestic consumers.
- *By encouraging efficiency and innovation through increased competition and interaction:* Businesses benefit from experience and knowledge gleaned from their competitors and are forced to apply new techniques and technologies to improve efficiency and quality in order to stay competitive. This discourages waste and redundancy and lowers overall prices for consumers.

A positive ancillary effect of freer trade is the necessity of countries to maintain, improve, or liberalise other policies in order to remain competitive in a global market. Countries with repressive economic policies will not be the relocation choice for investors or businesses, and the result will be lost jobs and potential growth in the restrictive country. These potential consequences create strong incentives for countries to adopt freer economic policies.

Real-world data support economic theory (Figure 1.1). Over the past four decades, total world trade (exports plus imports) as a

4. Ricardo, David, *On the Principles of Political Economy and Taxation*, par. 7.16, at *www.econlib.org/library/best.html.*

percentage of global GDP nearly doubled from 24.3 per cent in 1960 to 47.2 per cent in 2003. This trend has been accompanied by a more than doubling of global per capita GDP from $2,622 in 1960 to $5,786 in 2003 (in constant 1995 U.S. dollars).

Figure 1.1

Global Trade and World GDP Per Capita (1960-2003)

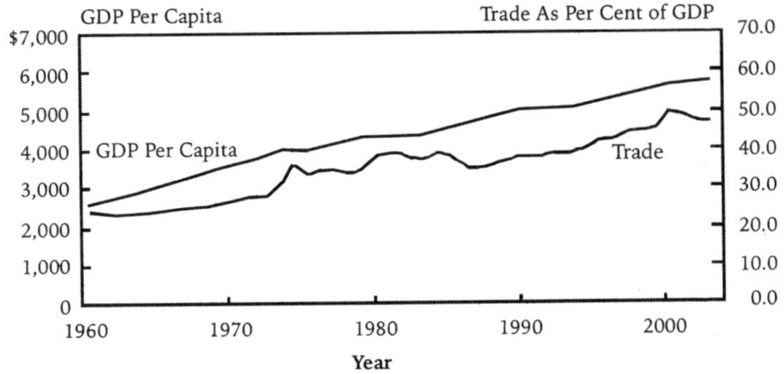

Sources: World Bank, World Development Indicators Online, available by subscription at *www.worldbank.org/data.*

Moreover, countries in every stage of development have benefited from this trend.

- Trade as a percentage of GDP in high-income countries increased from 24 per cent in 1960 to 44.4 per cent in 2003, and per capita GDP increased from $9,724 to $29,968 over the same period (in constant 1995 U.S. dollars).
- Trade as a percentage of GDP in medium-income countries as a group increased from 23.6 per cent in 1970 (the earliest year for which data on that group are available) to 65.9 per cent in 2003, and per capita GDP rose from $979 to $2,056 (in constant 1995 U.S. dollars).
- Trade as a percentage of GDP in low-income countries increased from 19.5 per cent in 1960 to 42.7 per cent in 2003, and per capita GDP increased from $216 to $452 (in constant 1995 U.S. dollars).[5]

Modern technology, knowledge, and data permit a far more precise analysis of the evidence. Most studies do not question the underlying

5. World Bank, *World Development Indicators Online*, available by subscription at *www.worldbank.org/data.*

positive benefits of freer trade, but they do question whether trade liberalisation alone can be beneficial if other areas of the economy remain restrictive or if institutions remain weak. For instance, some studies point out that the robustness of the relationship between tariff levels and economic growth declines when institutions, geography, investment, and other factors are taken into account.[6] Moreover, the quality of the data declines significantly the farther one goes back in time, undermining the overall effort to identify such a relationship.

However, the lion's share of economic analyses conclude that liberal economic policies, including low trade barriers, in developing and developed countries alike lead to lower costs and greater efficiency as entrepreneurs determine the activities in which they have a global or regional comparative advantage. These gains translate into increased economic growth and per capita income.[7]

---

6. Some more recent studies include David Dollar and Aart Kraay, *Institutions, Trade, and Growth: Revisiting the Evidence* World Bank, Development Research Group, January 2003; Juan Carlos Hallk and James Levinsohn, "Fooling Ourselves: Evaluating the Globalisation and Growth Debate," National Bureau of Economic Research, *Working Paper No.* 10244, January 2004; Bineswaree Bolaky and Caroline Freund, *Trade, Regulations, and Growth*, World Bank, March 2004; Robert E. Baldwin, "Openness and Growth: What's the Empirical Relationship?" National Bureau of Economic Research *Working Paper No.* 9578, March 2003; and Pinelopi Koujianou Goldberg and Nina Pavcnik, "Trade Inequality, and Poverty: What Do We Know? Evidence from Recent Trade Liberalisation Episodes in Developing Countries", National Bureau of Economic Research, *Working Paper No.* 10593, June 2004.

7. Numerous economic studies conclude that economies with low trade barriers grow faster than countries with higher trade barriers. For instance, a 2003 study by Michael W. Klein, Scott Schuh, and Robert K. Triest found that the benefits of trade outweigh its costs by 100 percent, or two/one. Michael W. Klein, Scott Schuh, and Robert K. Triest, *Job Creation, Job Destruction, and International Competition* (Kalamazoo, Mich.: W. E. Upjohn Institute for Employment Research, 2003). A 2002 World Bank study found that increased integration into the world economy from the late 1970s to the late 1990s by 24 developing countries with over three billion people led to higher growth in income. These countries achieved a five per cent average growth in income per capita per year during the 1990s. By contrast, the non-globalising nations experienced poor economic growth of only 1.4 per cent on average in the 1990s, and many saw negative growth. Paul Collier and David Dollar, under supervision of Nicholas Stern, *Globalisation, Growth, and Poverty: Building an Inclusive World Economy* (Washington and New York: World Bank and Oxford University Press, 2002), p. 5. A related World Bank study found that increased growth resulting from expanded trade "leads to proportionate increases in incomes of the poor" and that "globalisation leads to faster growth and poverty reduction in poor countries." David Dollar and Aart Kraay, abstract of draft, *Trade, Growth, and Poverty*, World Bank, Development Research Group, March 2001. Other studies include David Dollar, "Outward-Oriented Developing Economies Really Do Grow More Rapidly: Evidence from 95 LDCs, 1976–1985", *Economic Development and Cultural Change*, Vol. 40 (April 1992), pp. 523–544; Robert J. Barro and Xavier Sala-i-Martin, *Economic Growth* (New York: McGraw-Hill, 1995); and Jeffrey D. Sachs and Andrew Warner, "Economic Reform and the Process of Global Integration", *Brookings Papers on Economic Activity*, Vol. 1995, Issue 1 (1995).

The evidence offered by the *Index of Economic Freedom* on the impact of trade policy on economic growth supports the theory that trade liberalisation is indeed a factor in generating greater economic growth. Focusing exclusively on changes in *Index* scores for trade policy, countries that adopted freer trade policy from 1997 to 2005 experienced an average compound growth of 2.6 per cent in GDP per capita. Countries whose trade policy remained unchanged experienced an average compound growth of 2.0 per cent in GDP per capita. Meanwhile, average growth in countries whose trade policies became more restrictive was only 1.5 per cent on average (Table 1.1)

Table 1.1

Freer Trade Policy Associated with Higher GDP Per Capita Growth

*Trade Policy Score Change** *(1997 Index–2005 Index)*	*Compound GDP Per Capita Growth* *(1995–2003)*
Improved	2.6 %
No Change	2.0 %
Declined	1.5 %

Note: * Among 126 countries observed, 49 countries improved, 55 had no change, and 22 declined in their trade policy scores.

Sources: World Bank, *World Development Indicators Online*, available by subscription at *www.worldbank.org/data*; Marc A. Miles, Edwin J. Feulner, and Mary Anastasia O'Grady, *2005 Index of Economic Freedom* (Washington, D.C.: The Heritage Foundation and Dow Jones & Company, Inc., 2005), at *www.heritage.org/index*.

Contrary to those who suggest that only developed countries benefit from dropping barriers to trade or reducing government intervention, a liberal trade policy contributes to greater economic growth in both developing and developed countries. Evidence from the *Index* shows that between 1997 and 2005, both developed and developing countries experienced higher average compound GDP growth per capita if they improved their trade policy scores than would have been the case if they had not improved their trade policy scores (Table 1.2).

Developed countries stand to lose the most from resisting freer trade. The key to understanding this fact is overall economic freedom. Dividing these countries according to total economic freedom scores rather than levels of development reveals an interesting pattern. Quite simply, economically free countries in general benefit more (in terms of faster economic growth) than developed countries when barriers to trade are eliminated (Table 1.3).

Table 1.2

Freer Trade Policy Associated with Higher GDP Per Capita Growth in Both Developed Countries and Developing Countries

Trade Policy Score Change (1997 Index–2005 Index)	*Compound GDP Per Capita Growth (1995–2003)*	
	*Developed Countries**	*Developing Countries***
Improved	2.3 %	2.6 %
No Change	2.2 %	1.8 %
Declined	n/a	1.5 %

Notes: * Developed countries include high-income OECD members and high-income non-OECD members. The following are 29 developed countries whose GDP per capita and trade policy score in the *Index of Economic Freedom* are available for this table: Australia, Austria, Barbados, Belgium, Canada, Cyprus, Denmark, Finland, France, Germany, Greece, Hong Kong, Iceland, Ireland, Israel, Italy, Japan, Luxembourg, Netherlands, New Zealand, Norway, Portugal, Singapore, Slovenia, Spain, Sweden, Switzerland, United Kingdom, and United States. Among these countries, 4 countries improved in their trade policy scores while 25 showed no change.

** 97 developing countries whose GDP per capita and trade policy score in the *Index of Economic Freedom* are available. Among those countries, 45 countries improved, 30 showed no change, and 22 declined in their trade policy scores.

Sources: World Bank, *World Development Indicators Online*, available by subscription at *www.worldbank.org/data*; Marc A. Miles, Edwin J. Feulner, and Mary Anastasia O'Grady, *2005 Index of Economic Freedom* (Washington, D.C.: The Heritage Foundation and Dow Jones & Company, Inc., 2005), at *www.heritage.org/index.*

Table 1.3

Changes in Trade Policy by Overall Level of Economic Freedom and GDP Per Capita Growth by 2005 Index of Economic Freedom Category

Trade Policy Score Change (1997 Index–2005 Index)*	*Compound GDP Per Capita Growth (1995–2003)*		
	*Free***	*Mostly Free****	*Mostly Unfree and Repressed*****
Improved	4.2 %	2.5 %	2.4 %
No Change	2.5 %	2.3 %	1.4 %
Declined	n/a	2.5 %	1.3 %

Notes: * 126 countries whose GDP per capita and trade policy score in the *Index of Economic Freedom* are available. Among those countries, 45 countries improved, 30 showed no change, and 22 declined.

** Within 17 "Free" countries, 2 countries improved and 15 declined in their trade policy scores.

*** Within 45 "Mostly Free" countries, 21 countries improved, 19 showed no change, and 5 declined in their trade policy scores.

**** Within 64 "Mostly Unfree and Repressed" countries, 26 countries improved, 21 recorded no change, and 17 declined in their trade policy scores.

Sources: World Bank, *World Development Indicators Online*, available by subscription at *www.worldbank.org/data*; Marc A. Miles, Edwin J. Feulner, and Mary Anastasia O'Grady, *2005 Index of Economic Freedom* (Washington, D.C.: The Heritage Foundation and Dow Jones & Company, Inc., 2005), at *www.heritage.org/index.*

These results are to be expected. Individual factors of economic freedom are complementary. As noted by Richard Roll in the *2004 Index of Economic Freedom*, all of the 10 factors measured in the *Index* have a relatively equal relationship to a country's overall level of economic freedom.[8] In freer countries, more markets can respond positively to opening trade, producing a more positive growth response.

Combined with the proven relationship between greater economic freedom and increased economic growth, the lesson is that good policies are mutually reinforcing in their impact on growth. In other words, not only does trade liberalisation enhance growth by compelling businesses to reduce costs, but the positive impact of trade liberalisation can more easily engender responses in other, free complementary areas.

Paths to Free Trade

As the evidence illustrates, expanding free trade offers net benefits to economies, consumers, and businesses and should be pursued. There are three traditional methods for pursuing trade liberalisation: bilateral, regional, and multilateral.

Ideally, free trade should be pursued multilaterally: i.e., among many countries. Broad trade liberalisation minimises the potential impact of trade diversion over trade creation and maximises the growth opportunities of trade.[9] The original forum for such negotiations was the 1948 General Agreement on Tariffs and Trade (GATT), which eventually, in 1994, formed the core of the World Trade Organisation (WTO). With 147 members accounting for 97 per cent of the world's trade, successful negotiations in the WTO would apply liberalisation across most of the world in one swipe.

Over the past five decades, the GATT/WTO framework has dramatically reduced global barriers to trade; but even though GATT/WTO has been very effective in lowering trade barriers, its members

---

8. Roll, Richard (2004) "Weighting the Components of the *Index of Economic Freedom*", Chapter 3 in Miles, Feulner, and O'Grady, *2004 Index of Economic Freedom*, pp. 39–42.

9. Indeed, one study found that regional trade agreements offer far fewer benefits to than broad liberalisation. See Athanasios Vamvakidis, "Regional Trade Agreements or Broad Liberalisation: Which Path Leads to Faster Growth?" International Monetary Fund *Staff Papers*, Vol. 46, No. 1 (March 1999), pp. 42–68.

are not required to engage in free trade. Members merely agree to lower existing barriers on specified products, not to eliminate them.[10]

Moreover, the combination of a membership and rules requiring that changes be adopted through consensus means that negotiations in the WTO are difficult, slow, and often prone to avoidance of the more controversial aspects of trade liberalisation. Each of the concluded eight rounds of negotiations on trade liberalisation under the GATT has taken progressively longer to complete.[11] The most recent, the Uruguay Round of GATT negotiations that led to the creation of the WTO, lasted nearly a decade from 1986 to 1994. The current Doha Round of negotiations began in 2001, and despite progress made in the July 2004 meetings, prospects for reaching a final agreement by 2005 appear dubious.[12]

While free trade is best pursued globally to minimise barriers and distortions in trade, the slow pace of negotiations in the WTO has led many nations to pursue free trade through bilateral and regional agreements, creating a spotty network of free trade around the world. To their credit, bilateral and regional agreements have the virtue of greater flexibility than multilateral agreements. They allow a country to pick and choose among prospective trade partners and customise individual agreements based on the needs and concerns of individual countries. This is particularly true for bilateral negotiations that allow talks to move forward at the speed that best suits both trade partners rather than being held hostage to the slowest-moving party involved in the regional or multilateral negotiations.

However, the flexible nature of bilateral negotiations is also a weakness because it permits countries to exclude entire economic sectors, such as agriculture, from the scope of the agreements. These negotiations are also limited in that they extend free trade incrementally, one nation at a time, rather than broadly as is the case through regional and multilateral agreements.

Regional agreements offer opportunities to negotiate with multiple countries, broadening the impact of the agreement, but can proceed

10. World Trade Organisation (2003), Chapter 2, "The Agreements," in *Understanding the WTO*, 3rd ed., at *www.wto.org/english/thewto_e/whatis_e/tif_e/utw_chap2_e.pdf.*

11. World Trade Organisation (2003), *Understanding the WTO*, p. 16, at *www.wto.org/english/thewto_e/whatis_e/tif_e/utw_chap1_e.pdf.*

12. Paul Blustein (2004), "Accord Reached on Global Trade: Talks Aim to Cut Farm Aid, Tariffs", *The Washington Post*, August 1, p. A1.

only as quickly as the slowest member. This can substantially delay the process, as evidenced by negotiations on the Free Trade Agreement of the Americas, which have made little tangible progress despite years of effort. Additionally, a greater number of negotiating partners means that more diplomatic problems could constrain portions of the agreement, thereby undermining its effectiveness.

Circumventing These Problems: The GFTA

While bilateral and regional free trade agreements and the WTO offer useful means for pursuing free trade, their weaknesses should encourage nations interested in pursuing free trade to consider faster, more efficient options for achieving that goal. One solution that offers an impressive degree of promise is the Global Free Trade Alliance (GFTA).

A GFTA member would authorise other members access to its market, with no restriction through tariff, quota, or other trade barriers on the single condition that they reciprocate this access. Ideally, this authorisation would be a legislative initiative rather than a drawn out treaty. Such a route could speed adoption and expansion of membership. A possible model could be most favored nation (MFN) status, wherein countries legislatively lower barriers to an agreed level for a qualifying group of nations.[13]

The central tenet of the legislation should establish the principal membership criteria: a demonstrable record of both free markets and elimination of tariffs and quotas on goods from other GFTA members. Nations meeting these criteria could immediately approach existing GFTA members with proof of their qualification and willingness to eliminate remaining trade barriers. Existing members would then verify those policies and admit the country into the alliance.

The legislation should include an enforcement mechanism rescinding this special access to GFTA markets if a country ever (1) reinstates trade barriers in violation of the agreed GFTA requirements or (2) enacts policies that would cause it to fall short of the qualifying criteria. When members joined the alliance, they would stipulate that

13. Due to the GFTA's inclusive nature—the fact that members, regardless of other factors, are able to join when they meet the same objective standards—we feel that the GFTA does not violate MFN standards of treating all relevant nations equally. In addition, the GFTA is in line with the spirit of Article 24 of the GATT, which states that "A regional arrangement must facilitate trade among its members, and not raise trade barriers between its members and other nations."

if they fail to meet the numerical targets in the future, they would agree to leave the alliance if they could not again meet the criteria within one year.

Rather than having a standing secretariat, the GFTA would merely be a formalised meeting of the memberships' trade ministers, staffs, and technical experts. Specific technical working groups would exist only as long as their specific tasks (e.g., agreeing on common accounting standards) were being addressed. Additional decisions on trading initiatives would be made on a consensual basis in areas such as codifying uniform standards on issues like capital flows, regulations, or establishing GFTA rules for reducing subsidies and other non-tariff barriers to further minimise barriers within the alliance.

Who Would Qualify for the GFTA?

GFTA membership should be based on objective analysis of the country's commitment to free trade in goods, services, and investment of the sort that is employed in the *Index of Economic Freedom*, published annually by the The Heritage Foundation and *The Wall Street Journal*. The *Index* analyses 50 economic indicators in 10 independent factors: trade policy, fiscal burden of government, government intervention in the economy, monetary policy, capital flows and foreign investment, banking and finance, wages and prices, property rights, regulation, and informal (or black) market activity. These 10 factors are graded from 1 to 5, with 1 being the best score and 5 being the worst. The scores are then averaged to give an overall score for economic freedom. Countries are designated "free," "mostly free," "mostly unfree," and "repressed" based on these overall scores.

To measure a country's willingness to interact with the global economy, The Heritage Foundation developed a 'Trade Openness Index' from a subset of four of the 10 factors used in the *Index of Economic Freedom*: trade policy, capital flows and foreign investment, property rights, and regulation. These four factors, among all the 10 considered, were seen as exerting the greatest influence on decisions to engage in international transactions.[14]

---

14. John C. Hulsman, Ph.D., and Aaron Schavey (2001), "The Global Free Trade Association: A New Trade Agenda", Heritage Foundation *Backgrounder No. 1441*, May 16, at *www.heritage.org/research/tradeandforeignaid/bg1441.cfm*.

- *Trade Policy*: Obviously, a prospective GFTA member would have to have the fewest possible barriers to trade, including low tariffs and minimal import licenses, controls, quotas, and other non-tariff barriers.
- *Capital Flows and Foreign Investment*: Similarly, open international investment markets are important, including a transparent and open investment code, impartial treatment of domestic and foreign investment, and an efficient and speedy approval process.
- *Property Rights*: A central tenet for exchange of goods and services is an established rule of law—enforced by an independent, fair, and efficient judicial system—that protects private property and provides an environment in which business transactions take place with a high degree of certainty.
- *Regulation*: A GFTA member must not impose an undue regulatory burden on entrepreneurs or business. Key elements include an efficient, transparent licensing system that allows a business to be established quickly, equal application of regulations, and transparency.

To qualify for the GFTA, a country would need to be open to trade and investment and maintain a secure rule of law with low levels of regulation. Using the *Index*, countries receiving a score of either 1 or 2 on trade policy, capital flows and foreign investment, property rights, and regulation would qualify. While only 13 countries currently qualify for the GFTA, another 18 countries from every region of the world could qualify by improving their scores in only one of these four factors.

What are the Advantages of a GFTA?

The GFTA has the potential to encompass all nations if they meet the criteria and wish to open their markets to goods and services from other GFTA members. However, this is unlikely to occur in the near future because fewer than three-dozen countries are currently within sight of GFTA membership. Therefore, bilateral, regional, or multilateral options for pursuing free trade should not be abandoned—particularly trade negotiations involving countries that are not eligible or willing to take advantage of the GFTA.

But the advantages of a GFTA merit support even if the short-term potential membership is measured only in the dozens. As proposed,

Box 1.1

Countries Qualifying for the Global Free Trade Alliance According to the 2005 Index

In the 2001 edition of the *Index*, three Heritage analysts proposed a plan for a global free trade association (GFTA).* This year, 13 countries qualify, while 18 are in the 'near-miss' category, falling short in only one factor by one point.

The qualifying countries, based on *2005 Index of Economic Freedom* data, are Australia, Botswana, Denmark, Estonia, Finland, Hong Kong, Iceland, Ireland, Luxembourg, New Zealand, Singapore, the United Kingdom, and the United States. All of these countries qualified last year except for Botswana, which improved its trade score to qualify this year.

Among the near-miss countries are examples that range from Switzerland to Bahrain to Trinidad and Tobago. Taiwan's foreign investment score improved this year, moving the country into the near-miss category. Burdensome regulation is keeping the country from qualifying. Cyprus fell out of the near-miss category because its trade score worsened.

Of the 18 near-miss countries, 15 fail to qualify because of their regulation scores; Canada does not qualify because of its foreign investment score; Bahrain does not qualify because of restrictions on trade; and El Salvador does not qualify because of weak property rights.

Membership in a Global Free Trade Alliance

Qualifying Countries	*Countries Next in Line*	*Policy Blocking Membership*
1. Australia	1. Austria	Regulation
2. Botswana	2. Bahrain	Trade
3. Denmark	3. Belgium	Regulation
4. Estonia	4. Canada	Foreign Investment
5. Finland	5. Chile	Regulation
6. Hong Kong	6. El Salvador	Property Rights
7. Iceland	7. France	Regulation
8. Ireland	8. Germany	Regulation
9. Luxembourg	9. Israel	Regulation
10. New Zealand	10. Italy	Regulation
11. Singapore	11. Netherlands	Regulation
12. United Kingdom	12. Portugal	Regulation
13. United States	13. Spain	Regulation
	14. Sweden	Regulation
	15. Switzerland	Regulation
	16. Taiwan	Regulation
	17. Trinidad and Tobago	Regulation
	18. Uruguay	Regulation

Source: Marc A. Miles, Edwin J. Feulner, and Mary Anastasia O'Grady, *2005 Index of Economic Freedom* (Washington, D.C.: The Heritage Foundation and Dow Jones & Company, Inc., 2005), at *www.heritage.org/index*.

Note: * John C. Hulsman, Gerald P. O'Driscoll, Jr., and Denise H. Froning, "The Free Trade Association: A Trade Agenda for the New Global Economy", Chapter 3 in Gerald P. O'Driscoll, Jr., Kim R. Holmes, and Melanie Kirkpatrick, *2001 Index of Economic Freedom* (Washington, D.C.: The Heritage Foundation and Dow Jones & Company, Inc., 2001), pp. 33–39.

Figure 1.2

Prospective Membership in a Global Free Trade Alliance

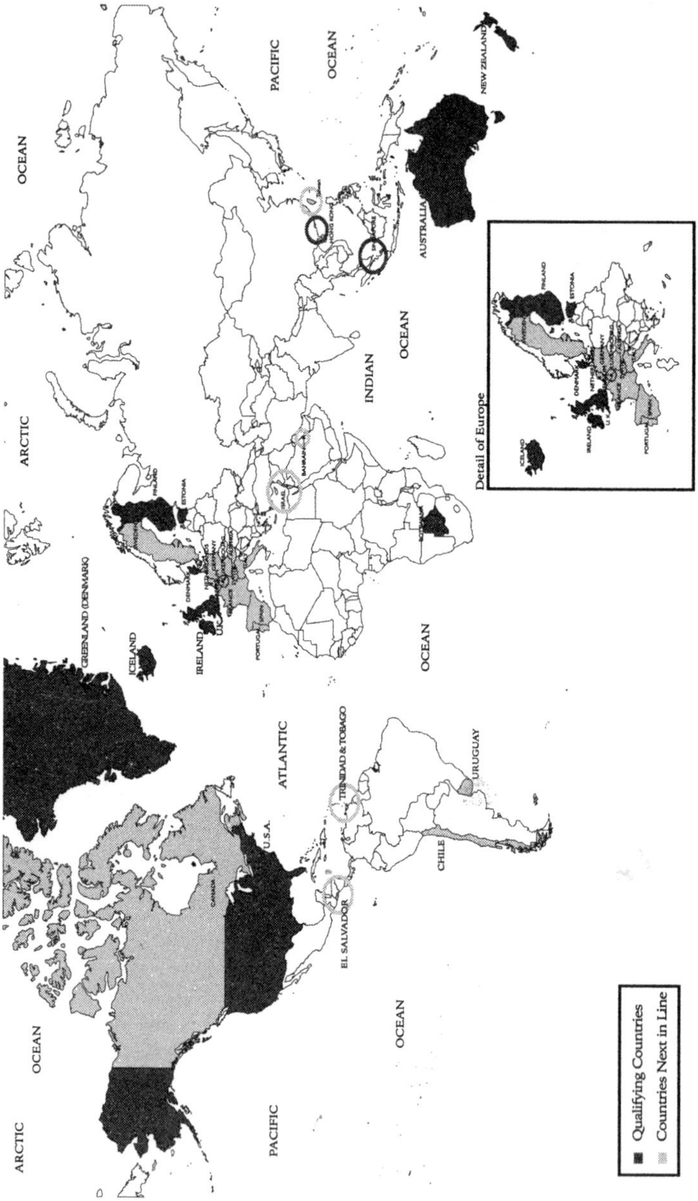

the GFTA would complement existing options for trade liberalisation by:

- *Sharply reducing negotiations*: As a coalition of the willing, the GFTA would involve minimal negotiation. Membership would be based on existing policies, not negotiated concessions. It would secure the benefits of increased trade and investment among members without their having to undergo any new major policy reforms. It would reward nations for their commitment to economic freedom by securing a coalition of the willing determined to maximise trade liberalisation.
- *Leaving sovereignty intact*: The GFTA is voluntary, and nations would be free to adopt policies in violation of the GFTA at any time—with the understanding that such actions would cost them privileged access to other GFTA markets. Its numerical target methodology allows for self-selection and gives the whole policy initiative a self-governing aspect it would otherwise lack.
- *Becoming more attractive over time*: There is a tipping point here; as membership grows, the organisation becomes increasingly more attractive, giving non-member countries an incentive to make market-friendly reforms in order to reap the benefits of membership. Such an incentive has long been missing in trading regimes.
- *Offering a speedy means for global free trade*: Unlike bilateral or regional free trade agreements, the GFTA is not bound to a finite number of partners or a specific region. In theory, it could include all nations. However, unlike the WTO, it would expand free trade rather than simply pursue incremental reduction in trade barriers.

Everything else aside, the notion of a Global Free Trade Association would merit support based only on the beneficial impact of the criteria on economic growth. As noted, freer trade policy as measured by the 'Index' is associated with increased growth in per capita GDP. This positive relationship is enhanced when the four GFTA criteria are considered as a group.

Averaging these four scores together yields a 'trade openness' score, with one being 'open' and five being 'closed'. Analysis of the relationship between trade openness (as measured by the average *Index* score in the four factors discussed above) and per capita GDP reveals that open economies have an average GDP per capita twice that of mostly open economies, that mostly open economies have a GDP per capita over seven times that of mostly closed economies on average, and that mostly closed economies have a per capita GDP over twice that of closed economies (Figure 1.3).

Figure 1.3

Trade Openness is Associated with Higher GDP Per Capita

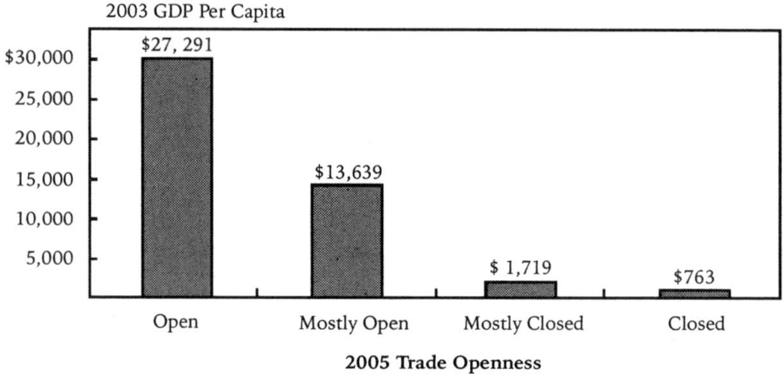

Note: Trade Openness is based on the *2005 Index of Economic Freedom* by averaging the score for the trade policy, property rights, capital flows and foreign investment, and regulation factors.

Source: World Bank, World Development Indicators Online, available by subscription at *www.worldbank.org/data*; Marc A. Miles, Edwin J. Feulner, and Mary Anastasia O'Grady, 2005 *Index of Economic Freedom* (Washington, D.C.: The Heritage Foundation and Dow Jones & Company, Inc., 2005), available at *www.heritage.org/index*.

The relationship between trade openness as measured by the *Index of Economic Freedom* and higher per capita GDP actually provides a stronger incentive for change than does analysis of the trade policy factor alone. Countries with improved trade openness scores experienced compound GDP per capita growth of 2.8 per cent. Those countries whose score remained unchanged experienced growth of 2.4 per cent. Countries where trade openness scores declined experienced compound GDP per capita growth of only 1.4 per cent. (Table 1.4). Moreover, there is a positive relationship between per capita GDP growth and changes in trade openness: the higher the growth, the more the trade openness score improves. (Figure 1.4).

Table 1.4

Trade Openness and GDP Per Capita Growth: An Incentive Just to Move toward Qualification for GFTA

Trade Openness Change (1997 Index–2005 Index)*	*Compound GDP Per Capita Growth (1995–2003)*
Improved	2.8 %
No Change	2.4 %
Declined	1.4 %

Note: * Trade openness is based on the Index of Economic Freedom by averaging the score for the trade policy, property rights, capital flows and foreign investment, and regulation factors. Among 126 countries observed, 43 countries improved, 34 made no change, and 49 declined in their trade openness.

Sources: World Bank, *World Development Indicators Online*, available by subscription at *www.worldbank.org/data;* Marc A. Miles, Edwin J. Feulner, and Mary Anastasia O'Grady, *2005 Index of Economic Freedom* (Washington, D.C.: The Heritage Foundation and Dow Jones & Company, Inc., 2005), at *www.heritage.org/index.*

Figure 1.4

Improving Trade Openness Means Higher Economic Prosperity

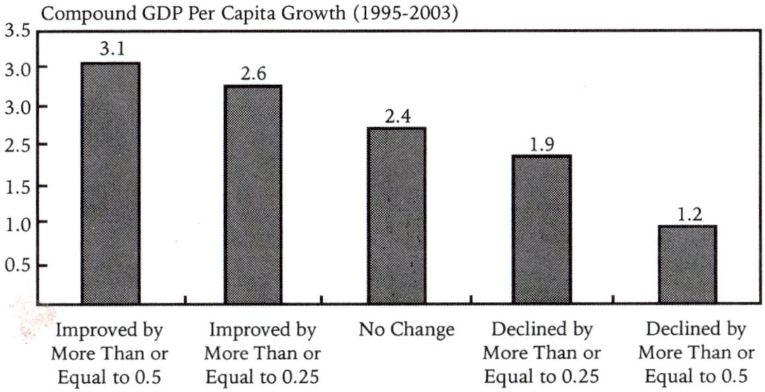

Change in Trade Openness (1997 Index-2005 Index)

Note: Trade Openness is based on the Index of Economic Freedom by averaging the score for the trade policy, property rights, capital flows and foreign investment, and regulation factors. Among 126 countries whose GDP per capita and trade policy score of the Index of Economic Freedom are available, 14 countries "improved by more than or equal to 0.5;" 29 countries "improved by more than or equal to 0.25;" 34 countries "no change;" 15 countries "declined by more than or equal to 0.25;" 34 countries "declined by more than or equal to 0.5".

Source: World Bank, World Development Indicators Online, available by subscription at *www.worldbank.org/data;* Marc A. Miles, Edwin J. Feulner, and Mary Anastasia O'Grady, *2005 Index of Economic Freedom* (Washington, D.C.: The Heritage Foundation and Dow Jones & Company, Inc., 2005), available at *www.heritage.org/index.*

What is the lesson? Even without actually qualifying for the growth-generating possibilities of free trade from GFTA membership, countries that simply adopted more liberal policies (as proposed for membership in the GFTA) would benefit through increased per capita GDP growth. Thus, even countries that fail to qualify immediately for the GFTA would be doing their economies and citizens a service by working toward that goal.

Conclusion

The Global Free Trade Alliance offers a new, innovative means for pursuing free trade. The GFTA can change the way people and countries think about free trade. Wrangling over 'concessions' to further global trade liberalisation is eliminated. Instead, free trade will be seen for what it is: a policy that gives countries a massive economic advantage. As the advantages of such an alliance become apparent, the GFTA can serve as a practical advertisement for the enduring global benefits of free trade.

2

The Changing Nature of Trade Diplomacy[1]

STEPHEN WOOLCOCK

Introduction

The conventional wisdom with regard to trade policy is that it has undergone a number of major changes. First, the progressive increase in the coverage of trade policy (or a deepening) to include new issues. This deepening is seen as bringing about an internationalisation of policy areas (such as services, investment, environmental regulation, consumer protection, food safety etc.) with a resultant increase in the number of actors or interests concerned with trade policy. Civil Society groups, some times organised at a 'global' level are challenging the existing decision making processes, the legitimacy of 'the WTO' and the assumption of progressive liberalisation of trade and investment in a rules-based international order. As a consequence trade policy makers must now deal with a wider range of 'domestic' actors. As a result trade policy has become more complex and more transparent.

Second, there has been an increase in the number of countries actively participating in the international trading system, or a widening of the trading system. Not only are many developing or newly industrialising countries now seeking to play a more active role, but also transition countries including China are now members, making the trade regime a truly global regime. This means that the US, EU or the OECD countries together are no longer able to shape outcomes. If agreement between the US and EU was sufficient during the Tokyo Round, and necessary during the Uruguay Round, it is now

---

1. The chapter has been re-printed from the document archive of the International Trade Policy Unit of the London School of Economics, available at - *http://www.lse.ac.uk/collections/internationalTradePolicyUnit/*. An earlier version of the paper has been presented at the BISA Panel on "Economic Diplomacy in the 21st Century", London School of Economics and Kings College, December 2002. We thank Prof. Stephen Woolcock for granting the necessary permission.

necessary but not sufficient to ensure the successful conclusion of the Doha Development Agenda (DDA) negotiations of the WTO. As the Seattle WTO Ministerial Meeting showed, a number of developing countries are now willing and able to veto agreements, which they feel have not been negotiated without their participation or are against their interests. As a result there has been a discussion of institutional reform in the WTO and much debate (and some action) taken to enhance the capacity of developing countries to actively participate in trade and investment negotiations.

This deepening and widening of the trading system raises some important questions for trade diplomacy. For example, is it possible to make trade policy making more open and transparent in order to satisfy the demand for greater accountability, without politicising the policy process and heightening the risk of capture by protectionist interests? Is it possible to make decision-making within the WTO more inclusive, by providing scope for the active participation of a large number of countries, without a system—which is based on consensus decision-making—becoming incapable of reaching conclusions to difficult issues? Developments since the conclusion of the Uruguay Round of trade negotiations suggest a mixed picture with regard to the apparent ability of policy makers to cope with these challenges. The failure of the Seattle WTO Ministerial appeared to suggest that trade diplomacy was not coping well. This also followed the collapse of the Multilateral Agreement on Investment (MAI) which global civil society saw as a sea change in the 'fight against globalisation'. On the other hand, the Doha Development Agenda (DDA) negotiations were successfully launched in November 2001, albeit with a text that—in the best traditions of the GATT—was open to various interpretations. Despite the start of a new multilateral round, however, regional and bilateral trade diplomacy has continued apace, with all major (and lots of minor) WTO members actively engaged in negotiating regional or bilateral free trade agreements. Does the remarkable growth of regional trade diplomacy could reflect scepticism that trade diplomacy will really be able to deal with the challenge of deepening and widening?

What Did Trade Diplomacy Used to be Like?

In order to discuss whether trade diplomacy has changed, it is necessary to have some reference point against which to measure the recent developments. Most comparisons are today made with the period after the establishment of the GATT in 1948. If one takes a period between the foundation of the GATT and the mid to late 1980s, one can say that—despite a good deal of change—the broad features of trade diplomacy remained fairly constant.

Trade Policy was Relatively Narrowly Defined

Trade policy consisted primarily of border measures, even though the Tokyo Round codes had sought to tackle non-tariff and regulatory barriers such as subsidies, government procurement and technical barriers to trade. US leadership shaped the GATT, with a growing role for the European Community/Union especially from the mid 1970s onwards. Under this leadership an international regime had been established in the GATT, which was able to continue and indeed become stronger even when US leadership was more equivocal as was the case from the early 1970s. Few developing countries played an active role in the GATT. Although many DCs were Contracting Parties few had the inclination or capability to be involved in all GATT activities. Even the active DCs such as India and Brazil 'benefited' from had Special and Differential Treatment. A fact that tended to diminish their ability to shape the course of negotiations and the rules of the organisation. Most developments in trade policy were therefore shaped either in the USA at the beginning or in the OEEC and OECD.

The GATT system was based on what became called 'embedded liberalism', in other words the system promoted liberalisation and above all required non-discrimination, but granted the Contracting Parties to the GATT considerable national policy autonomy. This was achieved by the non-discrimination principles of the GATT based on most favoured nation and national treatment, which allowed governments to pursue domestic policies on tax or regulation, provided they did not discriminate against imports of like products.

In this period concerned trade policy remained relatively insulated from political pressures. The lessons of the 1930s, when a politicisation of trade policy had led to protectionism and a decline in trade and growth, were still fresh in the minds of policy makers (in administrations and legislative branches of government). So there was a clear consensus on the need to insulate trade policy making from protectionist pressures as far as possible. The insulation was less enduring in the United States, where Congress began to reclaim greater control over trade policy. This brought about an end of what might be seen as an exceptional period following the Reciprocal Trade Agreements Act of 1934 during which the US administration had considerable scope and flexibility to negotiate international agreements. The shift towards a greater politicisation of trade in the US began in the 1974s but increased markedly in the mid 1980s with the 'fair trade' debate and the passage of the Omnibus Trade and Competitiveness Act in 1988. In Europe trade diplomacy has been less politicised, in part because policy is largely shaped by the interaction between national trade officials and the European Commission within the framework of the EU (formerly EC and EEC). The additional level of policy making in which national policy preferences are reconciled at the EU level before the joint position is carried forward into international negotiations by the Commission, made trade policy much more remote for most national politicians. This enabled European trade diplomacy to remain more insulated from national politics, although not from sector interests as agriculture and textiles testify. National parliaments rarely got involved in detailed debates on trade policy and governments tended to report to parliaments rather than seek their approval for negotiating positions. The same applied for the European Parliament, which had no powers under the Article 113 of the Treaty of Rome provisions that set out how EU trade policy was to be determined.

Trade policy in Europe, as elsewhere was therefore shaped predominantly by interest group politics rather than majoritarian politics. In other words policy makers tended to engage those interests with a direct interest in trade, whether they were seeking protection or liberalisation, as opposed to the voting public. For most voters the costs and benefits of trade were too small or too remote to be of much importance. Trade policy analysts have reflected this approach to trade policy in the application of rational choice to trade policy decision-making.

In Europe therefore trade diplomacy retained its 'technocratic' character for long with national bureaucracies and the European Commission effectively running the show. The European Parliament was not permitted much of an active role and most national parliaments were not too interested in providing close scrutiny of the EU policy process. Democratic accountability was ensured through the General Affairs Council control over trade policy, but much of the detailed work was done in the Article 133 Committee, which brings together the top national trade officials.

This separation of trade and domestic politics was in line with the basic principles of the GATT. The GATT was based on non-discrimination, in the shape of most favoured nation status and national treatment, but allowed scope for a wide range of national policy autonomy. This was the consensus, of 'embedded liberalism' as it has been described by scholars.

A further feature of trade diplomacy during the period up to the mid 1980s was that it was shaped by a limited number of leading GATT members. Initially one could say that the GATT was based on US hegemonic leadership. As this leadership faded the regime was supported by the EU and other OECD countries. Although developing countries were members of the GATT, they had little influence.

Finally, trade diplomacy was focused on the multilateral trading system. There was the major exception of the EU, but other regional approaches that sought to emulate the EEC during the 1960s and 1970s failed to make much progress.

How Has Trade Diplomacy Changed?

A deepening and widening of the international trading system has brought about an accentuation of the tension between democratic accountability and effectiveness in trade diplomacy. This challenge for trade diplomacy is the result of the success over the past half century in liberalising trade and investment through successive rounds of trade negotiations.

Deepening

The deepening of the trading system has taken the form of increased coverage of international rules governing trade and investment. This has steadily eroded the original 1948 design of the system. The early rounds of trade negotiations were almost entirely concerned with tariffs. Here the concept of most favoured nation treatment served the purpose of reducing tariff protection. Once tariffs affecting large percentages of international trade began to come down—at least in the developed countries—attention shifted to non-tariff barriers to trade, such as subsidies, government procurement (which had been excluded from the GATT, but which accounted for 10-15 per cent of GDP at the time) and technical barriers to trade. The Tokyo Round (1973-79) codes on these topics, were essentially efforts to extend national treatment to these policy areas and therefore retained much of the original GATT design. But national treatment was soon proved to be ineffective in dealing with, for example technical barriers to trade. National technical regulations that were on the face of it non-discriminatory, could in practice discriminate against foreign suppliers. But the application of national treatment to technical barriers to trade and government procurement had next to no impact on this type of non-tariff barrier. The perception that open markets required more than national treatment was reflected in the efforts of the European Union to harmonise regulations and standards and in pressure for more effective multilateral provisions.

The Uruguay Round was a watershed in trade diplomacy for a number of reasons. It represented a shift towards 'deeper integration', or greater policy harmonisation/approximation as a means of enhancing market access. This change took the trading system beyond national treatment and begun to erode the consensus of 'embedded liberalism.' For example, the Uruguay Round provisions on non-tariff barriers being more comprehensive, the agreement on technical barriers to trade sought to strengthen the rules, encourage the use of international standards and promote mutual recognition. The Agreement on Sanitary and Phytosanitary Measures went a little further in requiring the use of agreed international standards for food safety, except in clearly defined circumstances. The Uruguay Round also included trade in services (including investment in service activities), a logical step given that services accounted for a far larger share of the economies in almost all countries than manufactures. Although the General Agreement on Trade in Services (GATS) provided a framework of rules based on national treatment, sector agreements in telecommunications and financial services required a degree of regulatory harmonisation. Without such harmonisation there was little prospect of real market opening. For example, obligations to provide national treatment for foreign telecommunications services providers has no impact whatsoever when a service is provided by a national monopoly, as was the case in some national telecommunications markets.

The Uruguay Round also sought to extend the rules further into investment. Again this was a logical step given that investment was becoming a major, if not the most important means by which international competition was being increased. But the agreement on Trade Related Investment Measures (TRIMS) was modest and only resulted in rules on a few performance requirements such as local content requirements on inward investors. The agreement on Trade Related Intellectual Property Rights (TRIPS) did however require conformance with agreed international standards for the protection against counterfeit trade and patents. This took the WTO a good way down the road towards policy harmonisation.

In addition to a shift from national treatment towards policy harmonisation (with some rather vague encouragement for mutual recognition) the Uruguay Round facilitated access to an enhanced—legalistic—dispute settlement procedure. Trade diplomacy would henceforth have less scope to resolve disputes through negotiation. National governments struggling to reconcile domestic political imperatives with the rules of the trading system, would in future find there were fewer safety values or means of ducking out of WTO commitments. The WTO itself has stopped short of the kind of legal constitution for liberal trade and investment favoured by some writers. But trade diplomacy is under increasing pressure because the leading WTO members have put in place domestic mechanisms that channel private complaints against other countries. In the USA, for example, Section 301 provides the means by which private parties can effectively initiate action by the US Administration against governments that deny the US companies concerned market access or otherwise frustrate trade and investment. The EU has also introduced similar legislation that provides EU legal persons with a means of raising their concerns with the European Commission and Council. Trade diplomats therefore have less scope to reject calls from sector interests for bilateral negotiations and/or dispute settlement cases to be initiated in the WTO. In the past policy makers could more easily weigh the sector interests in remedies against the wider costs of acrimonious trade disputes.

Post 1994 the trend towards deepening has continued, with environmental issues being placed on the agenda as early as 1994 and competition and investment tentatively placed on the agenda in Singapore in 1996 and more firmly in Doha in 2001. The trade regime has now come to have a clear integration agenda or characteristics. As a result the old certainties about what was trade and what was not can no longer be relied upon. This change has not come about rapidly, but has been the result of the evolution of the system over the past 50 years. The definition of what is trade and what is a non-trade issue has clearly shifted over time as a result of the evolution of markets and pressure from sector interests to extend the scope of the GATT/ WTO rules.

The greater intrusiveness of the trade and investment rules in the WTO (and other international regimes) has awakened a wider domestic interest in trade and investment policy. More and more 'domestic' policy preferences are affected by trade diplomacy, and more interest groups perceive trade diplomacy as important. In many cases such domestic interests have been critical of the 'remoteness' of trade diplomacy or have openly criticised its lack of transparency. Civil society initiatives have in part rejected the formal channels of democratic accountability and legitimacy, which gave trade diplomacy scope to negotiate, as being ineffective. Hence the shift to more direct action by coalitions of civil society groups, which seek to bypass national channels of accountability and act directly at the international or global level. Civil society groups have also helped to increase awareness of the implications and impact of trade diplomacy among voters. This has resulted in trade diplomacy becoming less of an 'interest based' policy and more concerned with public opinion and majoritarian politics. Trade diplomacy is therefore faced with the challenge of working under much greater constraint. The growth in domestic expectations and demands makes it harder to reconcile domestic preferences in international negotiations and the tighter rules-based structure of the trade regime means there is also less opportunity to avoid conflicts by exploiting ambiguities in how the trade regime functions.

The deepening of the trade agenda has also had an impact on the application of reciprocity, another central principle of the post 1947 trading system. The complicated nature of the scheduling rules in the GATS reflect the greater complexities of ensuring reciprocity in services. More generally reciprocity in the field of regulatory policy may take the form of mutually recognising another countries regulatory norms. In this context unilateral liberalisation would take the form of accepting products or services regardless of the regulatory standard with which they comply.

Widening

The second major factor that has brought about a change in trade diplomacy has been the widening of the world trading system. The GATT was negotiated by a group of 23 men around a table in Geneva over the summer of 1947. By the Dillon Round of 1960-61 there were 39 Contracting Parties (CPs) to the GATT, by the beginning of the Kennedy Round there were 74 and the Tokyo Round brought together 99 CPs. Most of this growing number of Contracting Parties was newly independent and often small developing countries. Their impact on the balance of power and influence in the trading system was not great. Even the large developing countries with the will and resources to shape negotiations were held back by their—self imposed— second-class membership of the system in the shape of special and differential treatment.

An increase in the obligations on developing country WTO members and the end of the two-tier membership of the trading system that existed up to the 1990s also means they are more fully-fledged members of the 'club'. When the OECD countries sought to extend the scope of GATT rules in the 1970s, developing countries effectively opted out by maintaining special and differential treatment under Part IV of the GATT and not signing the qualified most favoured nation codes that were used to extend GATT coverage to non-tariff barriers in the Tokyo Round. In the Uruguay Round however developing countries signed the Single Undertaking that included the results of the round and thus agreed to, ultimately, adopt the same rules as the developed countries. Transition provisions and other forms of special and differential treatment meant, however, that there remains a difference in the level of obligations on developed and developing members of the WTO. The Uruguay Round also saw a growing number of predominantly newly industrialising countries seeking to play a more active role in the system.

The end of the Cold War also resulted in a large number of transition countries joining the WTO including in 2001, China. The result has been the transformation of the trading system from a 'club' of OECD members led by the United States in the 1950s to a global regime in which power structures are much more heterogeneous. As with the deepening process, this widening has been going on for some time. But the changes since the mid 1990s have had a profound impact on trade diplomacy. In the 1950s the international trade regime was reasonably accurately described by a system shaped by US hegemony. In the 1970s the EU emerged as a key player with the result that agreement between the US and EU became a necessary condition for the success of any negotiation. With the creation of the WTO, developing countries began to expect a greater say in what happened, with the result that US-EU agreement is now necessary but not sufficient for agreement. This was perhaps most clearly illustrated at the WTO Ministerial meeting in Seattle in 1999.

Trade diplomacy, which was once the preserve of a limited group of countries, has therefore now become global in nature. So that in addition to the greater constraints imposed by growing domestic expectations and demands (for transparency), the new fully paid up members of the WTO also want to be fully included in decision-making. Widening and deepening of the international trade/ investment system has therefore not unexpectedly resulted in increased tensions. On the one hand there is growing pressure from domestic interest groups and public opinion to make trade policy more transparent and accountable. On the other hand, the increased scope of trade policy makes negotiations and the larger number of countries involved and the absence of an economic hegemon able to shape outcomes makes the policy process much more complex. There is therefore a need for effective decision-making, but greater transparency, political accountability and inclusiveness can on the face of things be excepted to make it harder to reach agreements that will be ratified by national parliaments.

Policy Options

Given these challenges facing trade diplomacy, what are the broad policy options?

Stop the World—I Want to Get Off

Perhaps the most obvious option would be to slow the pace of change and thus the pressures on trade diplomacy. The question here is at what point should one stop. One option would be to hold things where they were at the end of the Uruguay Round in order to allow the implications of the developments in the round to be assimilated and for the agreements to be properly implemented. This option would find support from those who believe that the WTO has gone too far. These include, for example, those domestic interests who perceive the trade rules as threatening national policy preferences, including sections of civil society movement. Many trade economists also argue that the WTO has gone too far by extending into 'non-trade' issues and seeking policy approximation or harmonisation. Policy harmonisation according to this view threatens to undermine comparative advantage as 'northern' standards are imposed on all countries. For many trade economists harmonisation is likely to fail as government failure—to find the right policy to harmonise—is much more likely than market failure. Consequently there should be policy/institutional competition between national policies and the emulation of successful policies rather then the imposition of common policies.

This *status quo* option does not appear to reflect what is happening. The Singapore Ministerial meeting of the WTO was shaped by an assumption that investment and to a lesser degree other issues such as competition, the environment—but not labour standards —should be included in the rules. Retaining the *status quo* would also mean choosing which–if any–of the issues included in the in-build agenda should be dropped. The Uruguay Round included an agreement to start further negotiations on agriculture and services in 2000. This in-built agenda also included less important commitments to review various other agreements. For real progress in the sensitive market access issues of agriculture and services trade negotiators need to build a domestic coalition strong enough to counterbalance the obvious protectionist pressures. Building such a coalition effectively meant adding further issues to the agenda and thus a new round of multilateral negotiations, hence the move to launch the Millennium Round in Seattle.

A standstill on further trade negotiations is also problematic in the sense that even the Uruguay Round agreements were full of ambiguities. Given the improved dispute settlement procedures, WTO members unhappy with how agreements are being interpreted, could easily bring cases in order to clarify the interpretation of the text. This opens up the prospect of decisions on the scope of trade rules being determined in legal proceedings in the WTO, which would tend to accentuate the criticism of the WTO legitimacy.

A third difficulty with a standstill option is that there is no agreement on what constitutes an optimal set of trade rules. In short there is no agreement on the issue of 'global subsidiarity'. Why should there be harmonised international standards for food safety and the protection of intellectual property, as was agreed in the Uruguay Round, but not health and safety in general, environmental standards, competition policy or even core labour standards? The existing scope of the WTO has been determined by multilateral negotiations in which trade-offs have been made. The scope of the trade regime has not been determined by any set of logical economic, legal or political criteria. In other words the current coverage does not represent a steady state or even a defensible position.

Finally, market integration is unlikely to stop and bilateral, regional and or plurilateral agreements are likely to fill the vacuum left if the WTO does not keep pace with market developments. Ever since the conclusion of the Uruguay Round, which represented a significant advance in multilateralism, bilateral and regional agreements have continued a pace. To retain the *status quo* in multilateral negotiations would therefore increase the risk of regional agreements undermining the multilateral trading system.

Re-establish a Clear Set of Criteria for Determining the Scope of the Trade Regime

A more radical option would be to revert to a system in which the WTO dealt only with 'trade' issues. The logic for this option is elegant and compelling. It is that there should be a clear set of principles underlying the trading system and that these should be national treatment and MFN along with comparative advantage. The trading system should not venture into 'non-trade' issues because harmonisation can undermine comparative advantage. Trade liberalisation would occur from below through the unilateral liberalisation of trade and investment, rather than from above as a result of pressure to approximate policies in reciprocal trade negotiations. One benefit of this approach is that one could re-establish clear criteria for the trading system. One difficulty would be that this approach would require a number of established agreements to be unwound, in particular the TRIPS and SPS Agreements in the Uruguay Round. As these agreements have been the main focus of criticism from developing countries and consumer NGOs, there might be some advantage in this. Such a move would also reduce the risk of the trade regime becoming overburdened. Policy harmonisation could be dealt with in the respective specialist organisations, such as WIPO and the WHO as they were before the Uruguay Round. Other specialist organisations could also deal with policy areas such as environmental protection. The trade regime would again deal with trade matters and leave the rest to such specialist bodies or to domestic policy.

The downside of this approach is that one would in effect move trade diplomacy back to the 1980s, and the 1980s was the period when unilateral imposition of 'fair trade' (by the United States primarily) was a major threat. Indeed it was the threat of unilateral imposition of US intellectual property right standards that led most DCs to sign up to the TRIPS agreement. Those interest groups that have sought the inclusion of IPR, food safety, the environment or labour standards in the WTO have done so because the specialist organisations were seen to be ineffective. There would therefore inevitably be pressure to impose such standards unilaterally.

In short this option is not really politically feasible, even if it might make economic sense. An agreement could be reached to bind WTO members from taking unilateral trade policy measures, but that would be unlikely to hold. If major WTO members break such an agreement the credibility of the system would ultimately be damaged more than with a muddling through option.

Enhance Transparency and Inclusiveness in Policymaking

A third option would be to enhance the transparency of trade diplomacy in order to correct the perception that trade diplomacy is not legitimate or accountable. There was much rhetoric on enhanced transparency after the Seattle Ministerial and some measures have been taken. At the WTO level, documents have been made more generally available, so that most position papers of the WTO members and secretariat papers are made public within a reasonable period of time. The WTO Secretariat has also organised consultation sessions with Non-governmental organisations, both business and other civil society NGOs. At the WTO Ministerial meetings there are parallel conferences organised by civil society, business and other interests. These have perhaps had some effect in reducing the degree of suspicion about the WTO, but the scale of the events means there is little scope for any close dialogue. The WTO has not been selective in its invitation policy so that NGOs that can afford to participate do so. This contrasts with the UN, which does set criteria for participation and limit the number of NGOs that it recognises.

Increased involvement of NGOs in the workings of the WTO would raise some serious questions, such as how representative and accountable are the NGOs and whether they are adding to the legitimacy of the organisation or simply undermining the role of the (in most cases) elected member governments. The main impediment to any greater involvement of NGOs is opposition from developing country members. The DCs (as well as developed country governments) argue that they represent all interests, including civil society NGOs. Some direct involvement of NGOs in WTO committees has come in the form of NGOs on national delegations.

At the national level views differ about whether NGOs should be included. Some developing countries have included NGOs in their delegations in order to enhance their negotiating capacity. Developed countries also now tend to include NGOs, both from business and civil society, in their delegations to major conferences, such as the WTO ministerials in order to enhance the transparency and accountability of trade policy. But there must be some doubt that the presence of NGOs has any real bearing on negotiations. For example, in the EU the decisions are still taken in the Article 133 Committee or the EU General Affairs Council, where national governments only have a vote. The respective national government positions are determined by interdepartmental consultations in which NGOs play a role but probably not a decisive role. At an EU level the European Commission also organises consultations with NGOs (business and non-business), which involve a large number of NGOs. Participation is open—and as with the WTO meetings—tends to be determined by the ability of the NGOs to pay for someone to attend. There are also more select meetings between the major NGOs and Commission officials.

One cannot therefore help but feel that that enhanced transparency measures taken to date have been more for show than effect. Or to put it more positively, they are aimed at helping to create a perception that trade policy is transparent and legitimate, but without any major changes to the existing channels of legitimation and accountability. In short the scope for civil society to play some role in filling the democratic deficit in trade policy by direct lobbying at the WTO or WTO members is probably limited. Arguably the main impact that civil society NGOs have on trade diplomacy is in shaping public opinion. Public opinion will in turn shape views in national (and the European) parliaments on trade issues.

If there is democratic deficit in trade diplomacy it is because national parliaments, the most suitable and likely bodies to provide effective scrutiny have, with a number of notably exceptions, been largely ineffective. But opening the policy process to national parliaments runs the risk of politicising trade diplomacy and rendering it ineffective. National parliaments are generally not well-equipped to deal with the detail of trade policy. National (and the European) parliament could assume a greater role in ratifying the results of trade negotiations as the US Congress does. Indeed, with the greater awareness of trade policy among the voting public other legislatures are likely to be willing to exercise ratification powers. The European Parliament is, for example, likely to want to give its assent to any agreement negotiated by the EU in the Doha Development Agenda. If public opinion can be mobilised against ratification of the results there could well be cases of 'involuntary' defection or an inability of the EU or other major WTO members to get an agreement ratified. In the past it has always been US trade negotiators who have stressed the need for more concessions from it's trading partners in order to ensure that Congress ratifies the agreement. In the next round of negotiations other WTO members, most notably the EU, could well be in a similar position. Thus, whilst some involvement of NGOs and a greater involvement of national parliaments could well fill the 'democratic deficit' in trade policy, such closer democratic accountability will reduce the scope of trade negotiators and make the conclusion of significant agreements more difficult.

Institutional Reform of the WTO

Whilst the US and some other developed WTO members have been preoccupied by enhancing the transparency of trade diplomacy, developing countries have been concerned about making it more 'inclusive'. After Seattle there was much debate about the need for institutional reform of the WTO to make it more inclusive and transparent, whilst retaining its effectiveness. A number of proposals were made including one to establish a formal Parliamentary Assembly made up of elected representatives from national parliaments in order to bring these closer to the WTO process. In Seattle an informal assembly had been organised. There were also proposals for the creation of a Steering Committee of the WTO made up of major WTO members and rotating regional representatives, in order to provide a clearer leadership and direction for the WTO. There were also proposals for a formalisation of the so-called Green Room process, in which a small group of WTO members comes together to try and find solutions to deadlocks. The Green Room process had been especially targeted by developing countries because many saw themselves as unjustly excluded from the meetings. The old Green Room practice did not even include informing non-participating countries that the meetings were taking place. There were even proposals for the introduction of weighted voting similar to the voting in the IMF, but this was a non-starter given the oppositions from developing countries.[2]

Nothing has come of these proposals although the discussions on institutional reform have probably helped to clarify WTO members understanding of how the decision-making is supposed to work. Greater transparency has also been introduced into all procedures, which may have helped reduce the perception among developing countries that they were being excluded from the process. One area in which there has been much activity is that of providing technical assistance and capacity building for developing country WTO members. But this has not had a major impact on the number of developing countries that are able to maintain a presence across the board in WTO activities. This presence is limited by the limited size of developing country delegations in Geneva, or in many cases the absence of any delegation. The increasing number of committee meetings also means that even reasonably well-staffed delegations cannot attend all but the most important committee meetings.

Carry on Regardless

Another policy option is to continue with the established pattern of trade diplomacy, but with some modifications. Such an approach is the one that trade diplomats appeared to have opted for with the launch of the current Doha Development Agenda. The aim of this negotiation is to pick up on the in-build agenda and add to it in order to produce a package that will enable all WTO members to reflect their domestic needs. This means trade-offs in which further liberalisation (of agriculture and services, for example) is matched by the addition of other policies, such as something on the environment or multi-functionality in agriculture, that enables trade negotiators to build a domestic coalition strong enough to counterbalance continued protectionist forces.

This option is essential one carries on as before, although trade diplomacy has to be more transparent, the assumption being that

2. The WTO has carried over most of the decision-making procedures from the GATT even those there are more formalised provisions on decision making in the WTO. Decisions are thus by consensus except when decision affect principles such as MFN and national treatment, when they are to be by explicit unanimity (consensus is generally taken to be decision when there is no WTO member expressing opposition). There are also provisions for 2/3rd majorities on non-general principle issues and 3/4th for interpretations of WTO agreements. In other cases where there is no consensus and none of the voting rules apply decisions can be taken by a simple majority.

things will work out broadly as they have in the past. This option relies on the assumption that negotiators will as in the past be able to produce a package agreement with enough provisions for each party to ensure that national parliaments (and the European Parliament) will ratify the agreement. The difficulty with this approach is that developing countries are not very keen on any further extension of the WTO agenda to include sustainable development issues, investment or competition policy. A new round of negotiations was successfully launched in Doha, thanks in part to a more traditional ambiguous text, which leaves much to be decided still on the scope of the negotiations. Some of the failings in the run up to Seattle were also avoided, such as poor preparation and the production of a compromise draft declaration. Furthermore both the EU and US were clearly committed to launching a round, which was arguably not the case in 1999. The DDA has set a tight timetable for negotiations with completion scheduled for January 2005 and has to date not made very much concrete progress. Whilst the pace may pick up in 2003 there must be some doubt about the ability to conclude and agreement within the timetable. Failure to complete the round on time would not be as bad as negotiating an agreement within the deadline, which was not, ratified by one of the major WTO members. The odds must therefore be on a rather more lengthy negotiation than three years.

But have the Insurance Policy of a Multi-level Approach to Trade Diplomacy

A further policy option for trade diplomacy is to follow a multi-level approach. Given the risks associated with multilateral negotiations and the growing difficulties reconciling widening and deepening, it is not surprising that alternative levels of negotiation have been followed. Negotiations within a limited group of countries means that progress can be made on an integration agenda items or deepening without facing opposition from a large number of developing countries. Rather than negotiating on the multilateral level alone, therefore trade diplomacy has branched out into other levels. Again this is nothing new. Most of the multilateral agreements in the GATT were threshed out in the plurilateral OECD before hand. Indeed the whole structure of the GATT was one in which bilateral negotiations played an important role. Regional agreements have also been a feature of trade diplomacy for many years, and especially since the mid 1980s when the US shifted to a multi-pillar approach to trade diplomacy using multilateral, regional and unilateral pillars.

The regional or bilateral level offers an opportunity to more easily reconcile domestic policy objectives with wider liberalisation through policy approximation within the region. In other words, the difficulties caused by widening can be mitigated by concluding an agreement with a limited number of countries. Regional agreements between developed and developing countries may also offer more concrete benefits for both sides than wider multilateral negotiations can. For example, the developing countries can gain preferential, secure access to the more important developed country markets, whilst the developed countries concerned can more easily extend their regulatory standards across the region as a whole and thus avoid the problems of changing existing domestic policies. This may happen *de jure* through the adoption of common policies in regional agreements, such as in the extension of the EU axis across the whole of Europe or *de facto* through the effective extension of a dominant country's regulatory policies to its neighbours, as is happening with the extension of US norms to North America and possibly within the America as a whole. But as noted above there are also cross regional agreements being concluded between countries in different geographical regions. These appear to be motivated by a desire to set precedents or shape future trade negotiations as well as the more conventional motivations of enhancing market access for trade and investment. Geopolitical motivations also continue to play a role in the latest spat of bilateral and regional agreements. Thus for example, the US-Jordan bilateral agreement includes provisions on environment and labour standards, and the EU agreement with Tunisia includes provisions that envisage the ultimate application of European competition policy in Tunisia. Neither labour standards nor competition policies appear to be of immediate concern to the smaller countries concerned, but are important elements of the US and EU agendas for wider international trade regime.[3]

3. The US appears to have adopted a more consistent approach to such regional or bilateral agreements in that it is developing a template for all such agreements, which will no doubt reflect US approaches to regulation of markets, as exemplified in NAFTA. The EU which is also concluding a range of bilateral agreements does not yet seem to have adopted such a template. Indeed, the bilaterals/regional agreements concluded by the EU have varied quite considerably and not always reflected a set EU acquis. Another distinction is the fact that the EU policy appears to prefer region to region agreements (such as EU–Mercosur) in order to promote integration and economic development in the southern regions. The US on the other hand appears to prefer hub-and-spoke agreements, with the US as the hub, which can maximise negotiating leverage on the smaller spokes.

Conclusions

This chapter has set out a number of reasons for arguing that trade diplomacy has undergone fundamental changes since the mid 1980s. These changes have been largely brought about by the success of previous trade diplomacy in deepening and widening the international trade regime. Deepening and widening has created pressures to make trade diplomacy more transparent and accountable, but also requires effective decision making in very complex negotiations.

The chapter discusses a number of options that might be taken to ease these pressures, but finds that none of these have much prospect of succeeding apart from continuing with a somewhat modified form of the trade diplomacy that has been so successful to date. It remains to be seen whether trade diplomacy can succeed in concluding the current multilateral round of negotiations with an agreement that will be ratified by national parliaments and accepted by public opinion. In the event that the current round does not succeed, most countries seem to be taking out insurance in the shape of increased regional or bilateral agreements.

3

Developing-Country Coalitions in Multilateral Trade Negotiations

PETER DRAPER and
RAZEEN SALLY

Before the Uruguay Round (henceforth UR), most developing countries followed import-substitution and other trade-restrictive policies, and consequently were not very active in GATT forums in general. The scenario changed in the aftermath of UR: outward-oriented policies have made trade, and associated foreign investment, much more important in shaping national economic policies and performance. Thus developing-country participation across the range of WTO activities—in negotiations, dispute settlement, and in committees, working groups and review mechanisms handling the day-to-day administration of trade rules—is more important than ever.

The current chapter focuses on coalition-building by developing countries, which is a key indicator of their overall capacity and effectiveness in the WTO. We examine the issue in the context of national trade policies and trade negotiations on other tracks, particularly free-trade-agreement (FTA) initiatives. The chapter is organised as follows. Section 1 provides historical context on developing countries' participation from the GATT to the WTO, and assesses their current involvement in multi-country coalitions. It then discusses what form the WTO might take in future and the possible role of developing-country coalitions in this process, in the Doha Round (henceforth DR) and beyond. Section 2 describes the involvement of the developing-country majors (namely China, India, Brazil and South Africa),[1] in negotiating coalitions, and assesses implications for the present and future of the WTO.

1. India and Brazil are the long-standing developing-country 'big beasts' in the GATT/WTO. China has clearly joined this select rank with its accession in 2001. But is South Africa a developing-country major? It has neither the political nor economic weight of the other three, but it is by some measure the most important trading nation in Africa, ahead of Egypt, Nigeria, Morocco and Kenya. Hence, we think it worthwhile to add South Africa to the list, not least to shed more comparative light on the subject at hand.

SECTION 1

Developing-country Participation and Coalition-building from the GATT to the WTO

The GATT: Before and during the Uruguay Round

Developing-country participation in the GATT was relatively uncomplicated until the UR, as they largely excluded themselves from GATT negotiations.[2] They received unilateral tariff preferences from developed countries, in addition to tariff concessions negotiated among the latter in GATT rounds (through unconditional MFN treatment). But they were not obliged to reciprocate with own concessions, and had sweeping carve-outs from GATT disciplines (e.g. through the infant-industry and balance-of-payment provisions in GATT Article XVIII). These principles and measures were brought together under the rubric of Special and Differential Treatment (S&D) at the end of the Tokyo Round. The developing countries' restricted focus on tariff preferences and carve-outs made them dependent on uncertain and dwindling tariff preferences; it inculcated a begging-bowl culture; and their absence from the bargaining table allowed developed countries to exclude agriculture, textiles and clothing from multilateral liberalisation. Nevertheless, this stance was a logical fit with inward-looking, import-substitution policies in most developing countries. Brazil and India were seen to be the leaders of the developing-country block in both UNCTAD and the GATT during this period.

This pattern began to change visibly in the early 1980s, led by the unilateral liberalisation of several GATT members. Export-oriented economies like South Korea, Hong Kong, Singapore, and later other ASEAN countries, needed access to developed-country markets, but were increasingly facing protectionist policies there. Simultaneously, they were under pressure from the US to lower their trade barriers and strengthen IPR protection. This underlined the ineffectiveness of old-style S&D, and the compelling logic of being at the GATT bargaining table. At Punta del Este in 1986, East-Asian and Latin-American countries collaborated with the EFTA block in the 'Swiss-Colombian' coalition, overcame opposition from the developing-

2. Page, Sheila "Developing countries in GATT/WTO Negotiations", *Working Paper No. 20*, Overseas Development Institute, February 2002, pp. 9-10. *www.odi.org.uk/iedg/participation_in_negotiations/wto_gatt.pdf.*

country militant tendency led by India and Brazil, and brokered the compromise that launched the round.[3] Although India and Brazil remained, as before, vocal and active, for the first time a group of about 20 other developing countries became involved in the negotiating process of a GATT round, both formally and informally. Many Latin-American members were active in the Cairns Group on agriculture. Many East-Asian members were active in the International Textiles and Clothing Bureau. The ASEAN members, notwithstanding internal differences, cooperated effectively on several issues.

Thus, the UR witnessed the emergence of a minority of the developing world as active players at the multilateral level, in pragmatic, *à-la-carte* coalitions with other developing countries and developed countries to advance their positions on market access and rules. India resisted these developments right through the round. Brazil seemed to switch from Indian-style confrontation to pragmatism and flexibility in the second half of the round, coinciding with its unilateral liberalisation programme in the early 1990s. The vast majority of developing countries, mostly LDCs, remained passive and inactive. The Uruguay-Round Agreements reflected these dynamics. The active minority of developing countries made stronger commitments than the rest on market access, in addition to adopting a whole range of trade rules (such as TRIPS, TRIMS, SPS and TBT) for the first time as part of the Single Undertaking. In return they got extra market access to developed-country markets and stronger rules (e.g. on Voluntary Export Restraints and dispute settlement), though the options on agriculture, textiles and clothing, and disciplines on anti-dumping measures, were limited. This active minority gained from the round; the inactive majority did not. The latter did not get market access in products of interest to them, especially in agriculture, textiles and clothing.[4] S&D changed (*de facto* if not *de jure*) from an emphasis on non-reciprocity and blanket carve-outs to one where developing countries were expected to make market-access and rules commitments, though qualified by with lower liberalisation levels, longer transition periods for implementation, and (non-binding) promises of technical assistance. Old-style S&D seemed to be restricted only to least-developed countries (LDCs).

3. Croome, John (1999), *Reshaping the World Trading System: A History of the Uruguay Round*, Geneva: WTO/Kluwer, pp. 21-28.

4. Page, *op cit.*, p. 15.

From GATT to WTO

The UR agreements take the WTO wider, with broader sectoral coverage, and deeper into domestic regulations, all underpinned by much stronger dispute settlement. WTO membership has almost doubled over the last two decades. Three underlying trends need to be highlighted, all of which ring alarm bells.

First, the WTO has much more regulatory baggage compared with the GATT, with pressure to bring in even more detailed and prescriptive regulations on labour, environmental, food-safety and other product- and process-related standards. Second, the WTO has legalised considerably through dispute-settlement practice over the past decade. Third, the WTO is increasingly politicised. Externally, it is buffeted by a combination of old-style protectionist interests and new-style NGOs. Internally, the vast expansion of membership has made decision-making more unwieldy and snail-like. The 'UN-isation' of the WTO has gathered pace. Taken together, these pressures have virtually crippled the old GATT's traditional strength: its ability to deliver results through effective diplomacy and negotiation. Regulatory intrusiveness makes it more difficult to maintain political legitimacy with governments and interest groups (now including NGOs). Stalled negotiations increase the temptation to settle sensitive policy dilemmas through adversarial litigation, which further tests the political legitimacy of the system. The hyperinflation of membership also strains the workability of the system to its limits. For these reasons, the WTO as a 'negotiating' mechanism has severely malfunctioned since the late 1990s. This was evident at Seattle, between Seattle and Doha, and right through the DR. The only exceptions have been the Doha-Round launch and the July-2004 package, but neither delivered concrete results.

The activities of the individual players and coalitions in the WTO have evolved over time. Old and new features are worth mentioning. Looking at old features, the first observation is that the EU and US remain the two major players. Like the UR, the necessary but not sufficient condition for success in the DR and beyond is for both to contain domestic political difficulties, defuse bilateral conflicts and cooperate effectively. Second, following UR precedent, success in this round will require the effective participation of about 25 developed and developing members, already active in the WTO. Japan, Canada, Switzerland, Australia and New Zealand from the OECD and Brazil,

India, China and South Africa from the developing world need to be mentioned, apart from many other Latin-American and East-Asian countries. Third, multi-country coalitions will continue to be important. Broad-based, informal developed-developing country coalitions will be useful to share information and act as sounding boards for ideas (the 'chat-group' phenomenon); and even to resolve crises or give fresh impetus at strategic junctures, like the Swiss-Colombian coalition and the De-La-Paix Group during the UR. The drawback of these groups (such as Friends of the New Round and Friends of GATS) is they are too big and heterogeneous to forge common positions.

Perhaps more important will be small, discrete, issue-based developed-developing country coalitions. The Cairns Group is the pathfinder in this respect, although one cannot expect such formal and relatively tight-knit coalitions in other negotiating areas. Embryonic Friends Groups already exist, for example, in services, industrial goods, anti-dumping, subsidies and trade facilitation. These are noticeably weaker than they were during the UR. They need to be more coherent and proactive if the round is to advance. Not least, they are an important counter to the UN-isation of the WTO that threatens to stop all effective decision-making in its tracks.

Looking at new features, the first novel element is that the active, 'first-division' developing countries will be negotiating with each other and other developing countries, especially on the tariff and non-tariff barriers (henceforth NTBs) that throttle South-South trade. During the UR, the active developing countries tended to go head-to-head with developed countries but not with each other. That is changing—faster through bilateral and plurilateral FTA negotiations, and more slowly in the WTO. Malaysia and China, for instance, have their sights on the relatively high barriers that impede access to the Indian market.

The second novel element is the more active participation of many developing countries, including traditionally weaker ones, and even some LDCs, than during the previous rounds. These countries are too small or weak to sustain effective participation on their own, so they have been coming together in common-characteristic coalitions such as the Africa, ACP and LDC Groups, and the G90.

However, there are distinct limits to the active participation of 'second-division' and 'third-division' developing countries with limited-to-very-limited trade policy capacity, even in coalition-formation. True, their coalitions have been playing a more prominent role in the preparation for and at recent Ministerial Conferences. They were broadly constructive in Doha and in putting together the July-2004 framework, but were very negative in Cancun. They came to Cancun with a long list of demands, but without credible negotiating proposals of their own. Their tactics resembled those of the UN more than those of the old GATT. Given shortcomings in policy capacity, these countries are likely to remain followers, not initiators and proactive players, in future multilateral forums. This applies particularly to the LDCs, but also (though to a less extreme extent) to large low-income countries like Pakistan, Egypt, Kenya and Nigeria. All may have more 'negative' bargaining power than before, i.e. the ability and willingness to block agreement, but they will not have significant 'positive' bargaining power for the foreseeable future.

Third, smaller, defensive coalitions among developing countries have become more prominent. These include the G15 and Like-Minded Group (LMG), involving India, African countries and some ASEAN members. They took defensive positions in the run-up to Seattle and Doha, and prioritised implementation, S&D and TRIPS-and-public-health issues. Another example is the G33, formed on the eve of Cancun to campaign for the exemption of 'special products' from overall agricultural liberalisation. There is little doubt that these groups have made decision-making more complicated and halted the progress in core market-access negotiations.

Fourth, some regional coalitions that were effective during the UR (e.g. EFTA, the Nordic Group, ASEAN) are no longer extant or are much-weakened.

Fifth, the emergence of the G20 is clearly the big news in recent WTO coalition-formation. It was formed on the eve of Cancun and brought together India, Brazil, China and South Africa, as well as other developing-country members of the Cairns Group from Latin America and east Asia, plus Pakistan, Egypt and Nigeria. It was and remains a one-issue grouping whose central target is developed-country agricultural protection. Its position in Cancun was one of extreme offence and extreme defense: it pressed for significantly greater developed-country liberalisation as a precondition for meaningful liberalisation of own markets. Despite large internal differences, notably between Brazil's export interests and India's protectionist interests, the G20 has held together and become a major influence in the WTO.[5] Apart from putting extra pressure on trade-distorting farm subsidies in OECD countries, it played a crucial part in creating the July-2004 negotiating framework. Beyond this it has anchored the agricultural market access negotiations in 2005, with both the US and EU converging to its positions. It remains to be seen whether it will be similarly successful when it comes to domestic support.

Prospects for the Doha Round: The Longer-term Future of the WTO

To conclude the DR successfully, and to ensure the long-term relevance of the WTO, member-governments need to do two things: first, rediscover a core purpose; and second, revive an effective negotiating mechanism.[6]

To begin with, the WTO needs to rediscover a core purpose, something lost in the post-GATT transition. This should be the old GATT's *raison d'être*: the progressive reduction and removal of barriers to trade, underpinned by reasonably simple, transparent and non-discriminatory rules based on the Most-Favoured-Nation and National-Treatment principles (as embodied in GATT Articles I and III). At the same time, WTO members—especially the two majors, the EU and US—should stop overloading the negotiating agenda with multiple and conflicting objectives. This means steering clear of excessive standards harmonisation and regulatory intrusionism, nowadays especially on environmental and other product- and process-related standards. Excessive legalisation should also be avoided: dispute settlement should not drift into an exercise in judicial policymaking. Market access is (or should be) the bread and butter of the DR. Hence negotiations on core market access in

5. Narlikar and Tussie argue that the G20 has successfully combined developing country dissatisfaction with the dominance of developed countries in rule-setting in the multilateral trading system, and a single 'deal-breaking' issue, i.e. the agricultural negotiations. They raise the possibility (explored below) that, given these characteristics, and if the agricultural logjam is solved, it may morph into other areas. See Amrita Narlikar and Diana Tussie "Bargaining Together in Cancun: Developing Countries and Their Evolving Coalitions", 2003, *mimeo*.

6. This section draws on Razeen Sally, "The End of the Road for the WTO? A Snapshot of International Trade Policy after Cancun", *World Economics* 5,1, January-March 2004, pp. 9-13. *www.world-economics-journal.com*; and "Trade Policy and International Order: Imperium, Dominium and the Limits of multilateralism", *mimeo*.

agriculture, non-agricultural goods and services are far more important for development than all other aspects of the DR put together and should be given top priority.

Mending the WTO's broken negotiating mechanism depends, in the first instance, on intergovernmental political will, not so much on the reform of formal decision-making procedures. This is crucial if the WTO is to refocus on market access, where the real development gains lie, and avoid further drift.

The spirit of the Doha Ministerial Declarations is that the developing countries can and should participate proactively in collective decision-making, with the help of technical assistance and associated 'capacity-building' provided by international organisations and national donors. This notion is fanciful, not to say Utopian. Many developing countries have intractable domestic problems, not least chronic misgovernment that often descends into ethnic strife, civil war and state collapse. Competent and experienced trade officials and negotiators are scarce. These countries might be able to join common-characteristic coalitions, but, given their membership of failed, failing and weak states, it is, frankly, starry-eyed to see these coalitions as a serious negotiating force in the foreseeable future.

The silver lining is that there are about 20-25 first-division developing countries with increasing trade policy capacity that are increasingly integrated into world trade-and-production networks and have accumulated considerable trade-negotiating experience dating back to the UR. They have high-profile permanent representatives to the WTO and well-staffed Geneva missions. They are active in WTO-committee work, negotiations and dispute settlement.

Pragmatically, the key liberalising and rule-making deals in the WTO must be done by the 30-plus countries (counting the EU as one) that account for around 90 per cent of international trade and foreign direct investment.[7] This core group must concentrate first on market access in agriculture, non-agricultural goods and services. After the DR, new issues (such as the Singapore issues and trade-and-environment) should be dealt with plurilaterally through opt-ins or opt-outs. This would give developing countries the flexibility to join negotiations only if and when they feel ready to do so. Within this

7. Wolf, Martin, (2003), "The Abominable No-men Menacing World Trade", *Financial Times* 24th September.

core of 30-plus, there is an inner core of the developed- and developing country majors: the US, EU, India, Brazil and China (with South Africa on the margin). Their constructive leadership is vital. Without it, nothing will move.

Post-UR, positions have shifted within this inner core. First, Brazil, India and China are becoming noticeably more powerful. Second, the old understanding of an EU-US duopoly driving the GATT/WTO enterprise no longer works. Its last gasp was the failed attempt to pass a joint EU-US agricultural framework before Cancun (which triggered the formation of the G20). The leadership credentials of the EU are on the decline owing to its too defensive position on agriculture and too offensive position on environmental standards and other issues. Up-front US leadership, but only in tandem with 'genuinely' two-way 'coalitions of the willing' could be a better outcome.

The remaining 100-or-so developing countries should be accorded generous S&D. Through MFN, they should have rights to whatever liberalisation is negotiated by others; and preferably duty- and quota-free access to OECD and leading developing- country markets. At the same time, they should not be obliged to reciprocate, nor should they be under pressure to sign up to other new obligations. There could be a 'peace clause' on dispute settlement: an understanding that they will not be taken to court, even if in breach of existing obligations. Finally, WTO members could settle on a 'graduation' principle: an understanding that if countries reached a certain level of development, they would be expected to participate in reciprocal negotiations and adhere to stronger rules and obligations. However, these terms should be conditional on the countries concerned not blocking overall negotiating progress. They must be left in no doubt that, as free-riders, they will be on the sidelines, not at the centre of decision-making.

Practical politics dictates that such a two- or multi-tier configuration should not be expressed in formal WTO decision-making procedures. That would be unacceptable to the majority of the membership outside the charmed circle. It would be needlessly divisive. Rather the key decisions must be taken 'informally' in smaller, self-selecting groups, followed by broader multilateral consultations and some (but not unlimited) diplomatic give-and-take. It is probably expedient to preserve a multilateral veneer, but it will take realpolitik, behind the scenes to revive decision-making effectiveness.[8]

The unexpected progress in attempts to revive the DR in July 2004 broadly reflects the small club-like pattern sketched above. First, the event took place through a US initiative, 'not' a joint EU-US initiative: without US Trade Representative Robert Zoellick's letter to WTO members suggesting ways of putting a negotiating framework together, nothing would have happened. Second, the key discussions were confined to a small coterie—essentially the major powers—well away from the WTO circus in Geneva. Agriculture has, as usual, been the centre of attention; and it was the US, EU, the G20 majors, especially Brazil and India, and Australia (on behalf of the Cairns Group) that dominated the discussions.[9]

Asymmetries in decision-making are already reflected in a new approach to S&D, with the EU offer to give the G90 a free ride in this round. Critics point out that the G90 has been miscategorised, including countries (such as South Africa and Mauritius) that are not in the least-developed or low-income brackets. Its classification also smacks of constitutional formality, which is unnecessarily divisive and may obstruct progress. An informal, flexible approach may be more savvy: the general principle of treating developing countries differentially should be accepted; but the extent of S&D given to particular countries could be left to negotiations. In sum, if the WTO as a negotiating forum is to retain relevance beyond the DR, its members must negotiate agreements that are specific, focused and enforceable, not ones that are all things to all constituencies.

The viability of many of the old and new coalitions mentioned above depends substantially on the behaviour of the developing-country majors: China, India, Brazil and (to a lesser extent) South Africa. The influence of the first three in the WTO is increasing all the time, which is but a reflection of their growing political and economic power in the world.

---

8. For a detailed consideration of controversies around this issue, and strong argument in favour of "mini-ministerials" as a crucial manifestation of this imperative, see Robert Wolfe "Informal Political Engagement in the WTO: Are Mini-Ministerials a Good Idea?", forthcoming in Ciuriak, Dan and John M. Curtis, (eds.) *Trade Policy Research*, 2004: Ottawa: International Trade Centre.

9. See the following *Financial Times* articles: "Zoellick's Letter: Key Points", January 13th; "Zoellick set to call for all-out effort on Doha Round", May 10th; "Doha redivivus", May 11th; "Hopes Rising for Restart of Doha World-Trade Talks", May 15th/16th.

SECTION 2

Developing-Country Majors in the WTO

In this section, we focus on the developing-country majors in WTO negotiations and their participation in multi-country coalitions in the light of their overall trade policies and policymaking capacities.

China (in East-Asian Context)[10]

The massive trade-and-investment liberalisation over the last decade, first through enormous unilateral liberalisation 'before' WTO accession, and later supplemented by WTO commitments, is worth mentioning. Astounding trade-and-FDI numbers (e.g. a trade-to-GDP ratio of 70 per cent, with 60 per cent of trade generated by affiliates of foreign-owned firms) indicate that China is in the unique position of being the world's most populous country but with the real-economy openness of a small-to-medium-sized country.

China's strong WTO commitments exceed those of other developing countries by a wide margin and are often comparable with developed countries. These comparisons hold not only for tariff ceilings on goods (including agriculture), but also for border and behind-the-border NTBs in goods 'and' services. The Chinese implementation record so far is reasonably good, notwithstanding understandable hiccups and teething problems. China's unilateral reforms and WTO commitments, its integration into the global economy, and its clear-cut comparative advantage in labour-intensive manufactured exports, give it a strong market-access focus in the WTO. Paradoxically, this puts it in select company with small, open economies like Hong Kong, Singapore, Australia, New Zealand and Chile—all strong unilateral liberalisers that have big stakes in open

10. This section draws on Razeen Sally, "China's Trade Policies and its Integration into the World Economy", paper prepared for the *IGD/SAIIA SACU-China Workshop*, Johannesburg, 28th-29th September 2004. Also see Wolf, *Why Globalisation Works*, op cit., pp. 144-145, and his excellent columns on the China phenomenon in the *Financial Times*; Nicholas Lardy, *Integrating China into the Global Economy* (Washington DC: Brookings, 2002); Elena Ianchovichina and William Martin, "Economic Impacts of China's Accession to the World Trade Organisation", *World Bank Policy Research Working Paper 3053*, May 2003; Elena Ianchovichina and Will Martin, "Trade Liberalisation in China's Accession to the World Trade Organisation", *World Bank Policy Research Working Paper 2063*, June 2001; both at *www.worldbank.org*; Report of the Working Party on the Accession of China, the Draft Protocol on the Accession of the People's Republic of China, and attached Annexes with schedules of concessions on goods and services, all in WT/MIN(01)/3 at *www.wto.org*.

markets worldwide, underpinned by well-functioning, non-discriminatory rules. China is least interested to get into endless griping about injustices perpetrated by the North or Third-World solidarity; its primary goal is to ensure increased market access for products in which it has export advantage.

China operated in the DR discussions quietly but efficiently. It has been particularly careful not to antagonise the US–plainly evident in the charged atmosphere of Cancun. Its overall negotiating position is that, having already made such extensive liberalisation commitments, and with a sizeable implementation burden, it is not willing to concede much more in this round. It argues that newly acceded members of the WTO should be given special consideration in multilateral liberalisation formulas. This is alluded to in the Doha mandate; and it is specifically recognised in the Annexes on agricultural goods and non-agricultural goods in the July-2004 framework for future negotiations.[11] China's negotiating positions on specific issues are mixed: offensive here, defensive there, and in between here-and-there. Also, China is still in listening-and-learning mode as a new member of the club. That is one reason why it does not appear as publicly proactive as India and Brazil.

In the non-agricultural market-access negotiations, China's interests are manifestly offensive: it needs greater access for its manufactured exports. This is by far the main area where it is looking for multilateral liberalisation by developed and developing countries. On the contrary, China's positions are mixed on agriculture. Domestic compulsions restrict it from committing to substantial extra liberalisation. On the offensive side, it needs lower developed- and developing country tariffs, NTBs and agricultural subsidies in order to boost its agricultural exports. Hence despite joining G20, it maintained a low-key operation. It plays defensive in services, with few export interests; and is reluctant to concede to significantly

---

11. See *Proposal on Flexible Provisions for Recently Acceded Members*, *WT/MIN(03)W/8*, September 4 2003; *Ministerial Declaration*, *WT/MIN(01)/DEC/W/1*, November 14 2001; *Doha Work Programme: Decision Adopted by the General Council on 1 August 2004*, WT/L/579, all at *www.wto.org* . In the latter document, Annex A (*Framework for Establishing Modalities in Agriculture*) para. 47 states that: "The particular concerns of recently acceded members will be effectively addressed through specific flexibility provisions;" and Annex B (*Framework for Establishing Modalities in Market Access for Non-Agricultural Products*) para. 11 states that: "We recognise that newly acceded members shall have recourse to special provisions for tariff reductions in order to take account their extensive market access commitments undertaken as part of their accession and that staged tariff reductions are still being implemented in many cases. We instruct the Negotiating Group to further elaborate on such provisions."

stronger GATS commitments owing to domestic political sensitivities (though this would still leave it free to liberalise unilaterally). However, in some cases its existing GATS commitments even exceed those of developed countries (e.g. in maritime and audiovisual services, transparency obligations, and cross-border movement of business personnel).

One of China's biggest priorities concerns anti-dumping. It is active in the anti-dumping component of the rules negotiations and has tabled proposals, mainly with a view to removing, or at least diluting, its non-market-economy status (covered by GATT Article VI:I second para). China is flexible on Special and Differential Treatment. It defends developing countries' right to be treated preferentially, but it is far from extreme or militant viewpoint on the issue. It is equally flexible on the Singapore Issues. It kept its distance from the developing country militant tendency, led by India and Malaysia, right up to Cancun. It is comfortable with the July-2004 compromise to proceed with trade facilitation while leaving the other three issues (investment, competition policy and transparency in government procurement) out of negotiations.

Once China gets over the post-accession listening-and-learning phase, it should be more proactive in tabling proposals, cooperating with other majors, participating in large and small coalitions (such as the G20 and issue-based Friends Groups), helping to overcome inter-member differences and breaking logjams, and coming up with creative solutions. Its practical, diplomatic, problem-solving, system-supporting skills should be used more vigorously. Stronger US-China collaboration in the WTO would be particularly welcome.

China also has an active FTA strategy, directed mainly at its east-Asian neighbourhood. Its ambition is to displace Japan as the leading regional political and economic power. The China-ASEAN FTA, initiated by Beijing, is likely to be in place by 2010 (2015 for the new ASEAN members). The mini-FTA with Thailand and FTA with Hong Kong are already in place and discussions with newer potential partners are ongoing. China recently announced its preference for a pan-east Asian FTA encompassing 'ASEAN Plus Three' (the three being China, Japan and South Korea). China has also launched FTA initiatives outside the region, notably with South Africa.

A key component of China's FTA strategy is to get wider acceptance of 'market-economy status', especially with anti-dumping actions in mind. As mentioned earlier, China is pushing hard for removal of non-market economy status in the WTO, and bilaterally with the EU and US. A number of countries, including Singapore, Malaysia, Thailand and other ASEAN countries, New Zealand, Australia, Brazil and South Africa have already accorded China market-economy status.[12] It is not accidental that China is in or talking about FTA negotiations with the countries that have conceded market-economy status.

The contrast between China's FTA strategy and those of other powers in the region is instructive. Japan seems to be reacting to China's advance, but without a real strategy. Unlike China, it is defensive on agriculture and appears not to be interested in ambitious market-access coverage. Also in contrast to China, it seems to prefer bilateral deals with individual ASEAN countries. South Korea's profile is similar to Japan's. India is also hardly ambitious on market-access coverage and is pushing for restrictive rules-of-origin requirements. In all, China, not Japan, India, South Korea or ASEAN, is making the running on FTAs in Asia, with words and deeds.

India (in South-Asian Context)[13]

India is the most protectionist of the four developing-country majors in the WTO. The comparison with China is revealing. China's WTO-bound simple average tariff is 9.6 per cent (13 per cent on agriculture), and its average import-weighted tariff is under 7 per cent (less than 6 per cent now for manufactured goods). In contrast, India had an average applied tariff of 30.4 per cent (before tariff reductions in the last two years), with considerable tariff dispersion and escalation. Its WTO-bound average tariff is 50 per cent (much higher on agriculture), with many tariff lines unbound. China's commitments on classic NTBs on goods trade (export and import licensing, quotas, specific tendering requirements), trading rights, state-owned enterprises and state-trading enterprises, industrial and agricultural subsidies, are all stronger than India's. China's GATS commitments are very strong compared with India's weak commitments. Equally

12. "China Full Market Economy: ASEAN", *Straits Times*, September 7, 2004.

13. This section draws on Razeen Sally, "ASEAN in the WTO: Prospects of Cooperation with India ," and Anwarul Hoda's companion chapter, "India in the WTO: Issues, Challenges and Prospects of Cooperation with ASEAN", in Nagesh Kumar, Rahul Sen and Mukul Asher (eds.), *India-ASEAN Economic Relations: Meeting the Challenges of Globalization* (RIS: New Delhi and ISEAS: Singapore, 2005). We have benefited much from Professor Hoda's seasoned and measured observations.

strong are China's transparency obligations (on notification, enquiry points, time for review and comment), buttressed by administrative- and judicial-review mechanisms.

While the other three developing-country majors are generally pragmatic and flexible, balancing offensive and defensive positions, but with discrete market-access priorities to advance, India is defensive almost across-the-board. Its one offensive position—on GATS Mode-4 commitments for the cross-border movement of skilled personnel—has been lost in a fog of inflexible, defensive positions on market access, implementation, S&D and the Singapore issues. It is perhaps the chief obstacle to meaningful South-South negotiations on market access, limiting flexibility in the G20's negotiating position on agriculture.

There are signs that this unflattering state of affairs may be about to change. Indeed, some of India's negotiating positions have budged a little. It has not taken an especially hard line on exempting Special Products from overall agricultural liberalisation (unlike Indonesia and the Philippines in the G33). It supported the Girard Formula for tariff cuts on non-industrial goods and crafted bold offensive positions in the GATS negotiations, on the back of new comparative advantage in services such as software and outsourced BPOs.

An optimist would argue that India is gradually shedding its traditional scepticism of multilateral liberalisation, which would fit logically with the progressive opening of the Indian economy since 1991, and the recent acceleration of trade, FDI and related economic reforms (such as privatisation and the deregulation of services sectors). Most visibly, the maximum industrial tariff has been brought down to 15 per cent, with the intention of streamlining it into three bands (0-5-15 per cent) in due course. One hopes that accelerating unilateral reforms will, in the not-too-distant future, lead to a decisive shift of positions in the WTO, bringing India closer to the flexibility and pragmatism displayed by the other developing-country majors. This would send powerful signals to other WTO members. It has the potential to change coalition dynamics between developing countries and across the developed-developing country divide. However, its track record of alliances in the WTO remains overwhelmingly defensive, e.g. on S&D and implementation in the Like-Minded Group and the G15, on the Singapore issues with Malaysia and others, and on emergency safeguards in services. These are marginally offset by its participation in the G20, and an emerging offensive coalition with the US on services.

India is pursuing a number of new FTA initiatives, and is more proactive in its south-Asian backyard, especially with SAFTA. An FTA with ASEAN is to be concluded by 2011; a Framework Agreement with Thailand already in place; and negotiations with Singapore are to be concluded soon. Exploratory talks are on with others, notably MERCOSUR and China. However, it is broadly unlikely that India would be more flexible on market access in FTA negotiations than it is in the WTO.[14]

Brazil (in South-American Context)

Despite being a GATT founder-member, Brazil until the UR played a defensive role. This was rooted in its ISI development strategy, from the 1960s to the mid-1980s, in accordance with which tariffs were high, and the state actively promoted 'winners' through targeted financial and infrastructure support. For much of this period Brazil's export profile was concentrated on a small basket of primary products, notably coffee and various minerals. Therefore Brazil did not have an identifiable set of offensive interests that could be traded off for access to the Brazilian market at the expense of the ISI strategy. Also support for South-South alliances with a view to altering the terms of economic engagement with the North was predominant, and Brazil actively sought out key allies in the developing world that shared its vision. Consequently Brazil's approach to the GATT negotiations, in tandem with India and Egypt and consecrated in the G10 alliance, was to seek S&D from the developed countries in the form of preferences and wholesale opt-outs from negotiated agreements.

The scenario changed after the Tokyo Round when the US insisted on reciprocity for developing countries and graduation for more advanced developing countries based on per capita GDP, which was strengthened in the UR.[15] Despite initial resistance, as their offensive

14. If the unfolding SACU-India FTA is any guide, India will not give much away. See Phil Alves "Understanding Indian Trade Policy: Implications for the Indo-SACU Free Trade Agreement", *SAIIA Trade Policy Report* No. 5, November 2005 available at *www.saiia.org.za*. Also see Julius-Sen "Negotiating Trade Agreements with India: The Reality Below the Waterline", *SAIIA Trade Policy Briefing* No. 8, November 2005 also available at *www.saiia.org.za*.

15. This paragraph is based on Marcelo de Paiva Abreu, "Trade Liberalization and the Political Economy of Protection in Brazil Since 1987", Inter-American Development Bank, *INTAL-ITD Special Initiative on Trade and Integration, Working Paper 08b*, April 2004, pp. 3-5.

interest in the inclusion of agriculture in the GATT grew, it joined the Cairns Group alliance with Australia on the understanding that provisions on S&D would be preserved. Furthermore, mounting domestic economic problems caused Brazil to move for FDI-attracting export-promotion as well as cheap imports, and so Brazil signed up to the UR's Single Undertaking, happy with the 'new style' S&D it contained. It also coincided with the brief, intense and successful liberalisation of the economy between 1990 and 1994. Strategic partnership in the South through regional consolidation, ultimately in the form of MERCOSUR,[16] was regarded as an important step. Three goals were identified:[17] a managed and balanced expansion of bilateral trade; promoting bilateral investment flows in key economic sectors; and promoting cooperation in areas of critical importance for joint economic development such as energy, transport and technology. Sectoral agreements were initially seen as the primary instrument for pursuing these goals, particularly the capital goods sector which was regarded as the strategic nucleus. However, MERCOSUR later became the regional vehicle for implementing the new agenda through wider and deeper tariff reductions.

The Brazilian liberalisation episode suffered substantial reversal from 1994, with successive financial crises in Mexico, Brazil and Argentina contributing to the anti-liberalisation backlash. This took the form of reassertion of powerful sectoral interests mediated through sectoral chambers coordinated by the Industry Ministry. They were successful in rolling back liberalisation gains in particular sectors, notably the automotive industry and sub-sectors of agriculture.[18]

Accordingly, MERCOSUR has not progressed towards further trade liberalisation since 1995, but focuses on external relations and building internal coordination mechanisms. In its external engagements, the bloc now rejects special treatment for less developed countries, sustaining the principles of symmetry and reciprocity, and rejects 'WTO plus' commitments—especially in the unfolding Free Trade Area of the Americas (FTAA) negotiation.[19] So far, therefore,

16. Formally created by the Treaty of Asunción, signed on March 26th, 1991.

17. Alcides Costa Vaz, *Trade Strategies in the Context of Economic Regionalism: The Case of Mercosur*, Centre for Latin American Studies, University of California, Berkeley, June 2003, Paper No. 4, pp. 4-5.

18. Abreu, *op.cit.*, p. 26.

19. Vaz, *op.cit.* p. 21.

the FTAA (and to a lesser extent MERCOSUR'S negotiations with the EU) has not undermined processes of regional integration in South America as some critics had feared; rather it may be reconfiguring an arrangement that may well have blown apart in the absence of powerful external impulses.[20]

Crucially, the primacy of agricultural exports to Argentina and Brazil[21], and the unwillingness of both the US and the EU to consider reforming their agricultural subsidy regimes outside the WTO context, underpin Argentinean-Brazilian participation in the G20. In fact the WTO is the most important vehicle for Brazil to achieve its goals regarding liberalisation of agricultural trade. The slow progress over agriculture in the DR is the primary reason why both the FTAA and EU talks have not advanced and are unlikely to do so until the Doha gridlock has been unravelled.[22]

From the early 1990s up to Cancun, Brazil's pragmatic diplomacy in the GATT/WTO concentrated on trading off defensive positions on industrial goods and services to gain concessions on agriculture. Coalition activity centred on the Cairns Group, in which Brazil played a very prominent role alongside Australia. This changed with the formation of the G20, which has taken centre-stage in Brazil's WTO diplomacy. Brazil's leadership of the G20 alliance at and beyond Cancun, in collaboration with India and, more recently, South Africa and China, should be seen as the culmination of a two-prong strategy: reinvigorating South-South cooperation with a view to changing the rules of the game and opening new markets,[23] and negotiation of agricultural trade concessions with major trading partners through introducing additional leverage.

So far the G20 has been successful in bringing agriculture to the forefront of the Doha agenda, although its ultimate results still have to be determined. Much depends on Brazil's leadership of G20, and

---

20. For more on this issue see Nicola Phillips, "Reconfiguring Subregionalism: The Political Economy of Hemispheric Regionalism in the Americas", IPEG Papers in *Global Political Economy* No. 4, April 2002.

21. See Marcos Sawa Jank, "The Risks of Success", 04th May, 2004, at *www.iconebrasil.org.br.*

22. For more details see João Bosco M. Machado and Galeno Ferraz, "FTAA: Assessments and Perceptions of the Brazilian Government and Production Sectors", *Red Mercosur FTAA Series Brief No. 8*, July 2003, *www.redmercosur.net*; and Alexander Zourabichvili, "Brazil's Position in the Free Trade Agreement of the Americas Negotiation Process", *SAIIA Trade Policy Briefing No. 5*, February 2004, *www.saiia.org.za.*

23. On the latter see "China Begins to Exert its Influence on Latin America", *Financial Times*, 26th September, 2003.

the interaction of the latter with the Cairns Group (the two having significant overlapping membership). Brazil's willingness to act pragmatically, to compromise and trade-off, will be critical to achieve a breakthrough.

South Africa (in Southern-African Context)

Despite having been a founder-member of the GATT, South Africa is a new actor on the global stage. During the pre-UR period, its application of the ISI model extended to establishment of strategic industries with paramount military and security considerations. Accordingly, openness to trade was not really on the agenda.[24] Consequently, South Africa's conduct in the GATT could best be characterised as defensive. This framework changed in the late 1980s as moves towards a political settlement gathered pace. These developments took place as the UR unfolded. South Africa committed to a major overhaul (simplification and liberalisation) of its complex tariff regime, and signed up fully to the Single Undertaking. Special and Differential did not play a role during this period owing to the fact that South Africa was regarded as a developed country and the Apartheid government firmly regarded itself as playing in that league. Under-girding South Africa's commitments and participation in the UR was the strong need to overcome the isolation of the 1980s and the need to promote economic competitiveness. This culminated in more rapid liberalisation of tariffs than required in terms of South Africa's GATT bindings.

Given that the UR was complete when the ANC came to power in 1994, the trade liberalisation trajectory turned to bilateral and regional tracks. Relations with the EU were high on the agenda, given the preponderance of EU markets in South Africa's export basket. When the government realised that the EU was not going to grant it full access to Lomé preferences, it decided to negotiate a comprehensive agreement covering trade, aid and political cooperation.[25] A four year-long negotiation resulted a final agreement covering 'substantially all trade' and was asymmetrical in two respects: EU markets were opened first, and to approximately 95 per cent of

24. For an overview of this period see Trevor Bell, "Trade Policy", in Jonathan Michie and Vishnu Padayachee (eds.) *The Political Economy of South Africa's Transition*. London: The Dryden Press, 1997.

25. Signed in October 1999, this was known as the Trade, Development and Cooperation Agreement.

South African exports *versus* 85 per cent in return.[26] This experience, and the new government's policy trajectory in support of developing countries, constituted a substantive shift from the previous government's general approach to trade negotiations. However, many ACP states were concerned about the precedent this agreement set for the future of their relations with the EU, given the unfolding Economic Partnerships Agreement negotiations taking place under the Cotonou Convention. This unfortunate situation sowed seeds of distrust in the Africa Group regarding South Africa's intentions with respect to its broader trade relations strategy.

The second pillar of the regional/bilateral strategy was negotiations with the countries of the Southern African Development Community (SADC) to form an FTA. Approximately one-third of South Africa's manufacturing exports go to SADC countries, hence locking in market access was a key motivation. Once again, these negotiations proved divisive, given the presence in the region of the Community of Southern And Eastern African States (COMESA) and associated overlap in memberships. South Africa's decision to opt for SADC over COMESA was widely resented by many countries in the region, which came to the view that South Africa simply wanted to work with a grouping it could dominate.[27] This experience, coupled with the new government's subsequent support for launching the new round of multilateral negotiations notwithstanding generalised resistance in the Africa Group, has bequeathed a legacy of mistrust of the South African government's intentions in the region. Nonetheless, the FTA was concluded in 2000, and was also asymmetrical along the lines of the negotiations with the EU, excepting that South Africa opened first and more comprehensively, with many countries in the region backloading their liberalisation schedules.

The third dimension was renegotiation of the Southern African Customs Union (SACU) agreement as the basis for the global strategy. Talks were concluded in 2001, and the agreement came into force in July 2004. This agreement is of historic significance as it commits South Africa to effectively ceding sovereignty over trade policy

26. For details and analysis see Talitha Bertelsman-Scott, Greg Mills and Elizabeth Sidiropoulos, "The EU-SA Agreement: South Africa, Southern Africa, and the European Union", South African Institute of International Affairs, January 2000.

27. In it's defense it is important to note that the region was, and remains, divided on which regional grouping was better suited to promote regional economic integration. Thus the situation was not of the South African government's making.

formulation and implementation to new inter-governmental institutions, which have yet to be established. In essence, all decisions over tariffs and trade remedies will be taken at the SACU level by a Council of Ministers, advised in turn by a new SACU tariff body and a commission of senior officials. If faithfully implemented, SACU decision-making will be democratised. However, it is worth recalling a saying: "MERCOSUR operates on the basis of consensus. But there cannot be consensus without Brazil!" Given South Africa's centrality to the new revenue sharing formula through which the BLNS (Botswana, Lesotho, Namibia, Swaziland) countries will continue to be subsidised, and its economic dominance in SACU, it is unlikely that anything substantially different will be obtained here.

The fourth dimension is negotiation of new FTAs. These are divided into two tracks. Track one is currently underway, and covers the US, MERCOSUR, and the European Free Trade Association. Track two targets Asian countries, including India, China, Singapore, South Korea, and Japan. Negotiations with the US in particular have run into serious difficulties concerning trade liberalisation in general and the latter's 'WTO-plus' approach to trade negotiations.[28] To some extent it also reflects the South African government's desire, in common with Brazil, to pursue strong alliances with key developing countries in order to balance US power. The G20 alliance in the WTO was therefore a natural geopolitical one for the South African government and may have served this purpose more than the desire to promote agricultural market access. The latter is important, but hardly critical, to South Africa's export trajectory, accounting for a small proportion (approximately 10 per cent) of the overall export basket, whilst agriculture constitutes a smaller proportion of GDP.

Of far greater importance is securing access to markets for South Africa's burgeoning intermediate manufacturing exports, and liberalisation of services sectors to enhance South Africa's outward investment thrust into African markets in particular. The manufacturing export interest pits South Africa directly against the G90 which favours continued preferential access to developed country markets.[29] The

---

28. See Peter Draper and Mills Soko "US Trade Strategy After Cancun: Implications, and Prospects for the SACU-US FTA", *SAIIA Trade Policy Report No. 4*, February 2004, *www.saiia.org.za* and Peter Draper "The SACU-US FTA: In Search of a Contract Zone", *The Exporter* (Business Day supplement), June 2004.

29. See Minister Erwin's speech to parliament on September 26th for a strong statement of this view.

services interest, on the other hand, somewhat perplexingly pits South Africa against the Africa group.[30] Meanwhile S&D and the implementation agenda—priorities for the G90 and associated common-characteristic coalitions—have received persistent rhetorical lip-service but little sustained support from South Africa. Overall, therefore, South Africa's offensive agenda pits it against the ACP-LDC and Africa groupings and places it firmly in the ranks of the G20 and, to a lesser extent, the Cairns Group.

Conclusions

Our overall picture is of drift and crippled decision-making in the WTO, at least since Seattle. The July-2004 framework is little more than a holding operation. A market-access focus and the restoration of businesslike decision-making are needed to conclude the DR and secure the WTO's future as a viable trade-negotiating forum.

Defensive, one-sided pan-developing-country alliances are wrong in principle and unlikely in practice. The G77-type diverse alliances were logical in a world of import-substitution policies and the Cold War, but are illogical and archaic in the present setting. Like the UN General Assembly and UNCTAD, they serve little purpose but to highlight Northern iniquities and otherwise indulge in rhetorical flourishes.

Common-characteristic alliances among poor income developing countries, such as the Africa group, have more utility and are a more important feature in the WTO, especially at Ministerial Conferences. They bring legitimate issues to light, especially on developed-country agricultural protectionism (cotton subsidies, for instance). But, there are distinct limits, owing to a combination of overwhelmingly defensive positions (on tariff preferences, implementation, aid, and more generally on S&D), lack of negotiating capacity, and, underlying everything, bad policies and weak-to-terrible institutions at home. They can contribute to the WTO's decline by blocking operations, but are unlikely to be central players in finding constructive solutions.

30. The Africa group, representing countries in desperate need of foreign investment in core infrastructure services, should be encouraging its members to unilaterally liberalise such services whilst welcoming any FDI it receives—especially from neighbouring South Africa. Instead persistent complaints are made that South Africa is the new colonist on the block; whilst defensive positions on services are adopted in the WTO.

That leaves the WTO with a core of 30-plus developed and first-division developing countries, with an inner core of developed and developing country majors. As for the developing-country majors, we detect signs of convergence. All have switched to outward-oriented trade policies as part of market-based policy reforms; integrated faster into the world economy; exhibit more mature, constructive relations with the developed world—particularly with the US; and are trying to cement new alliances in the developing world, notably with each other. Finally, all are playing more forward-looking, 'system-maintaining' rather than 'system-wrecking' games in international institutions. It is one fundamentally novel feature that distinguishes the politics of the WTO from that of the GATT.

Arguably, China has mastered this foreign policy strategy better than the others, and is remarkably quick in doing so. It has been an exemplary WTO citizen, building on its huge market-based reforms, global economic integration and WTO commitments. Brazil and South Africa, with very different regional backyards, are also well positioned to pursue multiple coalition strategies, but they do not play this game as skillfully or as coherently as China. Internal divisions, regional tensions and contradictions, and vestigial North-*versus*-South ideological baggage, sometimes put them on the backfoot. On these occasions they unjustifiably defend protectionist positions, consequently compromising legitimate offensive export-market concerns. India is the laggard among the four, although its market-based reforms have come far since the early 1990s. But, at least until very recently, it has played the old, defensive North-*versus*-South game in the WTO —often in surreal disconnection to economic policies at home and 'high-politics' foreign policy. However, there are incipient and promising signs of change, with marginally less defensive positions on agricultural and NAMA, and noticeably more offensive positions on services.

If a successful outcome on agriculture were achieved, then a G20 model could conceivably work in other areas. According to some commentators, Brazil, India and South Africa could then find common ground on the NAMA negotiations, specifically resisting deep cuts in their respective industrial tariffs. Notwithstanding its offensive interests China is similarly reluctant to make further commitments in light of its extensive accession obligations. So a replication of the G20 alliance in the NAMA negotiations cannot be ruled out, if the common need to counter US and EU economic power persists.

Services negotiation by the G20 is another major possibility, in line with Brazil's apparent deal with India: Indian support in the agriculture negotiations will be reciprocated through Brazilian support in the GATS mode 4 negotiations. The arrangement may also find support from the ACP group, although given its current anti-immigration stance South African support is unlikely. It may be more forthcoming from China, which has an offensive position on mode 4 in the current services negotiations.

In sum, issue-based G20 alliances beyond agriculture are conceivable. The easiest option would be to construct defensive alliances on an Indian-Brazilian axis, e.g. on industrial goods and S&D. But this would diminish bargaining power overall and further polarise politics in the WTO. China would be highly unlikely to clamber aboard—unless external and internal circumstances conspire to bring about a *volte-face* in its economic and foreign policies. South Africa too would be sceptical. Offensive G20 alliances are conceivable too, but would have to overcome big protectionist obstacles in India and Brazil. Ideally, flexible and overlapping G20-style friendly formations would emerge on market-access and rules negotiating issues, alongside a mutually reinforcing interplay with the Cairns Group on agriculture.

4

Whither Trade Policies in Southeast Asia? The Wider Asian and Global Context[1]

RAZEEN SALLY and
RAHUL SEN

SECTION 1

Introduction

This chapter analyses trade policies in Southeast Asian countries in their wider Asian and global contexts. In essence, it not only compares and contrasts trade policies in individual Southeast Asian countries, but also analyses these policies in the context of regional and global economic integration, as well as the economic emergence of two other major Asian economies, China and India. The chapter first looks at recent trends in trade and FDI patterns in ASEAN. Then it summarises key trade-policy features in ASEAN countries, especially to get a sense of policy variety in the region and to see how policies have changed since the Asian crisis. Then follows an examination of ASEAN countries in international trade negotiations and agreements: first within ASEAN; second on cross-regional FTAs; and third in the WTO, especially in the Doha Round.

The discussion is organised as follows. Section 2 analyses the economic performance of ASEAN-6[2] countries in Asia and the global economy, focussing on trade and FDI flows. This is compared with basic economic-performance indicators for China and India. This sets up some economic implications of China's and India's rise for ASEAN. Section 3 provides an overview of trade policies among the individual ASEAN-6 economies, highlighting key similarities and differences.

---

1. The chapter has been re-printed from *ASEAN Economic Bulletin*, Vol. 22, No 1 (April 2005), pp. 95-115. We thank the publisher, Institute of Southeast Asian Studies, Singapore for giving us the necessary permission to re-print the article.
2. ASEAN-6 economies refer to Indonesia, Malaysia, Philippines, Thailand, Singapore and Vietnam.

Section 4 provides an assessment of ASEAN economic integration in terms of trade-and-investment policies geared to regional liberalisation, while Section 5 assesses the state of bilateral trade liberalisation initiatives involving ASEAN as a whole. Section 6 provides an assessment of the ASEAN-6 countries in the WTO. The final section (Section 7) highlights policy implications for the ASEAN-6 in pursuing trade policies on multiple tracks.

SECTION 2

ASEAN-6 in the Global Economy: Trade and FDI Inflows

Although the ASEAN-6 economies were growing at an average rate of 7.3 per cent during 1996, the triggering of the economic crisis in mid-1997 with the devaluation of the Thai Baht, seriously affected its growth prospects with all the ASEAN-6 economies except Vietnam, registering a negative growth rate for the year 1998 (Figure 4.1). Although most of the ASEAN-6 economies have now recovered from the crisis, the average growth rate of in 2003 was 4.2 per cent, far lower than the pre-crisis levels.

Figure 4.1

GDP Growth Rates (1996-2003)

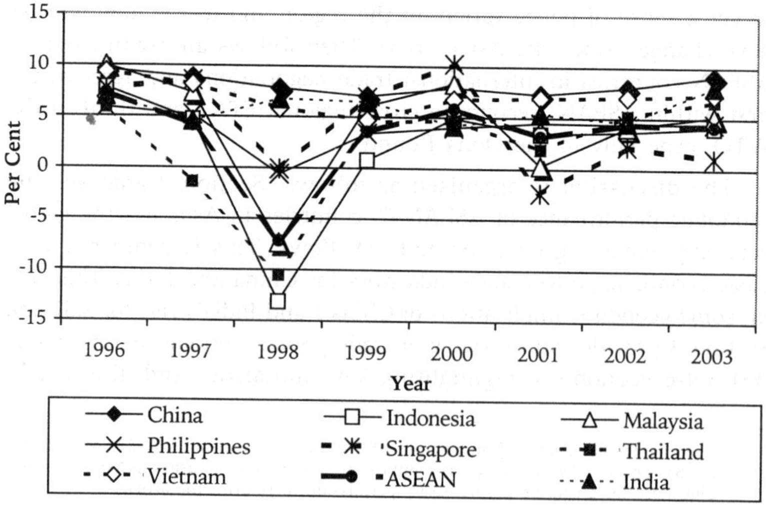

Source: ADB (2004).

In sharp contrast, the 1996-2003 period saw the economic emergence of China and the recent economic boom in India wherein two of Asia's largest economies registered a growth rate of 9.1 per cent and 8.1 per cent respectively in 2003. In particular, the average growth rate of the Chinese and the Indian economy over 1999-2003 was 7.9 per cent and 5.8 per cent compared to 4.2 per cent for the ASEAN-6 economies. Table 4.1 provides some selected macroeconomic indicators of the ASEAN-6 economies and also of China and India in 2003, given that economic developments in the latter are likely to have an indirect impact on the former. The following observations can be made:

(i) The ASEAN-6 economies constituted about 7 per cent of the world's population; and about 4 per cent of world income measured in Purchasing Power Parity (PPP) terms. However, on per capita basis, the income of these economies was close to quarter of the world's average in current value terms in 2003. In contrast, China accounted for more than a fifths of the world's population and about 12.5 per cent of the world's PPP GDP, but on a per capita basis, its income levels compared with the world average in current value terms was lower than that of the ASEAN-6 economies. The Indian economy constituted nearly 18 per cent of the world's population, but its PPP GDP was less than half of that of China in current value terms.

(ii) However, there are significant differences with respect to levels of economic development, domestic market size, and openness to the international markets among these ASEAN-6 economies, compared to China and India. Thus, while ASEAN-6 consists of a total population of about less than half of that of India it has the presence of one highly globalised entrepot, city-state economy, Singapore, which has a domestic market of only about 4 million, but with the highest level of per capita GDP.

(iii) The contrast is even more glaring when one observes the differences in the degree of openness of the ASEAN-6 economies and China and India, as indicated by the Trade/GDP ratio, and attractiveness to FDI inflows. It is observed that except for Singapore, which is a highly open-economy because of its entrepot status, five other economies in ASEAN are also significantly trade-oriented, with their trade ratios

Table 4.1

Important Economic Indicators of ASEAN-6, China and India in 2003

Countries	GDP (US$ bn.)	GDP Growth (%)	Population (mn.)	Per Capita GDP (US$)	PPP GDP (US$ bn.)	Merchandise Exports (US$ bn.)	Service Exports (US$ bn.)	Total Merchandise Trade (US$ bn.)	Services Trade (US$ bn.)	Trade/ GDP (%)	FDI Inflow (US$ bn.)	FDI/ GDP (%)
China	1409.0	9.1	1372.1	1026.9	6449.0	438.2	46.4	851.0	101.2	60.4	53.5	3.8
Indonesia	208.3	4.1	215.0	968.6	758.8	70.3	NA	112.4	NA	54.0	-0.6	-0.3
Malaysia	103.2	5.2	25.0	4118.5	207.8	117.9	13.5	217.0	30.8	210.4	2.5	2.4
Philippines	79.2	4.5	81.1	977.2	390.7	41.9	3.0	86.8	7.4	109.6	0.3	0.4
Singapore	91.3	1.1	4.2	21748.1	109.4	144.1	30.4	272.1	57.6	297.9	11.4	12.5
Thailand	143.2	6.7	64.0	2238.4	477.5	80.5	15.7	156.3	34.0	109.2	1.8	1.3
Vietnam	36.7	7.2	80.9	453.3	203.7	20.7	NA	45.7	NA	124.6	1.4	3.8
ASEAN-6	661.9	5.4	470.2	1407.5	2147.9	475.4	62.5	890.3	129.8	134.5	16.8	2.5
India	575.3	8.1	1073.0	536.2	3033.0	60.0	25.0	137.4	46.6	23.9	4.3	0.7
World	36252.7	3.8	6,379	5683.0	51480.0	7502.9	1796.5	15281.0	3578.9	42.2	560.0	1.5
Total	2646.2	–	2915.3	5627.3	11629.9	973.6	133.9	1878.7	277.7	–	74.6	–

Source: Computed from ADB (2004); WTO (2004).

almost close to or above 100 per cent of that of their GDP, compared to about 60 per cent in case of the Chinese economy. In comparison, the degree of openness in India has been about less than half of that of China's, indicating that the domestic market has largely driven the former's current economic surge.

(iv) The share of ASEAN-6 economies in total world FDI inflows was rather small (3.0 per cent) in 2003. In terms of FDI inflows, China attracted the highest amount of FDI inflows (about US $ 54 billion) among the Asian economies in 2003, with the ASEAN-6 (US $ 17 billion)[3] and India (US $ 4 billion) far behind. However, it is important to note here that the above data may not be directly comparable across these economies, as many of them report FDI inflows according to their country definitions, which may not necessarily be consistent with international standards.[4]

The remainder of this section briefly examines the economic interactions between ASEAN-6, China and India since the past decade, and briefly analyses the economic implications for ASEAN in the face of a rising China and a resurgent India.

Merchandise Trade

Figures 4.2a and 4.2b presents the shares of ASEAN-6 in world merchandise exports and imports compared to that of China and India over the past decade. It is observed that while the shares of ASEAN-6 have improved marginally in global merchandise exports, its share has declined by about a per cent in global merchandise imports, largely as a result of the crisis of 1997-98. In contrast, shares of both China and India have increased significantly over the period, with that of China's share in global merchandise exports more than doubling from 2.4 per cent to 5.8 per cent over the 1993-2003 period. However,

3. It is interesting to note that Singapore attracted nearly about US $ 11 billion in FDI inflows out of this total amount. The rest of it was directed largely towards Malaysia, Vietnam, Brunei, Philippines and Thailand.

4. For example, there are substantial differences with respect to reporting of FDI data by India and the above-mentioned economies. Thus, popular perceptions that China has been attracting nearly 20 times more FDI than that of India, needs to be carefully examined. Srivastava (2003) observed that FDI in China involves significant amount of round-tripping (and is thus overestimated), and the actual difference with Indian figures (which has been hitherto underestimated while comparing with IMF standards), could be just about 3-4 times. Notably, The Reserve Bank of India has recently revised India's FDI figures from the year 2001 to be consistent with IMF standards.

Figure 4.2a

Share in World Merchandise Exports (1993-2003)

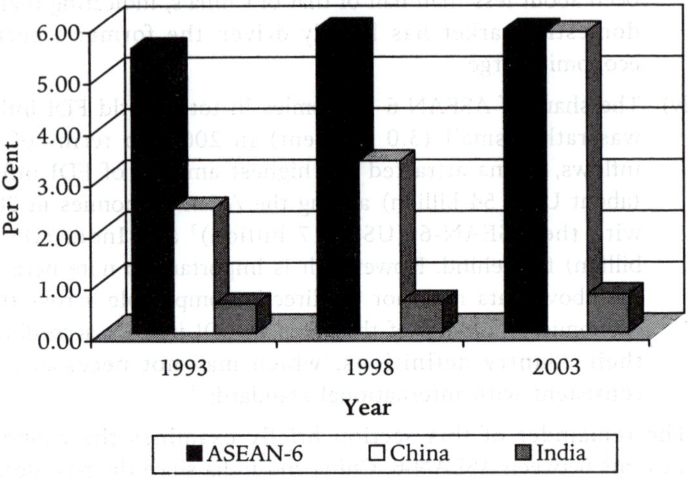

Source: WTO (2004).

Figure 4.2b

Share in World Merchandise Imports (1993-2003)

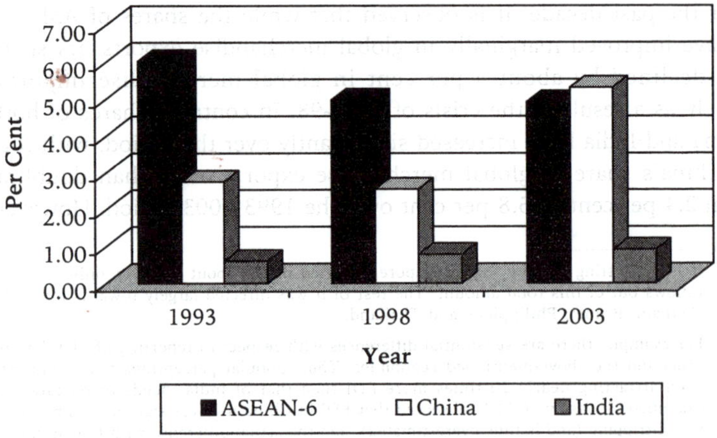

Source: WTO (2004).

Figure 4.3

Share of ASEAN's Exports and Imports with Selected Countries (1993-2003)

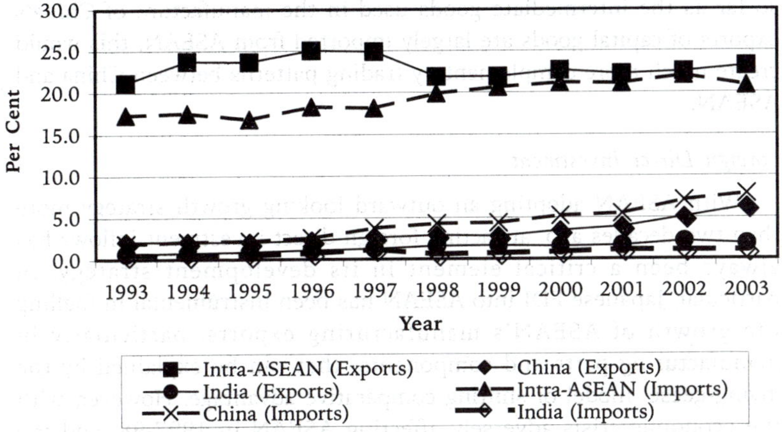

Source: ASEAN Secretariat (2004).

shares of India in global merchandise trade are still less than that of one per cent, indicating that its potential as a major player in global merchandise trade as yet remains underutilised.

Figure 4.3 analyses the trends in volume and share of bilateral merchandise trade between ASEAN, China and India over the period 1993-2003. It is observed that while the share of intra-ASEAN exports and imports have increased marginally over this period, there has been a significant growth in the share of ASEAN's trade with China and India. While China's share in ASEAN's exports has nearly tripled, its share in ASEAN's imports has more than quadrupled over the 1993-2003 period. Similar trends are also observed in case of ASEAN's trade with India, although the volume of its total trade in 2003 was only US $12 billion, compared to US $ 55 billion for ASEAN-China merchandise trade (ASEAN Secretariat, 2004). This indicates that with India's sustained economic growth and increased unilateral liberalisation, there is a huge untapped potential for expansion of ASEAN-India merchandise trade from the current levels.

In a recent study, Srivastava and Rajan (2004) observe that there has been a shift in composition of ASEAN-China merchandise trade towards manufacturing products during the past decade, and has led China to rapidly expand its production and export capacity in light manufactured products and in the assembly of parts and components of a limited number of capital goods, an area which directly competes with some lower and middle income ASEAN countries. However, in so far as the intermediate goods used in the manufacture of China's exports of capital goods are largely imported from ASEAN, this would create much more complementary trading patterns between China and ASEAN.

Foreign Direct Investment

With ASEAN adopting an outward looking growth strategy more than two decades ago, attracting foreign direct investment inflows has always been a critical element in its development strategy. In particular, Japanese FDI into ASEAN has been instrumental in fuelling the growth of ASEAN's manufacturing exports, particularly in manufacturing parts and components, that can be explained by the 'flying-geese' model of shifting comparative advantage. However, with the economic crisis adversely affecting ASEAN in 1997-98, and the Japanese economy experiencing prolonged periods of recession, Japanese FDI in ASEAN has declined significantly, which has led to an overall significant decline in FDI inflows into ASEAN. This is clearly shown in Figure 4.4 that presents the trends in FDI inflows into

Figure 4.4

FDI Inflows in ASEAN-6, China and India (1980-2003)

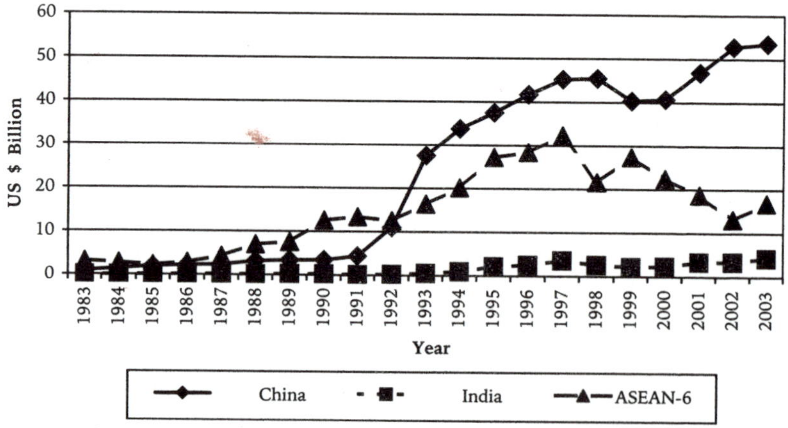

Source: UNCTAD (2004).

ASEAN-6 economies over the 1993-2003 periods, and compares it with similar trends in China and India.

It is observed that while ASEAN-6 economies experienced a surge of FDI inflows till 1997, the onset of the economic crisis in the region heralded the decline in FDI inflows to ASEAN-6 economies. Notably, the volume of inflows have nearly halved over the 1997-2003 period. While ASEAN-6 attracted more FDI inflows than China before 1993, the trend changed thereafter, with the latter now attracting more than triple the volume of FDI inflows than the former. However, it is to be noted that during the period 1993-97, while China's economic boom was in train, ASEAN-6 also continued to register an increasing volume of FDI inflows. It is only during the 1999-2003 period that ASEAN-6 is observed to experience a continuous decline in FDI inflows, while Chinese FDI flows have rapidly expanded. This leads one to believe that popular perceptions that China is gaining FDI at the expense of ASEAN may be suspect, since both economies were gaining up until the crisis hit the ASEAN economies.

While recording a comparably modest increase, the Indian economy has also begun to actively attract FDI inflows since economic reforms were introduced. Although the present volumes are much lower than that of ASEAN or China, further reforms could increase this volume significantly.

Available studies on bilateral FDI linkages between ASEAN, China and India indicate that while China is not a very significant investor in ASEAN, the reverse flows from ASEAN to China have increased significantly after the crisis of 1997-98. Available data on ASEAN's cumulative FDI into the PRC suggests a marked rise from about US$ 290 million in 1990 to over US$ 20 billion by 2000. Most of this has been directed towards the manufacturing sector, involving intra-firm trade by MNCs engaged in cross-border production sharing.

In contrast, the volume of FDI flows between ASEAN and India has been expanding only recently, with Malaysia and Singapore investors investing fairly aggressively in the Indian economy.[5] At the same time, with increased liberalisation of the external sector, Indian

5. Investments by ASEAN in India have been primarily in infrastructural projects such as roads and in the telecommunications, IT, ports, logistics, and the health care sectors (Sen, *et al.*, 2004).

companies are increasingly investing abroad. An important aspect to note is that since majority of FDI in India is directed towards the services sector, it is unlikely in the short-term to be a direct competitor of ASEAN for FDI in labour-intensive manufacturing industries. Further, with India being in a position to cooperate with ASEAN in diverse areas, from substantially lowering costs of essential drugs, including HIV-AIDS, to cooperation in food and energy security,[6] the huge potential for expansion of ASEAN-India investments is evident.

Economic Implications of China's Rise and India's Economic Resurgence for ASEAN

Although there has been several studies on the implications of the rise of China on the rest of Asia, including ASEAN, there continues to be sparse literature on the likely implications for ASEAN from the twin phenomenon of a continued rapidly growing Chinese economy, and the economic emergence of India. In this context, Srivastava and Rajan (2004) is one of the few studies that have attempted to examine these implications by analysing the comparative advantage positions of China and India not only in merchandise trade, but also in services trade. They have also examined the implications for FDI inflows in ASEAN. This section largely summarises some of their findings on this aspect, juxtaposing it with the existing literature.

First, it has been observed that there is indeed a high and growing degree of product overlap in the exports of China and ASEAN-5 to their major trading partners, *viz.* the US, suggesting increased export competition between the ASEAN-5 and China, in exporting to the U.S market. Further, studies using Revealed Comparative Advantage (RCA) indices at the 3-digit level over the 1992-98 periods have indicated that China's export structure appeared to be most similar to Malaysia in the final market for a number of 'finished' capital goods, *viz.* data processing equipment, telecommunications equipment and electrical machinery. In contrast, Thailand's export structure was found to be similar to that of China with respect to light manufacturing goods, *viz.* clothing, miscellaneous household equipment and electric machinery. In case of Indonesia, the only

6. See Sen, *et al.*, (2004) for further details on the range of possibilities for economic cooperation between ASEAN and India.

category that was found to exhibit export similarities with China was that of furniture (Shafaeddin, 2002, Table 9). However, these findings are insufficient to conclude that there is likely to be high export competition between ASEAN and China because of the fact that within each product category, traded goods are differentiated according to quality and brand or into sub-parts and components with differing factor intensities. It could well be that ASEAN countries have complementarities with China in production and export structures (i.e. vertical specialisation), while other parts are simultaneously competitive (horizontal specialisation). So far as India is concerned, comparative advantage patterns indicate that its manufacturing exports are more complementary than competitive with that of ASEAN, especially as it has hitherto not been a part of international division of labour involving exports of electronic parts and components in East Asia (Srivastava and Rajan, 2004).

Second, of particular concern is the impact on textiles and clothing exports from ASEAN, given that Chinese exporters are no longer going to be limited by the quantitative restrictions under the Multifiber Arrangement (MFA), which was phased out at the end of 2004. Indeed, studies using quantitative analysis have suggested that the removal of these quotas is likely to lead to a significant increase in the textile and clothing exports of both China and India at the expense of many Asian countries including those in ASEAN.[7] It is evident that will be non-negligible price pressures and adjustment cost effects on other textile and clothing exporting countries as a result of MFA abolition.

Third, China's continued economic rise is likely to trigger large shifts in comparative advantage for its other trading partners, thus necessitating large and sudden domestic adjustments. Hence, countries in ASEAN need to be aware of potential costs shifts in China and ensure constant industrial upgrading so as to remain competitive in the larger regional production network. Srivastava and Rajan (2004) therefore caution that a far more uncertain and competitive environment for ASEAN countries could develop, as China's western regions develop and labour intensive industries migrate to the inland regions, reducing the window of opportunity for lower income ASEAN members to upgrade to higher value added

7. See Adhikari and Yang (2002). Martin and Ianchoviachina (2001) and Francois and Spinanger (2001).

stages of production. Concomitantly, China's WTO accession commitments would also provide greater export-market opportunities for ASEAN countries.[8]

Fourth, increasing importance of international trade in commercial services presents a significant opportunity for ASEAN countries to gain from both China's WTO Accession and from India's economic resurgence, that has been largely fuelled by growth in its services sector. Notably, China's WTO accession is likely to fuel greater scope and demand for trade in services, and as it continues to rapidly urbanize and industrialise, there will invariably be vast opportunities for ASEAN businesses to be involved in major infrastructural development projects. Thus, richer and more developed ASEAN countries such as Singapore and Malaysia, which have growing strengths in these areas, should benefit significantly from the China's continued economic transformation. Travel and Tourism services are another major area of mutual gain for ASEAN and China, given the strong comparative advantage that most ASEAN economies enjoy in this area. A number of ASEAN countries such as Malaysia, Thailand and Singapore are taking specific steps to enhance their attractiveness as tourist destinations to Chinese residents. Studies such as Wu et al. (2002) have suggested that steps like ASEAN countries working in tandem or as clusters to promote the region as a whole would facilitate cooperation in tourism.

Concomitantly, India is increasingly becoming an important player in commercial services trade, both globally as well as in Asia. According to the WTO, India ranked the 6th and 7th largest exporter and importer of commercial services in Asia next only to China, and Singapore (among ASEAN-5 economies). Information and Communications Technologies (ICTs) and related services have been the main thrust of rapid expansion of services trade in India, accounting for three-fourths of commercial service exports in the year 2002 (World Bank 2004). Recent estimates have indicated that India enjoys a global comparative advantage in this area of service exports.[9] India's 2004-2009 Foreign Trade Policy envisages service exports to

8. This is be further illustrated by the argument by Adhikari and Yang (2002) that China's economic rise would fuel greater demand for agricultural and mineral products and raw materials—including energy products, forestry, agriculture and fishery and aquaculture products which is likely to benefit a number of resource rich countries in ASEAN *viz.* Indonesia.

9. See Srivastava and Sen (2004).

grow to US $ 150 billion by 2009, close to half of which is likely to be accounted for by software services. To the extent these targets are realised, India's global ranking in services trade is likely to improve further.

Indian companies are beginning to be globally competitive not just in ICT services. Indeed, recent years have seen more than 100 of the Fortune 500 companies setting up R&D or design centres in India. However, as noted by Asher and Sen (2005) and Sen *et al.*, (2004), firms from East Asia, including those from ASEAN, have been relatively less proactive in setting up such centres in India, and there are indeed significant economic opportunities to be tapped for firms from, Singapore, Malaysia as well as China to partner Indian firms in a wide range of commercial services from IT and logistics to tourism, healthcare, education and professional services.

Fifth, as shown in Figure 4.4, it would be incorrect to deduce that China's economic rise and India's economic resurgence will be the principal factors adversely affecting ASEAN's FDI prospects since FDI is not a zero-sum game that one country has to necessarily gain at the expense of the others. The possibility of direct competition between ASEAN and China on FDI inflows doesn't appear that significant, since the relatively sharp decline in ASEAN's FDI flows after 1998 was primarily due to the continuing economic crisis in Indonesia, the largest ASEAN member, where there was a sharp outflow of FDI between 1998 and 2000, due to domestic socio-political convulsions and investor uncertainty. Bhaskaran (2003) further states that stagnation in FDI flows to Malaysia in the late 1990s and early 2000 was also probably more due to policy uncertainty following the imposition of currency and capital controls in September 1998 than China's economic rise and its continued appetite for FDI. Thus, observed recent 'shifts' of FDI flows from ASEAN to China in relative terms is more likely due to the economic crisis in 1997-98 and resulting loss of confidence and structural weaknesses in the ASEAN economies.

It is however, important to caution that the current environment does involve a race for global FDI and if China and/or India are perceived by investors to be emerging as viable and promising investment alternatives, compared to other potential host countries with perceived economic and political weaknesses, the investors are likely to head towards the former. This implies that ASEAN economies would need to undertake domestic reforms to overcome its structural weaknesses in order to be more competitive and to be perceived globally as a comparable market for FDI *vis-à-vis* China and India.

Further, it is also important to note that the bulk of FDI inflows to ASEAN have been from Japan and the US, while in case of China, it has been overseas Chinese in Hong Kong and Taiwan who have been the major source of FDI inflows. In fact, a significant proportion of decline in ASEAN's FDI inflows has been due to decline in inflows from Japan, which was hitherto not an important investor in China. This also suggests that the possibilities of direct competition for FDI appears limited.

Finally, an important phenomenon that is likely to impact upon ASEAN's growth prospects would be the evolving economic linkages between China and India. Indeed, both countries are now focussing on opportunities for mutual gains and business interactions have intensified significantly in recent years. In fact, bilateral merchandise trade between India and China expanded more than four-fold from about US $ 1.7 billion in 1997-98 to about US $ 7 billion in 2003-04, with bilateral trade exceeding US $ 10 billion in the calendar year 2004. Further a joint study group has also been established to examine the feasibility of an economic partnership agreement between the two countries. These developments are likely to foster stronger economic ties between India and China, and ASEAN in the future will need to adapt its trade and other economic policies accordingly.

Last but not the least, is a distinct possibility of India following the Chinese strategy of aggressively attracting export-oriented FDI in its labour-intensive manufacturing sector in the near future. India is already emerging as an export hub for certain manufacturing products, particularly in auto parts and components, and is also likely to develop its capabilities in other areas of manufacturing as well. If that happens, ASEAN's competitiveness could well be adversely affected, as it would increase the possibility of direct competition for exporting from India and ASEAN to third countries that are its major trading partners, *viz.* US and the EU.

SECTION 3

National Trade Policies in ASEAN: Summary and Assessment[10]

Trade policy has become progressively more liberal in the last quarter-century as part of wider packages of economic policy reform. Indeed, a veritable trade-policy revolution has taken place across the developing world. However, this trend has been far from uniform. A minority of 'new globalisers' (the World Bank's terminology) has more liberal trade policies, improving institutions, greater global integration and higher growth rates. This is overwhelmingly an Asian phenomenon. In stark contrast, least-developed countries, mostly bunched in sub-Saharan Africa, have liberalised more modestly, and seen declining trade-to-GDP ratios as well as stagnant real incomes—all against the backdrop of failed or failing governments unable to provide even the most basic public goods.[11]

Southeast Asia clearly fits into the new-globalisation category. Major trade-and-investment liberalisation dates back to the 1980s, particularly in Malaysia, Thailand and Indonesia. Singapore and the Philippines were exceptions: in the former, export-led industrialisation and the return to liberal trade policies took place earlier; in the latter, substantial trade-and-investment liberalisation had to wait until the 1990s. Vietnam started opening its borders as part of its transition from Plan to Market from the late 1980s.

The Asian crisis changed matters somewhat. True, trade, FDI and other liberalisation measures were not reversed. Indeed, Singapore, Thailand and Indonesia went further in a liberalising direction—in the latter two countries induced by IMF structural adjustment programmes. But, with the exception of Singapore, government enthusiasm for further liberalisation declined markedly. This was reinforced by powerful interests keen to protect their markets against

10. This section draws on Razeen Sally, *Southeast Asia in the WTO* (Singapore: ISEAS, 2004b).

11. World Bank (2002). *Globalisation, Growth and Poverty: An Inclusive Agenda for the World Economy*, Washington DC/Oxford: World Bank/Oxford University Press, especially Table 1.1. Also see Wolf, Martin, Why *Globalisation Works*, New Haven: Yale University Press, 2004, pp. 142-143.

foreign competition, and a populist backlash of sorts against globalisation in general.

On the other hand, the rapid opening of China and its accession to the WTO have concentrated southeast-Asian minds. China's rise has led to fear that Southeast Asia will lose out, especially in the market for FDI. The emergence of India, though slower and less dramatic than that of China, has begun to exert a similar effect. That, to a large degree, explains the proliferation of FTA initiatives in the region. But will the China-and-India effect spark further substantial trade-and-FDI liberalisation and regulatory reform in Southeast Asia, akin to the liberalisation waves of the 1980s and early 1990s? That remains to be seen.

The remainder of this section focuses on the countries under discussion one by one.

Singapore

Singapore, after Hong Kong, has the world's most liberal trade policies and is the world's most globalised economy (Table 4.2). Unilateral liberalisation and domestic regulatory reform, especially since the Asian crisis, have reduced protectionist barriers in some services sectors.

Since 1999 bilateral, cross-regional FTAs have occupied centre-stage. Clearly, the Singapore government has a political and security imperative for its main FTAs: to cement long-term strategic alliances with major powers and trading partners. But it also views strong, 'WTO-plus' FTAs as a building block for regional liberalisation within ASEAN and multilateral liberalisation through the WTO.

Viewed less benignly, FTAs could divert political attention and negotiating resources from the WTO, in addition to creating a 'spaghetti-bowl' effect (overlapping FTAs with different and complicated rules of origin). Additional market-access gains seem to be rather modest. Finally, the logic of new FTAs with small, less developed, less market-oriented countries, e.g. in the Middle East, is at least open to question. These negotiations risk ending up in 'trade-light' agreements short on commercial substance but long on political gesture.

In all, Singapore has set an FTA precedent that other countries in the region, including ASEAN members, feel compelled to follow. But they have more complicated developing-country politics and

Table 4.2

Tariff Levels in ASEAN

Country	*Applied*	*Bound*	*% Unbound*
Singapore*	0	9.7	29.5
Malaysia**	9.2	19	35
Thailand***	16	29	36
Indonesia****	7.3	30.4	7
Philippines*****	5	28	40
Developing Countries			
Latin America/Caribbean	13	38	–
Asia	21	37	–
Sub-Saharan Africa	20	74	–
Middle-East/Mediterranean	23	46	–
Developing Countries Average******	19	49	–

Notes:

Applied = Simple average applied rate

Bound = Simple average bound rate at the end of implementation of Uruguay Round Agreements

% Unbound = proportion of total tariff lines unbound

**WTO Singapore Trade Policy Review* (TPR) 2000; *USTR National Trade Estimate Report on Foreign Trade Barriers*: Singapore 2003.

**WTO *Malaysia TPRs* 1997, 2001; *USTR National Trade Estimate Report on Foreign Trade Barriers*: Malaysia 2003.

***WTO *Thailand TPR* 1998; *USTR National Trade Estimate Report on Foreign Trade Barriers*: Thailand 2003.

****WTO *Indonesia TPRs* 2003, 1998; *USTR National Trade Estimate Report on Foreign Trade Barriers*: Indonesia 2003.

*****WTO *Philippines TPRs* 1995,1999; *USTR National Trade Estimate Report on Foreign Trade Barriers*: Philippines 2003.

******Average for 42 developing countries having had WTO TPRs

Sources: WTO Trade Policy Reviews; USTR National Trade Estimate Report on Foreign Trade Barriers, Michalopoulos 2001, pp. 48, 52 (Tables 4.1 and 4.3).

economics. The danger is that they may draw the wrong lessons from Singapore's FTA-pathfinder role, and end up with a messy patchwork of weak, market-distorting FTAs.

That said, Singapore retains a large stake in a rules-based multilateral trading system. It has a strong market access focus in the Doha Round (Table 4.3). Liberalisation of trade in industrial goods and services is the main priority, and trade facilitation is of keen interest. But what may have suffered is Singapore's 'honest-broker' role in the WTO. Traditionally, it has used its good offices to narrow

Table 4.3

The Doha Development Agenda: National Positions on the Issues

Country	*Market Access*	*Rules*	*Developing Country Issues*	*Singapore Issues*	*Trade and Environment*
Singapore	Top priority: industrial goods and services.	Stronger disciplines on anti-dumping.	No problems.	Comfortable. Trade facilitation a priority.	–
Malaysia	Top priority: industrial goods + palm oil exports. Defensive on services.	Stronger disciplines on anti-dumping.	Few implementation /SDT/TRIPS problems but promotes LMG positions. However, more flexible than LMG hardliners.	Defensive, especially on investment. More flexible on trade facilitation.	–
Thailand	Top priority: agriculture. Mixed on industrial goods. Defensive on services.	Stronger disciplines on anti-dumping.	No major concerns. Flexible.	Reasonably flexible.	Concerns about SPS+TBT barriers to agriculture and fisheries exports.
Indonesia	Defensive, particularly on agriculture, but also on services. Wants access for industrial and tropical product exports.	Stronger disciplines on anti-dumping.	Promotes LMG positions. But more flexible than hardliners.	Defensive but not hardline.	
Philippines	Defensive on agriculture. Also on services. Mixed on industrial goods. Wants market access for industrial and tropical product exports.	Stronger disciplines on anti-dumping and fisheries subsidies.	Defensive but not hardline.	Defensive but not hardline.	Concerns about SPS and TBT barriers to agriculture and fisheries exports.

differences between conflicting parties, especially across the developed-developing country divide. However, many developing countries now seem to trust it less as an honest broker because of its FTAs with developed countries, particularly with the US.

Malaysia

Malaysia is one of the world's most globalised economies with relatively liberal trade policies by developing-country standards (Table 4.2). However, there are peak tariffs, tariff escalation and assorted non-tariff barriers in politically sensitive goods sectors; and protection in services remains high. Protection must also be seen in the context of Bumiputera policies to discriminate in favour of the Malay majority. The result is a dualistic economy: competitive, FDI-driven manufacturing export sectors co-exist with inefficient, import-competing domestic sectors enjoying high rates of effective protection.

Malaysian leaders have usually reconciled the demands of globalisation and the dictates of Malay-dominated domestic politics through businesslike pragmatism. After the Asian crisis, however, Dr. Mahathir's government became more defensive, especially in the WTO. Policy oscillated unpredictably, though it has swung back somewhat towards businesslike pragmatism since Abdullah Badawi became prime minister.

Malaysia has mixed positions in the Doha Round (Table 4.3). Market access for its processed-palm-oil and industrial-goods exports—not least to other developing countries—is a top priority. Agriculture is of declining importance as a negotiating issue. Malaysia is defensive on services. It was defensive and inflexible on developing-country issues such as Special and Differential Treatment (S&D), and on the Singapore issues, but has shown more flexibility after Cancun.

Malaysia was late to join the FTA bandwagon. It is now negotiating bilaterally with Japan and India, and is of course part of collective ASEAN negotiations with third countries.

Malaysia's main trade-policy challenge is to liberalise pockets of protection through trade-and-FDI opening and domestic regulatory reforms. This is fundamentally a matter for unilateral action. But it can be complemented by a constructive, flexible, market-access-oriented stance in the WTO and by strong, WTO-plus FTAs. The danger is that an overly defensive, Third-Worldist stance in the WTO, combined with weak, trade-light FTAs, could distract attention from necessary reforms at home.

Thailand

Thailand retains relatively high protection by the standards of other old ASEAN members (Table 4.2). Its average tariff is significantly higher, with greater tariff dispersion and escalation; non-tariff barriers are not insignificant; and protectionism in services is considerable. No meaningful liberalisation of the economy has occurred under the present Thaksin administration.

Thailand was the first ASEAN member to follow Singapore on the FTA track. FTAs are now front and centre in Thai trade policy, dominating political attention and negotiating resources. But the wisdom and effectiveness of this policy is very much open to question.

Political will and symbolism is on abundant display, but economic strategy is less evident. Little thought and preparation have gone into assessing the costs and benefits of potential agreements, choosing the right negotiating partners, and formulating negotiating positions. There appears to be little idea of how FTAs fit into the broader national economic framework. Indications are that agreements concluded or taking shape will hardly advance on the *status quo*, perhaps delivering modest liberalisation in a few sectors but hedged about with restrictive rules of origin. The forthcoming negotiations with the USA may deliver something more substantial, given likely intense US pressure to further open Thai markets. But Thailand is not likely to get much in return. This is one among several reasons why the US-Thai negotiations have run into domestic political problems.

The present fixation with FTAs has manifestly diverted Thai attention away from the WTO. Thailand punches well below its weight in the Doha Round. Thai positions on the main negotiating issues are mixed but generally pragmatic (Table 4.3). Thailand's top priorities are market access for agricultural and some industrial-goods exports. But it also has defensive positions in all market-access negotiations due to protectionism at home.

Overall, the present FTA policy seems to be geared more towards partial sectoral deals than ambitious liberalisation. This diverts attention from both necessary domestic reforms and from multilateral liberalisation in the WTO.

Indonesia

Indonesian trade policies have swung from high protection to openness in a comparatively short period (Table 4.2). Its average unweighted tariff has come down to under 10 per cent. The IMF Structural Adjustment Programme agreed with the Indonesian government in 1998 significantly accelerated trade-and-FDI liberalisation and domestic regulatory reform in goods and services sectors. However, there are higher tariffs and tariff escalation, particularly in agriculture. There is also recent evidence of creeping protectionism through higher non-tariff barriers, particularly on agricultural products, textiles and steel. Overall, government enthusiasm for further liberalisation has clearly waned in recent years.

These trade-policy developments must be placed in the post-Asian crisis context of acute political and economic instability, with brittle institutions. The high-cost domestic regulatory and institutional environment—undependable enforcement of property rights and contracts, weak public administration, corruption, minimum-wage and other labour-market regulations, *inter alia*—now presents bigger obstacles to trade and FDI than formal market-access barriers. In addition, the fire-fighting atmosphere after the Asian crisis precluded a clear focus on trade and wider economic policy priorities. Thus, trade policy appears more *ad hoc* than it did before 1997.

Indonesia is less active than Singapore, Malaysia and Thailand in the WTO. Relatively weak trade-policy capacity and domestic fire fighting have prevented it from participating effectively in the Doha Round, not least given the latter's broad, complex and resource-intensive agenda. These factors, combined with increasing domestic protectionist pressures, have led to a defensive overall posture in the round (Table 4.3). Indonesia's top, overriding priority has been to exempt a list of 'special products'—mostly staples such as rice and sugar—from liberalisation in net food-importing developing countries. It has been relatively defensive on services, liberalisation of some industrial products, and on the Singapore issues. This has compromised its ability to promote market access for its tropical-product and industrial-goods exports to developed and other developing countries.

Indonesia is of course part of collective ASEAN FTA negotiations with third countries, and has also indicated an interest in negotiating bilateral FTAs. But the latter is in reaction to what Singapore and

Thailand are doing. Thus far, Indonesia's FTA policy appears reactive and *ad hoc,* with little sense of strategy.

Philippines

The situation in the Philippines is rather similar to that in Indonesia. Trade policies have swung from high protection to openness in the past decade (Table 4.2). The simple average tariff has come down to well under 10 per cent. But this co-exists with peak tariffs and tariff escalation in sensitive sectors, particularly in agriculture. There is recent evidence of creeping protection through higher non-tariff barriers, again concentrated on agricultural products. Backsliding has also occurred on AFTA commitments on petrochemical products. Protectionism is much higher on FDI and trade in services than it is on trade in goods. Restrictions on foreign ownership written into the Philippine constitution remain the most visible market-access hurdle. Overall, the government has displayed little enthusiasm for further liberalisation since the Asian crisis, and domestic protectionist pressures have increased.

As in Indonesia, a weak domestic regulatory and institutional environment is now perhaps a bigger obstacle to trade and FDI than formal market-access barriers. Trade and wider economic policies also appear less focused and more *ad hoc* post-Asian crisis than they were during the Ramos administration, when the main liberalisation measures were put in place.

The Philippines, like Indonesia, has never been among the most active of developing countries in the WTO. It suffers from relatively weak trade-policy capacity at home. It has been ambivalent about the Doha Round, complaining of the burdens of implementing Uruguay-Round agreements and exhibiting defensiveness on several negotiating issues (Table 4.3). It is a leading supporter of exempting Special Products from liberalisation in net food-importing countries. It has also been relatively defensive on services, liberalisation of some industrial products, and on the Singapore issues.

The Philippines is negotiating a bilateral FTA with Japan in addition to being involved in collective ASEAN FTA negotiations with third countries. Like Indonesia, Philippine FTA policy appears reactive and *ad hoc,* with little sense of strategy.

Vietnam

Vietnam's transition from Plan to Market has proceeded in stops and starts since 1986, but it has come far cumulatively—though not nearly as far as China. Liberalisation, including trade, has picked up since 2000, though domestic institutional reforms have lagged behind. Foreign trading rights have been liberalised extensively; quantitative restrictions and other non-tariff barriers have come down; and the average nominal tariff now stands at about 18 per cent, though the tariff structure contains higher tariffs on many products and high tariff dispersion. Protection in services remains very high. The government continues to discriminate heavily in favour of state-owned industrial enterprises and state-owned banks. Overall, Vietnamese protection in terms of tariffs, non-tariff trade barriers and FDI restrictions remains much higher than it is in the old ASEAN members. It also compares unfavourably with China, given the latter's huge external and internal liberalisation measures before and after WTO accession.

Vietnam's AFTA-CEPT commitments have contributed very little to overall trade liberalisation. The Vietnam-US Bilateral Trade Agreement, in contrast, has contributed much. It contains strong market-access commitments in goods and services, and has led to soaring Vietnamese manufactured exports to the US, especially in garments.

Vietnam's WTO-accession negotiations are in a critical phase. Before negotiations are concluded, differences will have to be narrowed on market access, particularly on tariff commitments, non-tariff barriers, domestic agricultural subsidies and services. Vietnam will also have to bring domestic legislation and regulatory procedures into line with all relevant WTO agreements, and put mechanisms into place to make sure these obligations are implemented satisfactorily after accession. It remains to be seen how strong Vietnam's WTO commitments will be compared with other newly acceded members—especially China. The strength of its commitments will largely determine how WTO membership will affect the domestic reform programme and Vietnam's further integration into the global economy. Stronger commitments on border as well as non-border regulatory barriers will likely spur domestic institutional reforms in addition to trade and FDI growth—as has happened in China. Weaker commitments, especially on non-border regulation, would indicate more foot-dragging by the Vietnamese leadership on structural reforms, e.g. on reforming state-owned enterprises, opening up the capital market, improving property-rights and contract-enforcement, and generally making the domestic regulatory environment more transparent and market-friendly.

Finally, Vietnam is involved in collective ASEAN negotiations with third countries but not in further bilateral FTA negotiations. This is probably wise. It should focus on domestic market-based reforms, WTO accession and ASEAN economic integration without getting distracted elsewhere.

SECTION 4

ASEAN Economic Integration: Opportunities and Challenges

China's and India's economic rise has driven home the realisation for ASEAN countries that it would be critical for them to restructure and integrate their economies in order to sustain their competitiveness. It has been envisaged that creation of an economically integrated ASEAN with a combined population of 500 million would strengthen competitiveness, not least by increasing its attractiveness as a host region for foreign investors. It was in this spirit that ASEAN leaders agreed to explore the possibility of creating an ASEAN Economic Community (AEC) by the year 2020. It was envisaged that the AEC could provide the necessary framework to enhance economic integration within ASEAN and will also facilitate in realising the economic component of the ASEAN Vision 2020 to create a stronger and prosperous ASEAN.

However, as observed in a recent study by Hew and Sen (2004), there exists a certain degree of ambiguity about the proposed AEC, and the way it is likely to be constituted. Although it has been advocated that in some ways, the formation of an AEC could possibly draw lessons from the European economic integration, ASEAN has to look for its own model of economic integration in a changing global environment. Thus, there could be two approaches for achieving an AEC: a) start off with sectoral integration with the number of sectors being extended at a later stage or b) go for broad-based economic integration wherein economic integration programmes are undertaken in a phased manner for all the sectors. The latter appears to be more feasible as ASEAN is already working to eliminate the intra-regional trade restrictions in goods *via* implementation of the ASEAN Free Trade Area (AFTA), and in services and investment, *via* ASEAN Framework Agreement on Services (AFAS) and the ASEAN Investment Area (AIA), all with the aim to achieve the ASEAN Vision 2020. However, given the vast level of diversity among ASEAN members, there would be a need to adopt the 'ASEAN minus X' principle wherein more developed ASEAN members can embark on economic integration, with a commitment from other members that they can join in as and when they are ready. Thus, the AEC should be more of an 'FTA-plus' arrangement that includes some elements of a common market, such as the free movement of capital and skilled labour. The AEC also needs to evolve a better institutional and legal infrastructure to facilitate greater economic integration.

Major challenges are likely to stand in the way of achieving ASEAN economic integration through the AEC. As noted:

> For the AEC to succeed, it would be critical to have a clear and comprehensive blueprint with action plans, deadlines and milestones to be achieved...there may be a need to consider making all economic commitments to realise the AEC to be legally binding ... the main concern would be whether ASEAN really has the political will to make the crucial decisions in the medium to longer term... also the general fear among ASEAN governments that sovereignty may have to be sacrificed for deeper economic integration ... the big question would be whether ASEAN has the ability to follow through with this bold and ambitious project.

SECTION 5

Emerging Bilateral Initiatives in ASEAN[12]

While ASEAN is grappling with the challenges of economic integration among its members, it is concomitantly embracing bilateral trade liberalisation initiatives for achieving deeper economic integration with its regional dialogue partners. Thus, there has been a rapid proliferation of bilateral Regional Trading Agreements (RTAs) between ASEAN and its major trading partners after the economic crisis in 1997-98, in spite of bilateralism being generally regarded by economists as being the 'third-best' option for global trade liberalisation, in terms of its welfare consequences. One of the prime reasons for emergence of bilateralism across ASEAN and in East Asia has been the slow progress in trade liberalisation at the multilateral

12. This section largely draws on Sen (2004).

level in the WTO. There is not only a perceived inability of the WTO to yield a multilateral consensus on major trade liberalisation issues, but also a perception that bilateralism could be a building block towards global free trade—though this depends on the appropriate design and 'WTO consistency' of the underlying agreements.

Besides individual ASEAN countries, *viz.* Singapore and Thailand, and now Malaysia, continuing to negotiate bilateral trade deals with their trading partners (as indicated in Section 4), there is also surging interest among the ASEAN members in negotiating bilateral RTAs (also commonly known as FTAs) with their major trading partners as a single grouping. To date, ASEAN as a group is negotiating bilateral FTAs with China, India, the Australia-New Zealand Closer Economic Relations (CER) grouping, Korea and Japan. The status of each of these initiatives is indicated in Table 4.4. Currently, all of them are in their initial stages of negotiation.

A comparative overview of all these initiatives clearly indicates that although crucial areas of negotiations haven't yet been undertaken, the coverage of all these initiatives as committed in the Framework Agreements or the Joint Declarations is far more comprehensive than just a free trade agreement and in many cases commit to liberalisation and facilitation of trade and investment in areas where not much progress has been made through the WTO. In that sense, all the above FTAs are WTO-plus in scope and potential. However, impending negotiations and eventual agreements will reveal whether that turns out to be the case in practice.

On a bilateral basis, these FTA initiatives could be beneficial for ASEAN members since they would provide greater preferential market access in goods and services due to reduction in trade barriers, increased investment opportunities in overseas markets, and reduction of business costs arising from dismantling of tariffs and non-tariff barriers. Further, as observed by Dayaratna Banda and Whalley (2005), these FTAs also provide opportunities for gains from bilateral bargaining in non-border trade-and-investment issues outside the WTO that might help facilitate in negotiations of these issues at the multilateral level in due course.

The above range of ongoing efforts on ASEANs-plus bilateral FTAs, in addition to individual initiatives of member countries, indicates that bilateralism is indeed gaining momentum as an integral part of the trade strategies of ASEAN countries. However, the extent

Table 4.4

ASEAN's Ongoing RTA Initiatives

RTA	*Status*	*Coverage Areas*	*Timeframe for RTA To Be Fully in Force*
ASEAN-China Comprehensive Economic Cooperation Agreement	Framework Agreement signed in November 2002; Agreement on Trade in Goods and Dispute Settlement Mechanism in force from January 2005.	Comprehensive: Trade in Goods, Early Harvest, Services, Investment, Dispute Settlement, Economic Cooperation.	2010 for China and original ASEAN-6 members, and by 2015 for the newer ASEAN Members, i.e. Cambodia, Laos, Myanmar and Viet Nam (CLMV).
ASEAN-India Comprehensive Economic Cooperation Agreement	Framework Agreement signed in October 2003; in March 2004, an ASEAN-India Trade Negotiations Committee (AI-TNC) established to negotiate the implementation of the Framework Agreement; now working on the provision of the Rules of Origin (ROO) and the Operational Certification Procedures for the ASEAN-India FTA.	Comprehensive: Trade in Goods, Early Harvest, Services, Investment, Dispute Settlement, Economic Cooperation.	2012 for India and original ASEAN-6 (except Philippines), and 2017 for Philippines and CLMV countries.
ASEAN-Japan Comprehensive Economic Partnership Agreement	Framework Agreement signed in October 2003; negotiations to commence in April 2005, to be completed within two years.	Comprehensive: Trade in Goods, Services, Investment, Facilitation and Economic Cooperation.	At most 2012 for ASEAN-6 and five more years for CLMV countries.

Contd. ...

...Contd. ...

RTA	*Status*	*Coverage Areas*	*Timeframe for RTA To Be Fully in Force*
ASEAN-Australia and New Zealand Free Trade Area	Agreed to launch negotiations in 2005, to be completed within two years.	Comprehensive: liberalisation of trade in goods, services and investment; trade and investment facilitation and economic cooperation measures.	Expected to be fully in force by 2015.
ASEAN-Korea Comprehensive Cooperation Partnership	Agreed to launch negotiations in early 2005, to be completed within two years.	Comprehensive: liberalisation of trade in goods, services and investment; trade and investment facilitation and economic cooperation measures.	Aim to have at least 80 per cent of products with zero tariffs in 2009, and with consideration for special and differential treatment and additional flexibility for new ASEAN member Countries.

Source: ASEAN Secretariat (2005).

to which it affects regional economic integration efforts in ASEAN, and is consistent with the multilateral framework, is indeed of concern.

One consideration is the extent to which such FTAs could complement the ongoing economic integration process in ASEAN, which was initiated through the ASEAN Free Trade Area (AFTA) in 1992. This concern is particularly pertinent given that prevailing economic diversity among ASEAN member's calls for a concerted approach towards economic integration. Further, the economic crisis of 1997-98 has made this task of economic integration more difficult, with resultant slow progress in the liberalisation of their economies in both goods and services. Although the AFTA has been implemented for ASEAN-6, tariff barriers on all goods are still not dismantled, while AFAS has not been able to significantly increase the pace of service sector liberalisation. In this context, comprehensive bilateral FTAs between ASEAN and third countries, involving goods, services and investment liberalisation could possibly encourage individual ASEAN countries to undertake domestic reforms to improve their global competitiveness, and hence complement economic integration at a regional level. This will depend crucially on ASEAN concluding strong, WTO-consistent and WTO-plus agreements with its negotiating partners.

Another important issue is the relationship of these FTAs to the WTO. Discriminatory preferences, complexities in the implementation of rules of origin, and the cost and time spent on the negotiation and implementation of these agreements, could well be market distorting as well as a burden on scarce administrative and negotiating resources. In sum, it could divert ASEAN's attention from the WTO. As further noted by Sen (2004):

> Since ASEAN is a diverse group of economies and individual countries are also involved in bilateral FTA negotiations with the same dialogue partners apart from the grouping itself, it is important to ensure a certain degree of consistency with respect to their terms of coverage of sectors, rules of origins, and the depth of tariff reductions, otherwise it can lead to problems for ASEAN in managing its external trade relationship and increase business costs instead, since it would have to deal with a wide range of rules and regulations and tariff measures ... involving exclusions for certain sectors and commodities with respect to preferential tariff treatment, ... this can indeed create a 'spaghetti-bowl' like situation wherein administrative and compliance costs of trade policy would be much higher.

What, then would be the ideal strategy to avoid such a situation? The best situation would be to adopt some kind of a Common

Framework Agreement among ASEAN countries that could form the basis for future FTA negotiations. The focus of such a framework should be on the sequencing and timing of the agreements, their nature and coverage of sectors, and the implementation mechanisms to be involved, as in case of the Pacific Economic Cooperation Council (PECC) proposal for a common understanding on PTAs[13] to achieve a degree of consistency. This would ensure its greater complementarity with regional and multilateral liberalisation efforts within ASEAN, so that FTA efforts in Southeast Asia end up in becoming a building rather than a stumbling block towards global free trade.

However, ASEAN member governments do not as yet regard the proliferation of FTAs as a looming problem. Hence it is unlikely that they will take these ideas seriously—at least for a while.

SECTION 6

Southeast Asia and the WTO[14]

None of the ASEAN members were particularly active in the GATT before the Uruguay Round. But that changed with their shift to more liberal, outward-oriented trade policies and their increasing integration into the world economy. ASEAN members also realised that, collectively, they would have more clout: they could bargain better by hanging together.

ASEAN cooperation, especially among the constituent national missions to the GATT, was reasonably strong and effective throughout the round. Effective participation in the negotiations was reflected in a broadly favourable outcome from the Uruguay-Round agreements, in terms of market access (substantial reduction of developed-country tariffs on ASEAN manufactured and tropical-product exports) and rules (abolition of VERs and marginal improvements in disciplines on contingent protection).

What is the state of ASEAN cooperation 10 years into the WTO's existence?

By developing country standards, the ASEAN-5—Singapore, Thailand, Malaysia, Indonesia and the Philippines—are relatively well

---

13. See Scollay (2004) for more details on the PECC proposal.
14. This section draws on Sally (2004b).

integrated into the WTO. They are among a score or so of developing countries with reasonably well-staffed missions in Geneva, who take an active part in WTO committees and working groups, are actively involved in formal and informal coalitions on particular issues, and have initiated anti-dumping actions and dispute settlement complaints (both complex tasks). All this pre-supposes a critical minimum of trade policy capacity, which the overwhelming majority of developing countries do not possess. Of course trade policy capacity among the ASEAN-5 varies with levels of development, ranging from Singapore at one end to Indonesia and the Philippines at the other.

The other three ASEAN members of the WTO are hardly active. Myanmar and Brunei have never been active; and Cambodia joined the WTO as a least-developed member only in 2004.

That said, ASEAN co-operation in Geneva has all but broken down. The reasons are manifold. Inter-country gaps have widened, leading to more distinct and different national trade (and wider economic) policy profiles. An enlarged ASEAN is more unwieldy and internally fractured. Trade policy responses to the Asian crisis diverged. AFTA has made next-to-no progress on non-tariff issues. Finally, the transition from GATT to WTO has compounded the problem. The WTO's work programme has vastly expanded, cutting deeper into politically sensitive domestic regulations. Its hyperinflation of membership, with so many more developing countries on board, has made decision-making more politicised and polarised—more along the lines of the UN General Assembly than the businesslike GATT of old.

This combination of trends in Geneva and back in the region has opened several cracks within ASEAN and made national differences more pronounced. Go-it-alone bilateral FTA initiatives are one response to intra-ASEAN divisions; going separate ways in the WTO is another.

Intra-ASEAN divisions on launching a new round and on the substance of its negotiating agenda were evident before Seattle and persisted into the Doha Round. Singapore and Thailand retained broadly pragmatic stances. They had 'offensive' (export market access) positions, and, in Thailand's case, 'defensive' (domestic protectionist) positions (hardly any for Singapore); but were generally willing to compromise and trade-off in order to ensure overall progress in the round. Malaysia, Indonesia and the Philippines, on the other hand, became increasingly defensive in critical areas such as agriculture,

Special and Differential Treatment, and the Singapore issues (Table 4.4).

Is there room for stepped-up ASEAN co-operation in the next—and decisive—phase of the Doha Round? And what of longer-term prospects for ASEAN co-operation in the WTO?

The Doha-Round negotiating framework put together in July 2004—especially with the removal of contentious Singapore issues—should help to narrow intra-ASEAN differences and perhaps encourage more ASEAN co-operation. Stepped-up but limited ASEAN co-operation could focus on rules, trade facilitation, SPS and TBT measures, and perhaps industrial goods. However, even to get to that stage would require more political will than is presently the case. To complicate matters, the entry of Cambodia to the WTO, and the prospective accession of Vietnam and Laos, are going to make it more difficult to find ASEAN common denominators on the issues. The switch of attention and resources to FTAs might make it extra difficult to revive even limited co-operation in the WTO. Given such political complications, perhaps one should not expect too much from ASEAN co-operation in the WTO anytime soon.

Taking the long view, Southeast Asia needs an effective WTO. The region's integration with the wider world economy gives it a long-term stake in a liberal, non-discriminatory, rules-based multilateral trading system: a patchwork of overlapping and discriminatory FTAs in Asia-Pacific and beyond is not enough. At the same time, east-Asian countries, with China centre-stage but also with an important southeast-Asian component, are well positioned to exercise considerable influence in the WTO. This will be especially important in the next phase of Doha-Round negotiations. They can and should contribute to setting the WTO on its legs again. That requires a stronger market-access focus, i.e. the progressive reduction of trade barriers according to transparent and non-discriminatory rules, and a return to effective decision-making.

ASEAN co-operation will likely not be a prominent feature in this scheme. But ASEAN members should be active and creative on an individual basis in forging multiple coalitions with other WTO members keen to promote market access and stronger multilateral rules, on discrete issues and across-the-board. The fulcrum of alliance formation could be strategic partnerships with the two major powers that favour a market-access-oriented WTO: the USA and China.

Economic and wider geopolitical shifts (a more assertive US on the global stage and a more assertive China on the regional stage), point in this direction. Especially encouraging is China's businesslike, pragmatic and generally constructive behaviour in the WTO after its accession—which flows from its massive unilateral liberalisation and very strong WTO-accession commitments.

Even India, traditionally defensive and inflexible in the GATT/WTO, has shown signs of pragmatism and flexibility in the last year or so, thus bringing its WTO activity closer into line with market-based reforms at home. If India does move farther in this direction, useful alliances between it, China and ASEAN countries in the WTO are conceivable. This could be reinforced by parallel FTA negotiations.[15]

SECTION 7

Conclusions: Whither Trade Policy in Southeast Asia?

Although ASEAN economies have largely recovered from the Asian economic crisis, their growth prospects are now challenged by the economic rise of China and the recent emergence of the Indian economy as one of the fastest growing economies in Asia during the past decade. Available data indicates that in spite of measures towards greater economic integration in ASEAN, the share of intra-ASEAN trade continues to be stagnant, while ASEAN's trade and investment linkages with China and India have been expanding at a much more rapid pace, especially for the developed ASEAN members. This growing reliance of ASEAN on China and India for its economic growth could reap rich dividends, provided that ASEAN countries pursue appropriate trade and wider economic policies to cooperate as well as compete effectively with the two major emerging economic powers.

As far as trade policies post-Asian crisis are concerned, the broad story for old ASEAN members, with the exception of Singapore, is

15. On China and India, their trade policies and WTO participation, see Sally (2004a), "China's Trade Policies and Its Integration into the World Economy", *mimeo*; Peter Draper and Razeen Sally, "Developing-country Coalitions in Multilateral Trade Negotiations," *mimeo*; Anwarul Hoda, "India in the WTO", and Razeen Sally, "ASEAN in the WTO", both in Rahul Sen, Mukul Asher and Nagesh Kumar (eds.), "ASEAN-India Partnership: Meeting the Challenges of Integrating World", RIS-ISEAS, forthcoming 2005.

that previous liberalisation has not been reversed, but its forward momentum has slowed down. Vietnam and Cambodia, on the other hand, have accelerated their opening to the world economy in the run-up to WTO accession. At the same time, China has dramatically narrowed the policy gap with ASEAN through its massive external liberalisation and domestic reforms. With China concentrating minds, India has also stepped up its liberalisation in recent years.

The ever-faster integration of first China and then India into the world economy presents vast opportunities to Southeast Asia in a more refined international division of labour. But it also exposes weaknesses within the region, especially in inefficient parts of agriculture, manufacturing and services cosseted by protectionist policies and protective domestic institutions. Southeast Asia's challenge is to further liberalise, deregulate and improve domestic market-supporting institutions. Only then can it maintain competitiveness and take full advantage of the historic global integration of China and India. How is that to be accomplished?

International and regional trade negotiations and trade agreements can be means to the desired end. But their importance should not be exaggerated: they have distinct limits. Despite visions and blueprints, plans for ASEAN economic integration have changed very few facts on the ground. Going on past experience, it would be naïve to expect speedy progress in the years ahead. Similarly, bilateral FTAs are unlikely to inject large doses of additional liberalisation. Worse, there is the prospect of weak, partial FTAs with large swathes of economic activity carved out, and with market access further restricted and red tape increased through rules-of-origin complications—not to mention the possible diversion of political attention from the WTO and unilateral liberalisation. Last, prospects for the Doha Round and the WTO's longer-term future are not rosy. The transition from GATT to WTO has produced a wider and deeper agenda, drilling down into politically sensitive domestic regulations. Hyperinflation of the membership has made even simple decisions elusive. The WTO is much more politicised than the old GATT, riven with internal divisions and buffeted by outside forces, including increasingly influential NGOs. All these factors make significant multilateral liberalisation and rule strengthening very difficult—perhaps almost impossible—to achieve, and the whole process is agonisingly slow.

Therefore, ASEAN countries cannot rely on external tracks 'from above' for meaningful trade policy reform. Rather they have to rely on themselves—'from below' as it were. The engine of liberalisation and regulatory reform has to be home-driven, with governments taking *unilateral* measures in response to internal and external conditions. China and India should concentrate minds within ASEAN countries; and it is up to them to follow the liberalisation train through competitive emulation. That is probably more important than relying overly on AFTA, FTAs and the WTO. This unilateral method was how liberalisation occurred in the 19th century, led by Britain. The World Bank estimates that unilateral measures have accounted for about 60 per cent of developing-country trade liberalisation since the 1980s.[16] This was how previous waves of east and southeast-Asian liberalisation, as well as more recent Chinese and Indian liberalisation, occurred.

Clearly, there is currently a multi-pronged approach to trade policy in Southeast Asia. However, if there is to be a fresh wave of unilateral liberalisation in southeast Asian in competitive emulation of China and India, then it can, as a second-order priority, be reinforced by sensible measures in AFTA, bilateral and plurilateral FTAs, and the WTO. But it is important to get priorities right and follow the process bottom-up, not top-down.

16. World Bank 2004 report on FTAs.

References

Adhikari, A. and Y. Yang (2002). "China's Increasing Openness: Threat or Opportunity?" ADB, Manila, *mimeo* (February 23).

ASEAN Secretariat, ASEAN Secretariat (2005). Website cited at *www.aseansec.org*.

ASEAN Secretariat (2004). *ASEAN Statistical Yearbook 2004*, cited at *http://www.aseansec.org/syb2004.htm*,

Asher, Mukul G. and Rahul Sen (2004). "India: An Integral Part of New Asia", *Lee Kuan Yew School of Public Policy Working paper no. SPP 63-04*, National University of Singapore.

Asian Development Bank (ADB) (2004). *Key Indicators of Developing Asian and Pacific Countries*, Manila: ADB.

Bhaskaran, M., (2003) "China as Potential Superpower: Regional Responses", *Deutsche Bank Research Report*, January 15.

Dayaratna Banda, OG and J. Whalley (2005). "Beyond Goods and Services: Competition Policy, Investment, Mutual Recognition, Movement of Persons, and Broader Cooperation Provisions of Recent FTAs involving ASEAN Countries", *NBER Working Paper no. w11232*, National Bureau of Economic Research, Massachusetts.

Draper, Peter and Razeen Sally (2004). "Developing Country Coalitions in Multilateral Trade Negotiations", paper presented at a conference on *India and Post-Cancun Negotiations in the Doha Round*, Jawarharlal Nehru University, New Delhi, October.

Francois, J. and D. Spinanger (2001). "With Rags to Riches but Then When?", paper presented at the *Fourth Annual Conference on Global Economic Analysis*, Purdue University, Indiana (June 27-29).

Hew, Denis and Rahul Sen (2004). "Towards an ASEAN Economic Community: Challenges and Prospects", *ISEAS Working Papers in Economics and Finance* no.1, Singapore: Institute of Southeast Asian Studies.

Martin, W. and E. Ianchovichina (2001). "Implications of China's Accession to the World Trade Organisation for China and the WTO", *The World Economy*, XXIV 1205-1219.

Michalopoulos C. (2001). *Developing Countries in the WTO*, Palgrave: New York and Hampshire.

Sally, Razeen (2004a). "China's Trade Policies and its Integration into the World Economy", paper presented at a *SACU-China Conference*, Institute for Global Dialogue/South African Institute of International Affairs, Johannesburg, September.

Sally, Razeen (2004b). "Southeast Asia in the WTO", *Southeast Asia Background Series no. 3*, Singapore: ISEAS.

Scollay, R. (2004). "Thoughts on Sequencing of Preferential Trading Initiatives in the Asia-Pacific Region", paper presented at the *APEC Study Centre Consortium (ASCC)/Pacific Economic Cooperation Council (PECC)* meeting, Vina del Mar, Chile, May 28.

Sen, Rahul (2004). "Free Trade Agreements in Southeast Asia", *Southeast Asia Background Series No. 1*, Singapore: ISEAS.

Sen, R., M.G. Asher and R.S. Rajan (2004). "ASEAN-India Economic Relations: Current Status and Future Prospects", *Economic and Political Weekly*, 39, 29, 17 July.

Shafaeddin, S.M. (2002). "The Impact of China's Accession to WTO on the Exports of Developing Countries", *UNCTAD Working Paper No.160*, UNCTAD.

Srivastava, Sadhana and Rajan, Ramkishen (2004). "What Does the Economic Rise of China Imply for ASEAN and India : Focus on Trade and Investment Flows", in H. Kehal (ed.), *Foreign Investment in Developing Countries*, Palgrave: McMillan, pp.171-204.

Srivastava, S. (2003). "What is the True Level of FDI Flows to India?" *Economic and Political Weekly*, 38, February 15, pp.608-611.

Srivastava, S. and R. Sen (2004). "Competing for Global FDI: Opportunities and Challenges for the Indian Economy", *South Asia Economic Journal*, 5, 2, pp. 233-260.

Wolf, Martin (2004). *Why Globalisation Works*, Yale University Press.

World Bank *(2002). Globalisation, Growth and Poverty: Building an Inclusive Agenda for the World Economy*, World bank/OUP.

World Bank (2002). *Regional Integration and Development*, World Bank/OUP.

World Trade Organisation (WTO) (2004). *International Trade Statistics 2004*, Geneva: WTO.

Wu, F., M.H. Toh, T.S. Poa, K.W. Seah and T.K. Lim (2002). "Potential of the Chinese (PRC) and Indian Tourism Markets for ASEAN", *Economic Survey of Singapore*, Second Quarter, Ministry of Trade and Industry, Singapore.

5

India's Participation in WTO Negotiations: The Changes in Attitude and Emphasis[1]

DEBASHIS CHAKRABORTY[2]

Introduction

The 10-year transitory phase of WTO has come to an end on 31st December 2004. However, it is evident from the recent trends in multilateral negotiation that the members are yet to arrive at a mutual agreement regarding the modalities on future reform for a number of WTO provisions.[3] Needless to add, the absence of mutual consensus on modalities (which, in other words, implies persistence of some trade barriers) affects the developing countries much more severely than their developed counterparts.[4] It has been argued that the level of market access realised by developing countries in the future would be a function of their negotiating skill, and they would be better off by adopting a joint negotiating agenda.[5] The statement also goes true

---

1. The chapter has been re-printed from *Taiwanese Journal of WTO Studies*, Vol. 1, No. 3, pp. 119-162, 2005. We thank the Editorial Board of the Journal (published from Center for WTO Studies, College of International Affairs, National Chengchi University, Taipei) for giving us the necessary permission to re-print the article.

2. An earlier version of the chapter has been presented at the Conference on WTO, FTA and RTA, organised by Center for WTO Studies, College of International Affairs, National Chengchi University on April 22, 2005. The author is grateful to Mr. Jack Chen-huan Hsiao and Dr. Dipankar Sengupta for their helpful comments on an earlier draft.

3. "... In general the negotiations did not move forward as far or fast as anticipated, with important spring deadlines in agricultural and non-agricultural market access and on dispute settlement being missed." *WTO Annual Report*, 2004, p. 2.

4. Stiglitz, Joseph E. (2001). "Two Principles for the Next Round or, How to Bring Developing Countries in from the Cold", in Bernard Hoekman and Will Martin (eds.) *Developing Countries and the WTO: A Pro-Active Agenda*, p. 23, Oxford: Blackwell Publishers. Also see Research and Information System for the Non-Aligned and Other Developing Countries, *World Trade and Development Report 2003: Cancun and Beyond*, New Delhi: Academic Foundation, 2003.

5. Das, Bhagirath Lal (2004). *The WTO and the Multilateral Trading System: Past, Present and Future*, Third World Network and Zed Books, The first Indian Reprint, New Delhi: Bookwell; Razeen Sally, "Developing Country Trade Policy Reform and the WTO", *Cato Journal*, Vol. 19, No. 3, Winter 2000, pp. 403-423.

for India, a developing country, and there is a need to assess whether its negotiating strategies are evolving accordingly over time.

The chapter is organised along the following lines. First, a brief account of Indian participation at all the GATT/WTO rounds is provided. The determinants behind the changing attitude of India towards multilateral negotiations are analysed next, followed by a discussion on the major features of its participation at WTO. India in the recent period has shown an increasing inclination towards entering into RTAs with other developing countries, and therefore a discussion on the future implications of this move is also attempted. Finally, the findings are summarised.

India at the GATT/WTO Rounds

Despite being a founder member of GATT, India was never very active in various negotiating rounds until late eighties. Since the Indian economy followed the import-substitution led growth strategy during sixties and seventies, gaining from the import liberalisation at principal export markets (the EU and US) was never a prime objective. In addition, a considerable proportion of India's trade was directed to the Soviet bloc countries, and the presence of this assured market weakened the incentive to search for newer outlets. On the other hand, opening the domestic market to foreign competition through progressive tariff cuts was perceived harmful for the local industries. Instead, the country was more willing to discuss trade and development related issues at UNCTAD forums in collaboration with other developing countries like Brazil (primarily through the G-77 network).[6] Despite adoption of a proactive approach at WTO, India still feels comfortable to discuss trade-related issues at UNCTAD forums for coalition building among developing countries on areas pertaining to mutual interest.[7]

During mid-eighties, a number of developing countries were willing in favour of launching of the new round, and India had no other option but to participate in the negotiating process. The

6. Draper, Peter and Sally, Razeen (2004). "Developing-Country Coalitions in Multilateral Trade Negotiations", paper presented in the Seminar entitled *WTO Negotiations: India's Post-Cancun Concerns* jointly organised by Planning Commission and International Trade and Development Division, JNU, October 18-19.

7. See *Developing Countries at UNCTAD Call for the WTO Doha Programme to Realise (not just Reflect) Development* 19 October 2004, available at, *http://twnside.org.sg/title2/twninfo171.htm*.

willingness to participate in the Uruguay Round (henceforth UR) increased in the post-1991 period, when India moved towards an export-led growth strategy.[8] However, in the initial years, India was quite uncomfortable with the future implications of including agriculture and TRIPS in the Dunkel Draft.[9] On the whole, during UR negotiations, the country was unsure about the full implications of the coming changes on the economy, and therefore did not adopt a proactive approach at the negotiating table. It however occasionally attempted to collaborate with other developing countries without any appreciable success.[10] Even after the Marrakesh Agreement (1994), the passive participation by India continued at the first two ministerial meetings of WTO at Singapore (1996) and Geneva (1998) respectively. At the Seattle Ministerial (1999), India came to the forefront for the first time, when it strongly objected to incorporation of labour and environmental concerns under the wings of WTO. Despite the apparent failure of the ministerial meeting, owing to differences among the member countries, India was quite satisfied with the fact that the developing and poorer countries were united for the first time to address a mutual concern.[11] It opined that any new topic should be put in the discussion agenda of the ministerial meetings in future only after realisation of the market access level promised during UR negotiations.

Since 2000, India started communicating with other developing countries through various forums,[12] although any conscious attempt to develop a formal negotiating block was still absent. Before the Doha ministerial, India called for discussion on the following issues at Doha in an urgent basis—(a) non-realisation of anticipated benefits (e.g. Agreement on Textiles and Clothing and Agreement on

---

8. Sengupta, Dipankar, Debashis Chakraborty and Pritam Banerjee, "Introduction and Editors, Note: India at the WTO: The Story So Far..." in Dipankar Sengupta, Debashis Chakraborty and Pritam Banerji (eds.) *"Beyond the Transition Phase of WTO: An Indian Perspective on Emerging Issues"*, New Delhi: Academic Foundation, 2006.

9. Sharma, Devinder (1995), *GATT-WTO: Seeds of Despair*, New Delhi: Konark Publishers Pvt. Ltd.

10. Chisti, Sumitra, *Restructuring of International Economic Relations: Uruguay Round and the Developing Countries*, New Delhi: Concept Publishing Company, 1991.

11. Government of India, Newsletter of Ministry of Commerce, *India and the WTO*, Vol. 1, No. 11-12, November-December 1999, pp. 4-5 (the Commerce & Industry Minister Murasoli Maran's reply to the short-duration discussion on the Seattle meet in the Rajya Sabha on 9 December 1999).

12. For instance, see *India and the WTO*, "India Reaffirms Position on WTO Issues at Mexico Meet," Vol. 3, No. 9, September 2001.

Agriculture), (b) inequities and imbalances in several agreements (e.g. TRIPS, Subsidies and Countervailing Measures, Anti-dumping Agreement etc.), (c) non-operational and non-binding nature of special and differential treatment provisions.[13] Furthermore, the country was particularly unhappy with the continuance of the traditional mindset of several developed countries towards freeing trade in agriculture.[14]

At Doha (2001), a number of developed and developing countries were keen to initiate a new round of negotiation as well as to discuss newer areas like Singapore issues, both of which was opposed by India. The importance of forming strategic alliances was intensely felt for the first time, as India was isolated on most of the issues brought at the ministerial.[15] The ministerial declaration, known as Doha Development Agenda (henceforth DDA), however pleased India by responding to several of its demands (e.g.—giving importance to implementation issues; discussion on market access issues in agricultural and non-agricultural products, with focus on special and differential treatment for developing countries; inclusion of a separate declaration on TRIPS and Public Health; acknowledgement of the importance of ensuring free movement of natural persons in service trade).[16]

Buoyed by the Doha experience, India started to participate actively in WTO negotiations from then on and advocated for reform in several areas during the next two years. Before Cancun (2003) particular emphasis was laid on the following areas for discussion at the ministerial—lowering of agricultural subsidy in the developed countries; improvement of non-agricultural market access;

---

13. *India and the WTO*, Vol. 3, No. 6-7, June-July 2001, pp. 3-5 (Letter of the Minister of Commerce of India to G-77 Trade Ministers dated 14 June 2001).

14. For an account of pre-Doha scenario see, Stefan Tangermann, (2001). "Agriculture: New Wine in New Bottles?" in Klaus Gunter Deutsch and Bernhard Speyer (eds.), *The World Trade Organisation Millenium Round: Freer Trade in The Twenty-First Century*, pp. 199-212, London: Routledge.

15. Developing countries like Egypt were in favour of launching of a new round, while countries like Chile supported discussion on trade and investment measures. Yashika Singh, "India at the Fourth Ministerial Meeting in Doha: Déjà vu – Again?" New Delhi: *RGICS Working Paper* No. 32, 2001.

16. The Minister of Commerce Mr. Maran commented in New Delhi that, "In Sum, the Doha Mandate Will Not in Any Way Harm Us; on the Contrary, We Have Substantial Gains." *India and the WTO*, Vol. 3, No. 10-11, October-November 2001, pp. 1-2 (Statement by Mr. Murasoli Maran, Minister for Commerce and Industry—in the Rajya Sabha on 21/11/2001 and in Lok Sabha on 21/11/2001—Regarding the Fourth Ministerial Conference of the WTO).

liberalisation of service trade (mainly movement of natural persons) and acknowledgement of public health concerns in developing countries.[17]

A few days ahead of Cancun ministerial, the EU and US joint proposal on liberalisation of agricultural trade displeased a number of developing countries (including Brazil, China and India) and they came out with an alternate proposition on the modalities for future reform (the G-20 proposal). The alternate proposal called for immediate action to end export dumping and production subsidies in agriculture and improvement of market access.[18] At Cancun, the revised declaration submitted by the EU and the US was again rejected by the developing countries, and the Ministerial Draft issued on 13 September 2003 (known as the 'Derbez Draft'; *Document No. JOB (03)/156/Rev.* 2) disappointed all concerned groups. While developing countries termed the Derbez Draft as another version of the EU-US draft, and insisted on considering the G-20 Draft as the basis of negotiation instead, the EU and US were uncomfortable with the Draft's proposals on domestic support. It was perceived that there exists tremendous scope for improving various aspects of the draft.[19]

India refused to accept the Derbez Draft as a basis for future negotiations primarily owing to three reasons. First, it believed that the draft did not properly acknowledge the developing country perspective on domestic support to agriculture. Second, while DDA assured that the future negotiations on Singapore issues would be initiated only after arriving at an explicit consensus, the Derbez Draft decided to do so without consulting the developing country members. Finally, the developing countries had been vocal on ensuring special treatment for their 'strategic' products for a long time and the extent of subsidisation of cotton cultivation in developed countries was at the forefront in that matter. However, instead of asking the developed countries to ensure WTO-compliance with respect to their cotton-subsidisation schemes, the Derbez draft adopted the long-route of promising advisory supports to the affected economies for crop diversification. All these issues prompted India to maintain a hard

17. India and the WTO, "Issues in the Run up to Cancun" (Replies given in Parliament during May, 2003), Vol. 5, No. 5, May 2003, pp. 3-8.

18. For the detailed proposal, see *India and the WTO*, Vol. 5, No. 8, August 2003, pp. 5-7.

19. International Food & Agricultural Trade Policy Council, (2004). *Twenty-Five Ways to Improve the Derbez Draft on Agriculture*, available at, *http://www.agritrade.org/Doha/Derbez/Assessment%20Paper.pdf*

stance against adoption of Derbez Draft.[20] Although the multilateral negotiation was stalled for almost a year due to these differences among member countries, India as a part of the G-20 initiative remained active in the process of reaching an agreement through informal negotiations during this period.[21]

When the deadlock in the negotiating process was broken in July 2004, India played a key role in the discussion along with Australia, Brazil, the EU and the US, which lasted for two weeks. The preliminary drafts prepared at the meeting did not reflect India's concerns on the need for setting disciplines on blue and amber boxes for the developed countries, inclusion of 'special safeguard mechanisms' and 'special product' provisions for developing countries, and it expressed dissatisfaction over these issues.[22] However, it declared at the end of the discussion that the finally agreed upon draft (known as July 2004 Draft), which formed the framework of future negotiations, is much more sensitive to developing country interests as compared to the Derbez Draft in terms of all three pillars of agricultural trade. In addition, the draft proposals on acknowledgement of developing country sectoral concerns (e.g. cotton) and enhancement of non-agricultural market access were also welcomed.[23] Furthermore, India was quite happy with the omission of three Singapore issues (barring trade facilitation) from the negotiating agenda for the time being. This is indeed ironic, as India was the only country opposing inclusion of trade facilitation in the negotiating agenda at Doha (2001).

The future negotiating strategy of India could be partly apprehended from documents of the recently concluded G-20 meet at New Delhi (18-19th March, 2005). The official declaration at the end of the meeting reaffirmed the G-20 position to be adopted the upcoming Hong Kong ministerial, "the need to observe necessary sequencing of issues identified in the July Framework so as to ensure

20. *India and the WTO*, Vol. 5, No. 10-11, October-November 2003, pp. 1-6 (Text of keynote address by the Commerce Minister Mr. Arun Jaitley at FICCI-UNCTAD Seminar on *Reflections on Post-Cancun Agenda: The Way Ahead*, 22 October 2003, New Delhi).

21. "On the Occasion of the Ministerial Meeting of the G-20 held in Brasilia, on December 11th and 12th, 2003, the Group had the opportunity to meet with Commissioner Lamy to discuss the present status of the Doha Round and how to move forward in the negotiations on agriculture." *India and the WTO*, Vol. 5, No. 12, December 2003.

22. "India Rejects WTO Draft", (2004) *The Hindustan Times*, July 31.

23. *India and the WTO*, Vol. 6, No. 8, August 2004, "Statement by Kamal Nath, Minister for Commerce and Industry, in Parliament on the WTO Framework Agreement", (New Delhi, 16 August).

progress in each of the three pillars... ."[24] The document also expressed concern over the pace of lowering of subsidies on cotton and elimination of tariff escalation in developed countries, and stressed the need to ensure special and differential treatment for developing countries for preserving food security, rural development and livelihood concerns within their territories. It is expected that the G-20 member countries would raise these issues at Hong Kong. However, various concerns regarding the group have been discussed in greater details at a later stage.

The Determinants of India's Increasing Participation at Multilateral Negotiations

The above discussion clearly shows that India broke away from the sceptical attitude of the early GATT years during late nineties and continued on a new course in the subsequent period. This change in emphasis was not fuelled by any single event, but was the result of a series of seemingly unrelated episodes, the cumulative effect of which provided the required thrust. At this juncture it is important to analyse the determinants of this changing attitude, both in order to appreciate India's performance at multilateral level in the following period and to form an idea about its future stances. Stated alternatively, it would be interesting to note, whether India has been able to address the initial concerns adequately. Furthermore, it needs to be focused whether India might revert back to the old submissive approach in the future, if the factors responsible for generating the proactive approach cease to exist in the long run. The determinants of India's changed attitude are noted in the following:

Firstly, the liberalisation exercise in early nineties resulted a double-digit export growth rate, which however declined in the post-WTO period instead of rising, as per expectation. The export growth rates during 1993-94 and 1994-95 were 20.0 and 18.4 per cent respectively, as compared to the corresponding figures of 5.3 and 4.6 per cent during 1996-97 and 1997-98 in that order. The export sector also felt the impact of the East Asian economic crisis, although the magnitude of it was much smaller in comparison with several other economies.[25] In all, the compulsion for enhancing export growth was

24. "G-20 Ministerial Declaration", available at *http://www.commerce.nic.in/wto_sub/g20/min_decln.htm*
25. The World Bank (1998), "What Effect Will East Asia's Crisis Has on Developing Countries?" *Prem Notes*, March, No. 1, available at *http://www1.worldbank.org/prem/premnotes/premnote1.pdf.*

felt intensely from 1998 onwards, and multilateral negotiation was rightly identified as a possible way out.

Secondly, despite reduction in tariff barriers in the post-WTO period; evolution of newer forms of non-tariff barriers (NTBs) substantially lowered the additional market access thus generated. While the trade flow of primary products was disturbed due to imposition of unnecessarily stringent SPS and environmental standards, the same of manufacturing products was disrupted due to frequent imposition of contingency provisions (anti-dumping investigations, countervailing duties and safeguard measures).[26] It could be seen from Figure 5.1 that the global share of India in world commodity export market hardly increased in the post-WTO period. India believed that the key implementation issues like special and differential treatment for developing countries or technical barriers to trade related matters were never seriously taken by the developed members, and this also contributed to the realisation of lower market access.[27] This particular realisation was another major factor behind adoption of a proactive approach.

Figure 5.1

India's Global Share in Goods and Services Trade

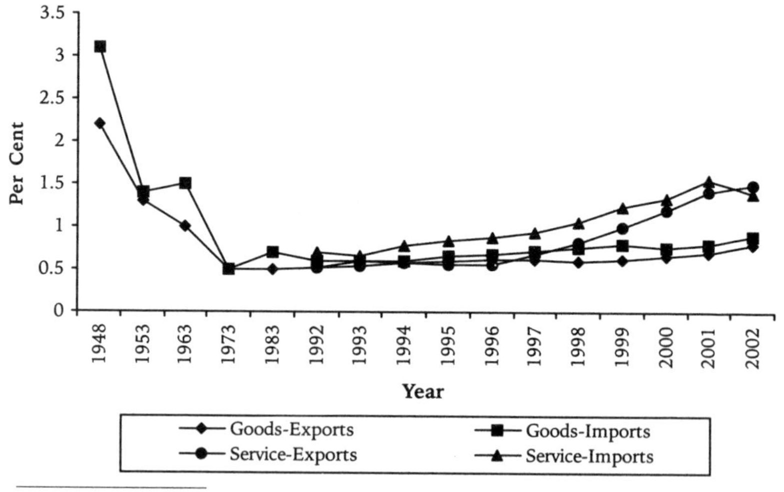

26. Bhattacharyya, B. (1999). "Non-Tariff Measures on Indian Exports: An Assessment", *Occasional Paper* No. 16, New Delhi: Indian Institute of Foreign Trade.

27. *India and the WTO*, Vol. 1, No. 4, April 1999, "Differential and More Favourable Treatment for Developing and Least Developed Countries in Various WTO Agreements —Concerns Regarding Implementation", pp. 1-7.

Thirdly, the service sector emerged as a major foreign currency earner in late nineties, and owing to the barriers on various components of this industry, the urgency to ensure free trade in this arena was intensely felt.[28] It could be observed from Figure 5.1 that the market share of India in world services export market increased significantly since 1997-98. Given the export of professional service providers to the developed countries from India, the major negotiating agenda became ensuring free mobility of natural persons (i.e., Mode 4 of service trade) right from the beginning.

Fourthly, the patenting of a variety of *Basmati* rice ('Texmati', by Ricetec Inc.) in US during late nineties and the indication of upcoming patent applications in traditional medicinal plants like *neem (Azadirachta Indica) haldi* (*Curcuma Longa*), etc. forced India to adopt a proactive approach in case of geographical indications.[29]

Fifthly, environmental and labour-standard related barriers affected a significant proportion of India's exports.[30] When developed countries started discussing inclusion of labour and environmental concerns under WTO purview, India had no other option but to oppose it actively at Seattle, as legitimatisation of these issues under WTO was completely contradictory to its interest.

Sixthly, a total of 13 cases were lodged against the WTO incompatibilities of several domestic provisions of India before Seattle, which had to be repealed after conceding defeat at the dispute settlement body (e.g. compliance with TRIPS—DS 50 and DS 79; removal of quantitative restrictions on imports of agricultural, textile and industrial products—DS 90–94 and DS 96; measures affecting the automotive sector—DS 146 and DS 175).[31] However, as evident by

---

28. For instance, see Dewang Mehta, "Non-Tariff Trade Barriers in I.T. Trade", paper presented in *WTO Information Technology Symposium*, 16 July 1999, Geneva, available at *www.wto.org/english/tratop_e/inftec_e/mehta.ppt.*

29. Khan, Amir Ullah and Debroy, Bibek (2004). "Intellectual Property Rights Beyond 2005: An Indian Perspective on the Debate on IPR Protection and the WTO", Kottayam: D C School of Management and Technology. Also see India's communication entitled, *Extension of the Protection of Geographical Indications for Wines and Spirits to Geographical Indications for Other Products*, Dated 29 March 2001 (*Document No. IP/C/W/247*).

30. Ministry of Commerce, "Non-Tariff Barriers Faced by India", *Preliminary Report*, GoI, New Delhi: November 1999.

31. Chaisse, Julien and Chakraborty, Debashis (2004). "Disputes Resolution in the WTO: In the Light of Chinese and Indian Involvements" in Bibek Debroy and Mohd. Saqib (eds.) *Future Negotiation Issues at WTO: An India-China Perspective*, pp. 377-432, New Delhi: Globus Books.

analysing the two Trade Policy Reviews on India (1998 and 2002), the Indian domestic regime became increasingly WTO-compliant from 1999 onwards.[32] However, the opening up of domestic economy to foreign competition was not matched with commensurate gains in the export markets, as expected by India, thereby further fuelling the urge for proactive negotiations at multilateral level.

Last but not the least, India was not a member of any vibrant trade bloc upto Doha Round and relied mostly on multilateral liberalisation for export growth. In the early days of WTO it had to bear the adverse impact of differential rules of origin requirements in various trade blocs, as the number of RTAs increased significantly in the post WTO period.[33] Scholars have pointed out in the nineties that the move towards regionalism might affect the pace of multilateral negotiation,[34] which was also subscribed by India. Therefore pro-active participation at multilateral negotiations was accorded utmost importance.

While the above-mentioned events led India to adopt a proactive strategy before Seattle ministerial, several other events before and after the Doha Round played a major role in its continuance. Firstly, on the face of HIV/AIDS epidemic in 2001, South Africa started importing a cheaper generic version of the patented medicines from an Indian firm Cipla, through The Medicines and Related Substances Control Amendment Act. However, rising protests from various quarters through legal and diplomatic channels caused South Africa to terminate this process.[35] This event led India to submit a proposal on 'TRIPs and Public Health' in association with several developing countries, which asked the WTO to ensure that the TRIPS Agreement does not infringe upon the sovereign right of the members to

---

32. Chakraborty, Debashis and Chaisse, Julien (2005). "Trade Policy Review Mechanism and Dispute Settlement System: A Cross-Country Analysis of Enforcing WTO Rules between Negotiations and Sanctions", in Bibek Debroy and Md. Saqib (eds.) *WTO at Ten: Looking Back to Look Beyond*, pp. 210-278, New Delhi: Konark Publishers.

33. *India and the WTO*, Vol. 1, No. 8, August 1999, p. 3.

34. Bhagwati, Jagdish and Krueger, Anne O. (1995). *The Dangerous Drift to Preferential Trade Agreements*, Washington D C: The AEI Press; Pravin Krishna, "Regionalism and Multilateralism: A Political Economy Approach", *The Quarterly Journal of Economics*, February 1998, Vol. 113, No. 1, pp. 227-251.

35. Dasgupta, Subhendu (2003). "Their Rules, Our Rights: Intellectual Property Rules and Right to Health", in Byasdeb Dasgupta *et al.*, (eds.), *WTO and TRIPS: Indian Perspective*, pp. 33-34, Kalyani: University of Kalyani, Ch. 2.

formulate their own public health policies and adopt measures for providing affordable access to medicines.[36] In addition, India raised the public health related concern in the post-Doha period at times.

Secondly, India emerged as a major victim of anti-dumping investigations in the post-WTO period, and the leading export-earning sectors like textile suffered in particular. India had to move to the Dispute Settlement Body (DSB) in a number of textile-related cases as complainant, and termination of the alleged measures after winning a couple of cases (for e.g. DS 33 involving US; DS 34 involving Turkey; DS 141 involving EU) encouraged it further to adopt proactive strategies. On the other hand, the defeat in a case on application of rules of origin on textile products (DS 243 involving US) forced India to focus more on market access concerns.[37] Thirdly, increasing participation at the DSB made India aware of the loopholes in the system, and negotiations on that front also took off from 2002 onwards. Fourthly, slow progress of MFA phase-out was another major concern area, which called for active negotiation by the developing countries.[38] It was observed that in the EU and the US market, quotas on most of the key products of India's export basket were to be liberalised only after 31 December 2004. Last but not the least, from mid-2003 onwards the negotiation pattern of the developing countries (including India) focused extensively on agriculture, which has been a direct consequence of the EU-US joint submission in that period.

On the whole, the above analysis suggests that although India's decision to opt for proactive approach was influenced both by domestic and export-market related concerns, the latter was the key determinant in the beginning, i.e., during late nineties. However, the urge for protecting the domestic market has been equally important behind the recent focus on agriculture from 2003 onwards. Given this observation, we turn to the major features of India's negotiation and participation at the WTO rounds.

---

36. India's Communication to WTO with African and Other Developing Countries dated 29 June 2001 (*Document No IP/C/W/296*).

37. India claimed that the rules of origin requirement in US on imports of textiles and apparel products were inconsistent with paragraphs (b), (c), (d) and (e) of Article 2 of the Agreement on Rules of Origin. However, the Panel ruled that India failed to establish its claims.

38. Commonwealth Business Council (2001). *Developing Countries and the WTO Trade Debate: Compelling Case for Full Participation in the New Round*, London.

India's Negotiation and Participation over Last Decade: Major Features

In the following, we note the major features of India's participation at the WTO forums over the last decade. The analysis suggests that while the approach towards 'request' has changed, the same on 'offer' is broadly following the old track.

First, the sectoral feature of India's negotiations and participation could be explained with the help of Table 5.1, showing its submissions to WTO over the last eight years. The primary focus of India's negotiating strategy becomes obvious from the table (agriculture, issues coming under general council, trade in services and intellectual property rights). During 1997-98, India had to respond to the various queries on agriculture by WTO members through notifications, and

Table 5.1

Analysis of India's Submissions at the WTO[39]

(Number of Submissions)

Subject Area	*1997*	*1998*	*1999*	*2000*	*2001*	*2002*	*2003*	*2004*	*Total*
Agriculture	7 (-)	7 (-)	0 (-)	5 (3)	6 (1)	1 (-)	6 (4)	2 (2)	34 (10)
Competition Policy	1 (-)	3 (-)	0 (-)	1 (-)	0 (-)	2 (-)	0	0	7 (-)
Dispute Settlement	0	0	0	0	0	4 (3)	1 (1)	0	5 (4)
Environment	2 (-)	2 (-)	0	3 (-)	0	0	1 (-)	0	8 (-)
General Council	0	4 (-)	29 (9)	1 (-)	7 (5)	1 (1)	8 (7)	1 (1)	51 (23)
Investment	1 (-)	1 (-)	4 (-)	1 (-)	1 (-)	4 (1)	0	0	12 (1)
Non-Agricultural Market Access	0	0	0	0	0	1 ()	4 (1)	0	5 (1)
WTO Rules	0	0	0	0	0	2 (-)	5 (-)	0	7 (-)
Services	3 (-)	1 (-)	0	2 (1)	1 (1)	1 (-)	5 (3)	5 (4)	18 (9)
TRIPS	0	0	2 (-)	7 (2)	4 (4)	4 (3)	1 (1)	1 (1)	19 (11)

Source: Compiled from documents in *http://www.commerce.nic.in/indian_wtopaper.htm*

Note: The numbers in the parentheses indicates the number of joint submissions in association with other developing countries for that category in a particular year.

39. Submissions under service trade include informal submissions to WTO as well.

the large number of submissions was actually defensive in character. However from 2000-01 onwards it started submitting proposals on export and domestic subsidy, market access and non-trade concerns like food security to the WTO. During 2003, the prime focus of the submissions was enforcement of special and differential treatment and identification of special products for developing countries, while in 2004; the focus shifted entirely on market access related issues. A wide variety of issues fall under the purview of general council, which explains the large number of submissions in that category. While in 1999 and 2001 Indian proposals to general council raised issues for discussion at the upcoming ministerial meetings, the communications in 2003 focused on future treatment of Singapore issues. Other concerns like anti-dumping investigations and market access in textile products were not ignored either. In case of services, the growing interest of the country becomes obvious from the increase in the number of submissions, and the stress was primarily laid on liberalisation of Mode 4. In the submissions focusing on TRIPS, India mainly concentrated on public health implications in strict IPR regime, protection of biological diversity and traditional knowledge etc. It is also observed that India did not put required thrust on non-agricultural market access related issues before the Cancun ministerial. In addition, a number of joint submissions on dispute settlement indicate that India is focusing on the need to improve the procedural framework as well.

Second, India always felt comfortable in a developing country grouping at various forums and WTO framework in recent period has not been an exception. After pursuing a submissive strategy in the first two WTO ministerial meetings, followed by a brief period of lone proactive policy at Doha, it is increasingly adopting a proactive approach in association with other developing countries in the recent period, which is likely to continue in coming future. The National Common Minimum Programme of the new Government (2004) clearly outlines its focus to be, "... Fully protect the national interest, particularly of farmers, in all WTO negotiations ... use the flexibility afforded in existing WTO agreements to fully protect Indian agriculture and industry ... play a proactive role in strengthening the emerging solidarity of developing countries in the shape of G-20 in the WTO."[40] The developing country G-20 group has further

40. *National Common Minimum Programme* in *http://www.nac.nic.in/ncmp.htm.*

expanded to G-23 with the entrance of Egypt, Indonesia and Nigeria in the forum, which shows the growing confidence of developing countries in this block. India is also member of the so-called G-33 group (with 42 developing country members), which is vocal on ensuring 'special products' and 'special safeguard mechanisms' for developing countries. The observation could be further stressed in light of the growing number of joint submissions made by India, as seen from Table 5.1.

Third, India's role in the WTO arena has completely reversed with respect to contingency measures in recent years. In the early days of WTO, India was quite unhappy with the high frequency of anti-dumping investigations against its manufacturing exports, especially on the textile and garment products. While from time to time India submitted its proposals to curb the increasing use of anti-dumping measures to WTO,[41] it has also successfully challenged a number of such cases through the dispute settlement mechanism. Although the Indian position was vindicated in a number of cases (for e.g. -DS 141 involving EC), it has also been defeated once (DS 206 involving US), while several others were mutually settled (DS 140 involving EC; DS 168 involving South Africa). However, as seen from Table 5.2, from mid-2001 onwards, India itself has emerged as a major initiator of anti-dumping investigations and concerns have been raised over it from various quarters.[42] Recently, Taiwan (DS 318), EU (DS 304) and Bangladesh (DS 306) have filed cases to DSB complaining against initiation of anti-dumping measures in India, and the results of these ongoing disputes are of immense relevance for all future cases on this provision.[43] It might be said that with respect to anti-dumping investigations, India has adjusted itself in the WTO forum in the

---

41. India's Communication dated 8 May 2003 (*Document No TN/RL/W/106*); Communication dated 17 October 2002 (*Document No TN/RL/W/26*); Communication dated 25 April 2002 (*Document No TN/RL/W/4*).

42. *WTO Annual Report* (2004), Geneva: World Trade Organisation, p. 47; *Trade Policy Review*, "India", World Trade Organisation, 2002.

43. Taiwan (DS 318) has complained that Indian measures are in violation of Article VI:1 and VI:2 of GATT 1994, and Articles 1, 2, 3.1, 3.2, 3.3, 3.4, 3.5, 3.7, 3.8, 4, 5, 6 (including Annex II), 7.4, 12.1 and 12.2 of the ADA. EU (DS 304) complained that Indian measures violate Article VI:1 of GATT 1994; Articles 1, 3.1, 3.2, 3.5, 6.6, 6.8 (including Annex II), 6.9 and 12.2 of the ADA. According to Bangladesh (DS 306) Indian measures are in violation of Article VI of GATT 1994, including Articles VI:1, VI:2 and VI:6(a); Articles 1, 2.1, 2.2, 2.4, 3.1, 3.2, 3.3, 3.4, 3.5, 3.7, 5.4, 5.8, 6.2, 6.4, 6.5, 6.8 (including para. 3 of Annex II), 6.9 and 12.2 of the ADA. The case lodged by Bangladesh is worth mentioning owing to the fact that for the first time a developing country has moved to DSB against India.

Table 5.2

Comparison of Anti-Dumping Cases—the EU, India and the US

Period	*India*		*EU*[44]		*US*	
	A	*B*	*A*	*B*	*A*	*B*
1 January 1995–31 December 1995	5	3	33	21	13	6
1 January 1996–31 December 1996	20	10	23	35	21	21
1 January 1997–31 December 1997	13	7	41	59	16	15
1 January 1998–31 December 1998	33	12	21	42	22	15
1 January 1999–30 June 1999	40	6	32	20	28	7
1 July 1999–30 June 2000	27	11	49	32	29	10
1 July 2000–30 June 2001	37	-	29	-	77	-
1 July 2001–30 June 2002	76	12	23	39	58	11
1 July 2002–30 June 2003	67	12	15	32	29	12
1 July 2003–30 June 2004	37	14	18	19	42	23

Source: *WTO Annual Reports* (various issues).
A – Anti-dumping investigations initiated by the country;
B – Anti-dumping investigations initiated against the country.

wrong way. It needs to be understood that increasing anti-dumping investigations (and imposition of final duties in a fair number of cases) not only hurt the consumers, but also the export industries depending on these import items as inputs; thereby hurting the competitiveness of the industry sector in the long run.

Fourth, Indian attitude towards RTAs has also changed significantly over time. Although it has been member of certain preferential arrangements under 'Enabling Clause' (for e.g. Bangkok Agreement), the emphasis was mostly on multilateral trade liberalisation for export promotion upto late nineties.[45] It has at several occasions expressed concern over the trade-distorting effect of the RTAs.[46] However, shortly afterwards, before Cancun it became interested in forming RTAs with a number of WTO members, spread over Asia, Africa and Latin America.[47] At present the country is

44. The data includes the anti-dumping measures imposed on individual EU member states as well.

45. Chakraborty, Debashis (2003). "Regional Trade Agreements and the WTO Framework: Reconciling Free Trade Objectives", *Policy Paper* No. 4, New Delhi: Liberty Institute.

46. See India's Communication dated 6 June 2003 (*Document No. TN/RL/W/114*).

47. Baru, Sanjaya (2003). "India Launches FTA Spree before Cancun", *The Financial Express*, Friday, June 20. Available at *http://fecolumnists.expressindia.com/print.php?content_id=36543*.

engaged in a couple of Preferential Trade Agreements (Bangkok Agreement; SAPTA, which will be converted into SAFTA). The Free Trade Area with Sri Lanka is already operational, and phasing out of customs tariffs with Thailand has recently started. The Comprehensive Economic Cooperation Agreement (CECA) with Singapore has recently (June 29, 2005) been signed. Negotiations on Indo-ASEAN FTA, Indo-GCC FTA, Indo-MERCOSUR PTA, and BIMST-EC are currently in progress. Furthermore, negations with Southern African Customs Union and Chile have recently started and joint study group on FTA with China is also functioning. Preferential arrangements with Egypt and Israel are also likely to follow in coming future. However, it needs to be mentioned this 'mushrooming' of the RTAs by India has been criticised by several scholars on the ground that the country is going to gain most by continuing on the track of multilateral liberalisation.[48] Given this argument, there is a need to look at the future implications of this move at greater details, and the next section is devoted for that purpose.

Fifth, a similar changing perspective has been noticed in case of trade and investment measures. India was not willing to include Singapore issues in the discussion at Doha ministerial, but later it modified its stance only for trade facilitation. However, in late nineties, it was willing to draw parallel of the freer investment regime (i.e. capital) with free mobility of labour. It noted in its submission to the Working Group on Trade and Investment (*Document No. WT/WGTI/W/39*, Dated 4 June 1998) that, "... Even if the Working Group considers ways for the mobility of capital, there is little or no guarantee that appropriate labour inputs would become available for utilisation of that capital.... For complementing immediate production purposes, the Working Group can suggest ways for selected labour to move from surplus regions to deficit regions." Submissions in the following period further advanced the argument (*Document No. WT/WGTI/W/72*, Dated 13 April 1999), "... mobility of labour should be inextricably linked with the discussions on trade-investment linkage if the WTO is to go beyond looking at delivery systems to look at production systems." However, in the following period, India started slowly moving away from this position citing the slow progress of technology transfer to developing countries, and argued it to be an

48. Agarwal, Manmohan (2004). "Regional Trading Arrangements in the Era of Globalisations: An Indian Perspective", *International Studies*, Vol. 41, No. 4, pp. 411-423, New Delhi: Sage Publications.

obvious reason for regulating FDI inflow (*Document No. WT/WGTI/W/105*, Dated 26 June 2001). India's apathy towards discussion of Singapore issues at Doha should be judged in the light of this changing perspective.

Sixth, it is widely believed that the Indian textile sector would come out as a major 'winner' in the post-MFA phase, although the estimated growth falls short of the same in case of China.[49] India from time to time stressed the importance of ensuring free trade in the textile sector for the developing countries from January 2005 onwards (*Document No. WT/GC/W/503*, dated 14 July 2003). It has also raised concerns over the increase in other form of barriers affecting trade in textiles (*Document No. WT/GC/W/502*, dated 14 July 2003). However, scholars have pointed out that owing to several internal problems (outdated technology, low labour productivity, etc.), which have not been effectively tackled over the last decade, the actual gains of India might be much lower as compared to the estimated one.[50] Clearly the enthusiasm at the external front has not been matched by well-chosen internal policies.

Seventh, TRIPS and public health provisions has always been a major point of debate in India, and the decision of introducing product patent regime has been delayed for 10 years on that concern. In 2005 however, in line with the WTO directive, India introduced the third amendment to the 1970 Patent Act, which allows filing of product patent applications in the area of chemicals, pharmaceuticals, agricultural chemicals and food products. It needs to be mentioned that scholars point out that the amendment goes much beyond India's WTO obligation and might create tensions in the future.[51] Clearly India failed to play its cards properly in this case.

Finally, despite the apparent success, several academicians are quite sceptical on India's claims about gains attained at the Doha Round and at the subsequent forums. It is widely held that the

---

49. Nordas, Hildegunn Kyvik (2004). *The Global Textile and Clothing Industry Post the Agreement on Textile and Clothing*, The World Trade Organisation.

50. Verma, Samar (2004). "How Big is the Bang for India: Market Access in Textiles Post 2004", paper presented in the Seminar entitled *The WTO and India: Issues and Negotiating Strategies* jointly organised by JNU, ICSSR and Cotton College, Guahati, August 11-12.

51. Dhar, Biswajit and C. Niranjan Rao, "Third Amendment to 1970 Patent Act: An Analysis", EPW Commentary, *Economic and Political Weekly*, December 25, 2004, available at *http://www.epw.org.in/showArticles.php?root=2004&leaf=12&filename=8076&filetype=html.*

negotiating stance is focusing too much on attainment of special and differential treatment. Anant (2001) had heavily criticised the official position on implementation issues, and blamed India for its failure at Doha by saying, "The consequence of the government's approach to the WTO and to trade negotiations is to create a self-fulfilling prophecy. Our flawed rejectionist approach to negotiations, with the absurd threats to leave, imply that we are unable to address our own immediate trading concerns ..."[52] Mattoo and Subramanian (2003) also described India's position at Doha as, "characteristically but perhaps not unjustifiably defensive."[53] Most of the scholars have acknowledged the changes in India's attitude towards participation at the multilateral negotiations since Doha, but believed its position in the subsequent period to be rather inflexible.[54] Thus, the qualitative change in India's negotiations is still less than adequate. Furthermore, it is argued that in spite of active participation by India, the 'July 2004 package' has left a number of unanswered questions and the material gains of it from the exercise has been quite questionable.[55] Given the current state of multilateral negotiations, it is highly unlikely that India would gain significantly at the Hong Kong ministerial to be held in December 2005.

The RTAs Involving India: Future Concerns

The considerable increase in the number of proposed RTAs involving India since Cancun could casually be linked with its growing dissatisfaction with the pace of multilateral liberalisation. However, given this explanation, a number of relevant questions arise. First and foremost, whether the RTAs would be able to provide a 'safe' export market for India? A related concern is whether the proposed blocs, once in force, be able to provide a sizable alternative to multilateral

---

52. Anant, T.C.A. (2001). "India and the WTO: Flawed Rejectionist Approach", *Economic and Political Weekly*, Vol. 36, No. 46& 47, pp. 4243-4245, Mumbai: November 24.

53. Mattoo, Aaditya and Arvind Subramanian (2003). "India and the Multilateral Trading System Post-Doha: Defensive or Pro-active?" in Aaditya Mattoo and Robert M. Stern (eds.) *India and the WTO*, p. 328, Washington, DC: World Bank and Oxford University Press.

54. Deardorff, Alan V. and Robert M. Stern (204). "Designing A Pro-Active Stance for India in the Doha Development Agenda Negotiations", paper presented in the Seminar entitled *WTO Negotiations: India's Post-Cancun Concerns* jointly organised by Planning Commission and International Trade and Development Division, JNU, October 18-19. Also see Draper and Sally (2004).

55. Chakraborty, Debashis (2004). "Recent Negotiation Trends on Agriculture under WTO", New Delhi: *RGICS Working Paper* No. 47.

negotiations. Second, is the bond among the members in these proposed trade blocs strong, i.e., do they have a cohesive force among them? Finally, given the fact that a number of the proposed partners are already members of G-20 network, is there any possibility of replicating the 'success' of agricultural negotiation in case of other areas, for e.g.—services?

It is easier to address the first question and the answer is in affirmative, at least in the short run. It has been observed that Indian export industries are enjoying economies of scale, while the same is on the decline for import-competing sectors.[56] In addition, the Intra-Industry Trade between India and East and South-East Asian countries are on the rise, which is expected to increase further in the future. Both these facts jointly indicate that Indian export industries would be able to reap the full benefits of the proposed RTAs. In addition, the agreements are 'extensive', i.e., they promise to liberalise trade in goods, services as well as the investment measures. Therefore, apart from the export industries, the import industries, which depend on raw material imports, would be benefited from the lowering of tariff barriers. Furthermore, several RTA-led reforms would be instrumental in enhancing the overall efficiency as well as the pace of future reform. For instance, the CECA with Singapore allow three Singaporean banks complete operational freedom in India, and in return consolidate the status of Indian banks there. This could well emerge as the first step towards full-fledged opening of financial sector.[57]

The argument could be further elaborated with the help of Table 5.3, where the trade scenario of India with the proposed partners is compared for the years 1996-97 and 2003-04, both in terms of trade ranks and market shares. A clear trend emerges from the analysis. First, barring a handful of exceptions like Brunei, Paraguay etc., the importance of proposed partners in India's trade basket is increasing (measured in terms of either export or import ranking of the proposed partners or both). Second, a number of countries, already negotiating partners of India at multilateral forums, are climbing up in the rankings both in terms of exports and imports (China, Sri Lanka,

---

56. Barua, Alokesh and Debashis Chakraborty (2004). "Liberalisation, Trade and Industrial Performance in India: An Empirical Study", paper presented in the Seminar entitled *WTO Negotiations: India's Post-Cancun Concerns* jointly organised by Planning Commission and International Trade and Development Division, JNU, October 18-19.

57. "Club Rules Apply", *Hindustan Times*, June 27, 2005.

Table 5.3

Analysis of Trade Scenario between India and Proposed Partners

Countries	Export				Import			
	1996-97		2003-04		1996-97		2003-04	
	Share	Rank	Share	Rank	Share	Rank	Share	Rank
West Asia								
Afghanistan	0.0679	78	0.2279	54	0.0078	100	0.0518	69
Bahrain	0.1875	55	0.1748	59	0.3393	37	0.0954	54
Kuwait	0.4623	37	0.4998	35	2.4253	12	0.1823	44
Oman	0.3495	43	0.4057	39	0.0309	79	0.0651	64
Qatar	0.0953	68	0.2012	56	0.3140	39	0.2394	41
Saudi Arabia	1.7245	16	1.7595	16	4.6500	6	0.9440	21
United Arab Emirates	4.4100	6	8.0285	2	3.3929	8	2.6358	13
South Asia								
Bangladesh	2.5962	10	2.7266	9	0.1590	50	0.0993	52
Bhutan	0.0657	81	0.1402	68	0.0863	60	0.0670	63
Maldives	0.0310	97	0.0663	90	0.0004	130	0.0005	156
Nepal	0.4951	33	1.0484	25	0.1637	49	0.3660	31
Pakistan	0.4697	36	0.4494	36	0.0924	58	0.0738	60
Sri Lanka	1.4264	20	2.0663	12	0.1095	57	0.2492	40
East and Southeast Asia								
Brunei Darussalam	0.0180	108	0.0072	159	0.0001	142	0.0004	158
Cambodia	0.0047	141	0.0291	117	-	-	0.0004	160
China, PR	1.8369	14	4.6287	5	1.9342	17	5.1865	3
Indonesia	1.7683	15	1.7656	15	1.5257	19	2.7154	11
Japan	5.9933	3	2.6773	11	5.5899	4	3.4136	9

Contd. ...

...Contd. ...

Countries	*Export*				*Import*			
	1996-97		*2003-04*		*1996-97*		*2003-04*	
	Share	*Rank*	*Share*	*Rank*	*Share*	*Rank*	*Share*	*Rank*
Lao People's Democratic Republic	0.0011	184	0.0007	201	-	-	0.0002	168
Malaysia	1.5869	17	1.3984	19	2.8194	11	2.6188	14
Myanmar	0.1350	61	0.1404	67	0.4528	34	0.5234	28
Philippines	0.5487	31	0.5036	34	0.0420	72	0.1563	46
Republic of Korea	1.5491	18	1.1980	21	2.2580	14	3.6202	8
Singapore	2.9204	8	3.3282	7	2.1494	16	2.6684	12
Thailand	1.3358	21	1.3027	20	0.5039	32	0.7793	25
Vietnam	0.3528	42	0.6429	32	0.0043	105	0.0489	70
Africa								
Botswana	0.0020	170	0.0105	145	-	-	0.0001	178
Mauritius	0.4820	34	0.3180	45	0.0102	92	0.0097	103
Namibia	0.0028	161	0.0120	143	0.0001	140	0.0001	173
South Africa	0.9447	26	0.8448	29	0.8204	25	2.4302	15
Swaziland	0.0086	130	0.0455	101	0.0182	84	0.0022	136
Latin America								
Argentina	0.1753	57	0.1368	72	0.5144	30	0.6705	27
Brazil	0.3959	41	0.4300	37	0.3900	35	0.4012	29
Chile	0.1974	53	0.1300	74	0.2495	43	0.2006	42
Paraguay	0.0186	107	0.0166	138	0.0004	129	0.0010	145
Uruguay	0.0480	93	0.0305	114	0.0038	106	0.0131	96

Note: Calculations on the basis of the data taken from the Ministry of Commerce, Government of India.

Singapore, Thailand, Brazil etc.). Furthermore, as of 2003-04, the total shares of the intended partners account for nearly 40 and 30 per cent of India's total export and import respectively. In this scenario, it is only logical to expect that preferential agreements would provide further boost to bilateral trade and investment among the partners. However, competitiveness is not time-invariant and in long run certain Indian products may face stiff competition from the other bloc members, and the future pace of internal liberalisation in that case would depend on the intensity of that competition.[58] Nonetheless the internal objection to the adverse impacts of liberalisation in the initial years is likely to be minimum, since negotiations in most of these proposed blocs would be completed over a period of ten years.[59] However, the incentive for multilateral negotiation would remain quite significant since at least for trade in services, India would still be looking towards liberalisation of the EU and US market, given its export pattern.

To analyse the second question, let us consider Tables 5.3 and 5.4. The idea is to check whether India's inclination towards regionalism has been a calculated affair, i.e., whether a drift towards 'natural' allies has taken place. As mentioned earlier, trade intensity with most of the partners is on the rise. Apart from the willingness to enhance bilateral trade further, the urge to extract higher market access from other markets (e.g. the EU and the US) is another major incentive. Given the dominance of developing countries and LDCs among the proposed partners, it is expected that the bond among them would be strong owing to the following grounds.

First, Table 5.4 attempts to identify the existing level of cooperation between India and the proposed partners at multilateral negotiations, where the number of joint submissions by India and a particular country is used as a suitable proxy. The level of cooperation

58. For instance, Draper and Sally (2004) note that MEROSUR has not been able to enforce further trade liberalisation since 1995 owing to an anti-liberalisation backlash following the financial crisis. In the course of the field survey of a EU-funded project entitled, "Globalisation and its Impact on National Firms and Public Governance: The Case of China and India", it has been observed that a number of Indian firms are uncomfortable with the future implications of the FTAs with the South-East Asian countries.

59. The tariff elimination on goods trade between India and ASEAN countries would be complete by 2016, starting from January 2006, although in case of some countries, it will be achieved by 2011. In case of BIMST-EC, the tariff elimination for developing country imports under normal track will be achieved by June 2012, starting from July 2007. In case of Indo-Thailand FTA, the zero-duty imports will be achieved by 2010.

Table 5.4

Analysis of Current Cooperation between India and Potential Partners at WTO Negotiations

Countries	*WTO Disciplines*						
	A	*B*	*C*	*D*	*E*	*F*	*G*
West Asia							
Afghanistan	-	-	-	-	-	-	-
Bahrain	-	-	-	-	-	-	-
Kuwait	-	-	-	-	-	-	-
Oman	-	-	-	-	-	-	-
Qatar	-	-	-	-	-	-	-
Saudi Arabia	-	-	-	-	-	-	-
United Arab Emirates	-	-	-	-	-	-	-
South Asia							
Bangladesh	-	-	8	-	-	-	1
Bhutan	-	-	-	-	-	-	-
Maldives	-	-	2	-	-	-	-
Nepal	-	-	-	-	-	-	-
Pakistan	5	2	15	1	-	8	5
Sri Lanka	4	2	11	-	-	1	7
East and Southeast Asia							
Brunei Darussalam	-	-	-	-	-	-	-
Cambodia	-	-	-	-	-	-	-
China, PR	3	-	5	1	-	5	-
Indonesia	4	1	21	-	1	5	1
Japan	1	-	-	-	-	1	-
Lao People's Democratic Republic	-	-	-	-	-	-	-
Malaysia	2	3	15	-	1	4	1
Myanmar	-	-	-	-	-	-	-
Philippines	4	-	5	-	-	5	1
Republic of Korea	3	-	-	-	-	1	-
Singapore	-	-	-	-	-	1	-
Thailand	2	-	5	-	-	5	4
Vietnam	-	-	2	-	-	-	-
Africa							
Botswana	2	-	5	-	-	-	1
Mauritius	2	-	4	-	1	-	4

Contd. ...

...Contd. ...

Countries	*WTO Disciplines*						
	A	*B*	*C*	*D*	*E*	*F*	*G*
Namibia	1	-	1	-	-	-	1
South Africa	2	-	1	-	-	-	1
Swaziland	1	-	1	-	-	-	1
Latin America							
Argentina	3	-	-	-	-	4	1
Brazil	3	-	2	-	-	4	4
Chile	3	-	-	-	-	4	-
Paraguay	3	-	1	-	-	1	-
Uruguay	1	-	-	-	-	-	-

Note: Compiled from India's Proposals to WTO

A – Agriculture; B – Dispute Resolution; C – General Council (Special and Differential Treatment, Singapore Issues, Anti-Dumping, Trade in Textiles, Modalities, Preparation for Ministerial Conferences etc.); D – Investment; E – Non-Agricultural Market Access; F – Services; G – TRIPS.

is quite appreciable with a number of African, South-East Asian and Latin American partners as well as two regional neighbours—Pakistan and Sri Lanka. The West Asian countries however are yet to enter into any negotiating collaboration with India, presumably owing to the dissimilarity in trade pattern.[60] The areas characterised by maximum cooperation are agriculture, issues under general council (mainly trade in textile and garments, increasing use of contingency measures, etc.) and services. Interestingly, regional neighbours like Pakistan and Sri Lanka have rallied heavily behind India on the TRIPS front, clearly owing to similarity in export pattern. Given the dominance of labour-intensive products in the export basket of the proposed partners, the cooperation is likely to be strengthened further in future.

Second, there exist a striking similarity between the NTBs imposed on exports of India and a number of ESCAP countries, who are currently in the process of becoming partners, in the EU and the US market.[61] This calls for adoption of a joint approach to deal with the major barriers applied on their exports.

60. India's decision to enter into RTAs with the GCC countries is more influenced by the economic need of mineral fuel importation from most of these countries.

61. Economic and Social Commission for Asia and the Pacific (2005). "Non-tariff Measures with Potentially Restrictive Market Access Implications Emerging in a Post-Uruguay Round Context", (New York, ESCAP, *Studies in Trade and Investment* No. 40, United Nations, 2000); Rajesh Mehta and J. George (eds.), *Food Safety Regulation Concerns and Trade: The Developing Country Experience*, New Delhi: Macmillan India.

Third, there is a growing concern among the developing countries that even after the removal of the MFA quota regime, the expected level of market access will not be forthcoming.[62] In other words, it makes sense for the major exporters of textiles and garments to collaborate on this issue.

Fourth, apart from material areas of cooperation, the importance of institutional areas of cooperation should not be undermined. The working of the dispute settlement system has been questioned by developing countries at times.[63] With the completion of the ten-year transitory phase, a stream of disputes is likely to be brought to the DSB. The developing countries would gain extensively by following a joint negotiating agenda for systemic reform of the Dispute Settlement Mechanism.[64]

Last but not the least, apart from demanding market access for exports, the developing countries have also been vocal on ensuring sufficient protection to their domestic entities, as evident from the joint submissions to WTO regarding 'special products', 'special safeguard mechanisms' and 'special and differential treatment'. Clearly, this is another area where India and most of the partners stand to gain extensively by pursuing a joint negotiating agenda.[65]

However, a critical point needs to be mentioned here. While India's recent decision of entering into trade blocs with other developing countries is economically justifiable; the selection procedure for identifying the potential partners is subject to questions. It is quite evident that the proposed blocs, once in force, would lead to overlapping RTAs. For instance, India is in the process

---

62. See the proposal submitted by India and other developing countries on 14 July 2003 (*Document No. WT/GC/W/503*). India already holds trade ties with Maldives and Pakistan and is in the process of entering in preferential arrangement with Indonesia, People's Republic of China, Thailand and Vietnam. Also the Commerce Minster recently has talked about the need to resist new forms of protectionism in post-MFA era at the India economic Summit Plenary Session on *International Trade: A New Voice of Emerging Markets*, organised by Confederation of Indian Industries and the World Economic Forum, New Delhi on December 6, 2004. *India and The WTO*, Vol. 6, No. 11-12, November-December 2004, available at *http://www.commerce.nic.in/nov-dec04/main.htm#KAMALNATHSAYS*.

63. Hoekman, Bernard M. and Mavroidis Petros C. (2001). "WTO Dispute Settlement, Transparency and Surveillance", in Bernard Hoekman and Will Martin (eds.) *Developing Countries and the WTO: A Pro-Active Agenda'*, p. 23, Oxford: Blackwell Publishers.

64. See Chaisse and Chakraborty (2004). So far Malaysia, Pakistan, Sri Lanka and Indonesia have jointly submitted proposals with India to WTO in this regard.

65. Chakraborty, Debashis and Arnab Kumar Hazra (2005). "Preferential Trade Agreements and India: A Review of Issues", New Delhi: *RGICS Working Paper* No. 48.

of entering into a FTA with ASEAN, in which case the need for separate FTAs with Thailand or Singapore is not as important. Similarly, going for BIMST-EC undermines the working of SAFTA, proposed Indo-ASEAN FTA and Indo-Sri Lanka FTA. One of the major allegations made by India against RTAs during late nineties was that the complexities of the overlapping blocs act against the exporters of the excluded member.[66] In future, India might as well attract criticism on the same ground from various quarters.

Now let us consider the final question, i.e., whether the G-20 solidarity (and several other potential partners as well) in case of agriculture is replicable in case of negotiations in services. Scholars have pointed out from time to time that developing countries stand to gain heavily by pursuing a joint proactive approach at multilateral negotiations.[67] At Doha, India came to realise the ineffectiveness of pursuing a solitary pro-active approach, and started collaborating with other developing countries on the issues pertaining to its key interest, as seen from Table 5.1. Given the limited 'success' India has experienced in case of agriculture through joint negotiations, its interest in extending the same level of collaboration towards trade in services and other areas of interest like TRIPS would be obvious. It seems the developing countries have already reached a tacit understanding, as Brazil is returning India's support in case of agriculture at negotiations on Mode 4 in services.[68] Needless to add, this type of cross-sympathisation of interests would strengthen the developing country alliance further. In addition, apart from regional neighbor Pakistan; China, Indonesia, Thailand and the Philippines are fast emerging as strong negotiating partners in case of trade in services and an explicit focus is on liberalisation of mode 4, where India's prime interest lies.[69]

---

66. For overlapping RTAs, see World Bank, *Trade Blocs Policy Research Report*, Oxford University Press, August 2000, *http://www.worldbank.org/research/trade/pdf/trade_blocs2.pdf*

67. Mattoo and Subramanian (2003); Sally (2000).

68. Draper and Sally (2004).

69. See the developing country joint proposals entitled: *Review of Progress in Negotiations, Including Pursuant to Paragraph 15 of the Guidelines for Negotiations*, Dated 29 September 2004 (*Document No. TN/S/W/23*); *Informal Paper on Mode 4-Transparency Issues*, Dated 29 September 2004 (*Document No. JOB(04)/142*); *Review of Progress as established in Paragraph 15 of the Guidelines and Procedures for the Negotiations on Trade in Services*, Dated 31 March 2004 (*Document No. TN/S/W/19*); *Implementation of Paragraph 15 of the Guidelines and Procedures for the Negotiations on Trade in Services*, Dated 25 July 2003 (*Document No. TN/S/W/16*) and *Proposed Liberalisation of Mode 4 Under GATS Negotiations*, Dated 3 July 2003 (*Document No. TN/S/W/14*).

However, two quick facts need to be borne in mind. First, the export interests of the G-20 members vary widely, and hence arriving at a consensus on any issue would be difficult. It needs to be noted that although the G-20 Ministers at New Delhi in March 2005 have discussed issues relating to services export and non-agricultural market access, these provisions were not mentioned in the final declaration.[70] To put in a different way, the G-20 consensus in case of agriculture was achieved through an external shock, the EU-US joint proposal before the Cancun Ministerial. The consensus thus achieved was 'negative' in character, and was easier to form. Replicating the same in case of services through 'positive' measures, i.e., through offers by consensus among the members of the group would not be so easy. Scholars are already sceptical about the collective bargaining ability of the group in future.[71] Furthermore, India itself did not adopt a proactive approach towards liberalising trade in services 'across-the-board' upto Cancun, and the focus was primarily on Mode 4. The hesitant 'offer' approach by India in services negotiations has often been criticised. In addition, it is unlikely that in the post September 11 period, the number of visa applications granted by the US could be drastically raised. Furthermore, the Mode 4 process is partly victim of India's success in BPO, which is also being threatened in certain US states on the ground of domestic job losses.[72] This caused India to focus more on liberalisation of Mode 1 of services in the recent period (*Document No. JOB(04)/87,* Dated 28 June 2004).

Moreover, the level of support from proposed partners (including G-20) in India's pursuit in other areas like Mode 4 would significantly depend on the level of access realised by them in Indian market. While India has been vocal on the prevalence of NTBs in the developed country markets for quite some time, the same at its domestic market is not at all insignificant and might trigger dissatisfaction among the proposed partners in future.[73] To maintain

70. The Hindu (2005), "G-20 Adopts New Delhi Declaration", March 20, available at *http://www.thehindubusinessline.com/2005/03/20/stories/2005032001810300.htm*

71. See Ranjan Prabhash, "How Long can the G-20 Hold Itself Together? A Power Analysis" *Working Paper* No. 1, Centre for Trade and Development, An Oxfam GB Initiative, New Delhi, February 2005.

72. Hindustan Times (2004), "California Senate passes Anti-BPO Bill", August 25.

73. See Deb Kusum Das, "Quantifying Trade Barriers: Has Protection Declined Substantially in Indian Manufacturing?" New Delhi: *ICRIER Working Paper* No. 105, July 2003. Also, for an account of the current status of barriers on trade in various services in India, see United States Trade Representative, "Foreign Trade Barriers", 2004, pp. 213-226, available at *www.ustr.gov.*

a successful proactive strategy at the multilateral forum in case of services, India needs to liberalise the domestic market further.

In Lieu of Conclusion

India has indeed come a long way from the initial years of UR negotiations, when in association with Brazil and Egypt it actually opposed the US move for liberalisation of services trade.[74] The scenario has also tremendously changed in comparison with the early days of WTO, when India had at best 'stances' on various issues of national concern, rather than focused 'strategies'. Since the Doha ministerial, there has been a conscious attempt on India's part to address the major concerns effectively. The newly adopted proactive approach has allowed India to jointly negotiate on liberalisation of trade in agriculture and the recent enthusiasm on RTA formation is also expected to benefit the economy, although the selection of potential partners is subject to questions. The policymakers have understood the ineffectiveness of the submissive approach, and chances of re-adopting such a policy at a future date are practically nil. However, the WTO-compliance of several domestic policies (e.g., contingency measures) is likely to come under fire in coming future, and they might impede India's chances of success in future negotiations. The limitations of certain WTO-induced reforms (e.g., the Patent Act amendment in 2005) might also turn out to be harmful for the country. Furthermore, despite the outward changes in attitude towards negotiations, the attachment towards special and differential treatment and the hesitation in making offers at negotiation table is also likely to affect its potential gains. In addition, India's current uneasiness towards opening the agricultural and certain services sectors at negotiations is unrealistic.[75] Therefore, the need of the hour is to adopt a true 'request-and-offer' approach, in association with other developing countries at the future negotiations.

---

74. Chisti (1991), p. 103.

75. In late nineties, after India conceded defeat in DS 90 against the US, it had to remove import restrictions on agricultural items, and it was widely believed that the agricultural sector might be ruined. See Binu S. Thomas, *Flood of Food Imports could Destroy Indian Agriculture*, available at *http://www.twnside.org.sg/title/flood-cn.htm*. However, contrary to popular belief, the opening up of imports did not create any major problem for the agriculture sector.

6

Trade in Agriculture and India: Any Lesson to Learn from the Textile Sector?

DEBASHIS CHAKRABORTY and
PAVEL CHAKRABORTY

Introduction

Since the Cancun Ministerial (2003), agriculture has taken the hotspot at multilateral negotiations. While a number of developing countries under the wings of G-20 are actively negotiating for reduction in the farm subsidies in their developed counterparts, the other side is not too willing to go for immediate reforms. The negotiations based on the modalities arrived at the July 2004 discussions is yet to be concluded and clearly despite some progress the discussions at the Hong Kong Ministerial (2005) could not solve most of the concerns.

Much has been said about the negotiating stance of India, as a part of the G-20 framework, towards removal of agricultural subsidies. The current chapter wants to focus on the preparedness of India on agricultural trade from a slightly different perspective. The Uruguay Round discussion had created a beautiful set of inter-linked arrangements, by dint of which the first 10 years of WTO emerged as the transitory phase. While the developing countries were given 10 years time to introduce the system of product patents (under TRIPS) and implement the reduction commitments in case of agriculture;[1] the removal of the quota system on textile and clothing products was also delayed by the same period. It was quite obvious right from the beginning that the consessional phase of 10 years is not a solution by itself for developing countries, and there is an urgent need to enhance the competitiveness of their domestic industries in order to reap the benefits of the multilateral trade regime.

1. Agreement on Agriculture, Article 15, "Special and Differential Treatment", GATT Agreement.

The MFA regime has been phased out from January 1, 2005 onwards, for which India should have been reasonably well prepared, as the certainty of this event was known for the last 10 years. However, the relative gains of India *vis-à-vis* China in the post-MFA phase are subject to questions. A parallel could be run between textile and agricultural sector, as both the sectors in India are characterised by predominance of small players. The problems of market access in both sectors has been acknowledged by WTO at times (WTO, 2001). Furthermore, these two sectors jointly accounts for a significant proportion of workers in the economy. Although the exact date of 'freeing' (or practically speaking, reasonably reducing export and domestic subsidies) trade in agriculture is uncertain, the preparedness for that event for any developing country is no less important. The current analysis wants to comment on the possible outcome for India in case of a liberalisation of farm subsidies in developed countries, on the basis of its current level of preparedness.

The chapter is arranged along the following lines. First the pre- and post-MFA concerns of the MFA regime are discussed. The negotiating scenario in the agriculture front is analysed next, followed by the concerns at the domestic front. Finally, the conclusions are drawn.

Textile: The Pre- and Post-MFA Concerns

A number of *ex-ante* analyses on the likely impact of MFA phase-out had suggested that China and India would emerge as the major beneficiaries, while the brunt will be borne by several South-East Asian and Latin American countries (Spinanger and Verma, 2003; Nordas, 2004). Various other studies have also pointed out the potential gains of Indian textile sector in the wake of MFA phase-out (Exim Bank, 1995). However, there is a perceptible difference between having a potential for any sector and successfully harnessing it. The bottlenecks as well as the systemic problems faced by the Indian textile and clothing industries has been pointed out by various studies from time to time (Banik and Bandopadhyay, 2000; Verma, 2002; Carver *et al.*, 2004; Chakraborty, 2004b). The problems faced by the sector includes lower penetration of mechanisation at various stages of production, absence of shuttle-less looms in a major segment of the industry, abysmally low investment per machine[2] and low capacity utilisation trends, all of which low labour cost alone cannot

2. While the investment per machine is around US $ 250 in India, the comparable figures are around US $ 3000 in South Korea and Hong Kong.

compensate for. Most of these scenarios resulted from the government decision to reserve the sector as a small-scale industry until recently, which never allowed the firms to enjoy economies of scale in stark contrast with their Chinese counterparts. The net result was that India remained moderately (and not highly) competitive in various product segments as seen from the following table:

Table 6.1

Competitiveness of Indian Textile Industry at Various Stages

Process	*Determinants of Competitive Advantage*	*India's Competitive Position*	*Emerging Competition*
Spinning	Quality, Cotton Price	Medium	Indonesia, Turkey
Weaving	Technology, Automation, Power, Finance	Low	Vietnam, Philippines
Processing	Scale Economy, Technology, Environment Issue, Finance	Low	China, Vietnam, Philippines
Garmenting	Labour Cost, Productivity, Brand Fashion Design	Medium	Bangladesh, Sri Lanka, Morocco, East Europe, Mexico

Source: Verma (2002).

Nordas (2004) notes the Revealed Comparative Advantage (RCA) trends in textile and clothing industry for a number of countries. It is observed from the analysis that in case of textile, India (4.67) is quite in a poor position *vis-à-vis* a number of developing countries like Pakistan (18.35), Nepal (10.37), Cambodia (8.84), Bangladesh (8.74) and Egypt (5.44). A similar scenario is observed in case of clothing, where India's RCA (3.90) again looks quite modest in comparison to Macao (19.97), Bangladesh (18.63), Cambodia (18.06), Sri Lanka (14.36), Nepal (11.66), Hong Kong (10.09) and Pakistan (6.53).

It could be argued that since the textile and clothing products were subject to quantitative restrictions, RCA might not be the right indicator for measuring competitiveness. Through a GTAP analysis, Spinanger and Verma (2003) noted that in case of trade in textiles, China (PRC), Chinese Taipei, Japan and Bangladesh register a major growth in the post-MFA phase, while virtually all other economies experience losses (including India and Mexico). In case of clothing exports, the study observed that while PRC's share in total world trade would reach over 25 per cent in the base year, India's gains because of quota phase-out gain would be partly nullified due to Chinese accession into the WTO.

The market-wise detailed projections are quoted here from Nordas (2004) in Figures 6.1–6.4 in the following, which shows a favourable outcome for India, mostly in clothing. It is observed that in the EU market, both India and China will increase their market share, while African countries, the United States/Canada, Turkey, Central and Eastern European countries, Republic of Korea and Chinese Taipei will lose market share. In case of textile, while the pre-quota phase-out and post-quota figures for China are 10 and 12 per cent respectively, the figures for India are 9 and 11 per cent in that order. However for clothing products, China's gains from quota removal (18 to 29 per cent) are much higher as compared to the same for India (6 to 9 per cent).

A mixed scenario is repeated in the estimations for US market, where China and India stand to gain most from the MFA phase-out. However, the gains are almost nil in case of trade in textile where India's share remains unchanged at 5 per cent, while China increases its share from 11 to 18 per cent. India fares much better in the clothing segment, where its share increases from 4 to 15 per cent, although it looks far too modest in comparison with the same for China (16 to 50 per cent). African countries and would bear the maximum losses originating from MFA phase-out in the US market.

There is a need to focus on the determinants of the seemingly poor performance of the textile firms. In Table 6.2, a comparative account of the top and bottom firms of the sector is provided through an analysis on the basis of the data obtained from the CMIE PROWESS database. It is observed that while the sales and exports of the top 50 firms in the sector were increasing over the years that were hardly the case with the bottom 50 companies. Furthermore, the cash profit is quite low and the proportion of the firms with high profitability declined over 1995 to 2001, which partly explains the abysmally low R & D expenditures throughout the period. Even the number of firms undertaking R & D expenditures among the top 50 firms had declined over 1995 to 2001. While the possibility of under reporting by the firms cannot be denied, the trend is indeed noteworthy.

On the external front, it has been observed that the process of integration has been very slow, and developed countries often deliberately delayed it. During the first three years, the US and the EU eliminated only a handful of quota items (Verma, 2004). After eight and a half years the following number of quotas still remained operational—851 out of 932 in the United States, 222 out of 303 in the EU, and 292 out of 368 in Canada respectively (Government of

Figure 6.1

Market Shares before and after Quota Elimination (Textiles–EU)

Before

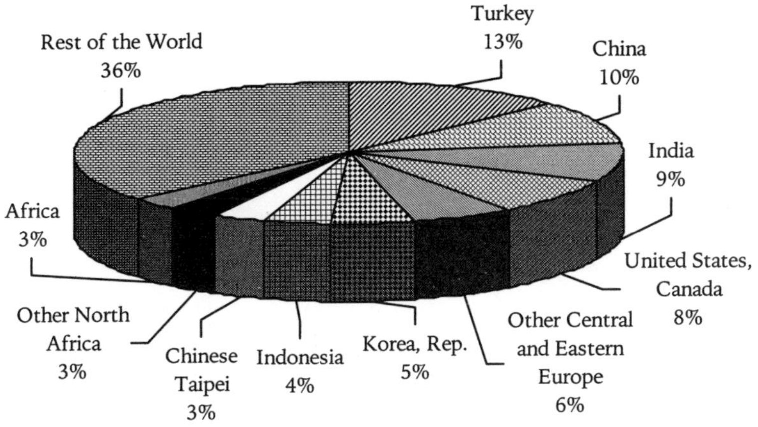

After

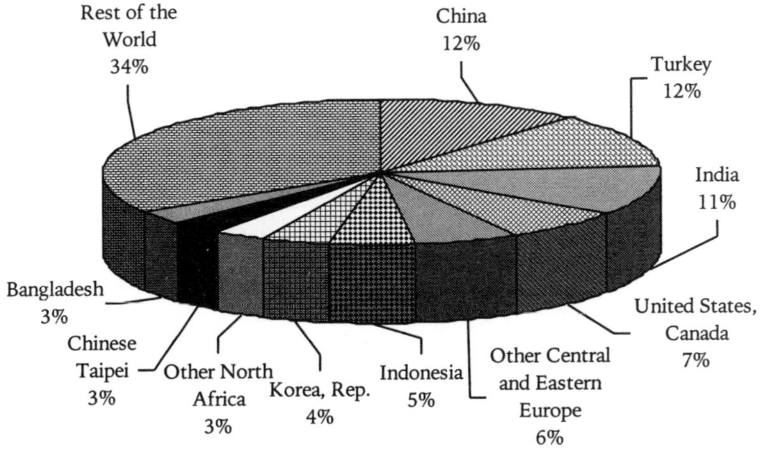

Source: Nordas (2004)

Figure 6.2

Market Shares before and after Quota Elimination (Clothing–EU)

Before

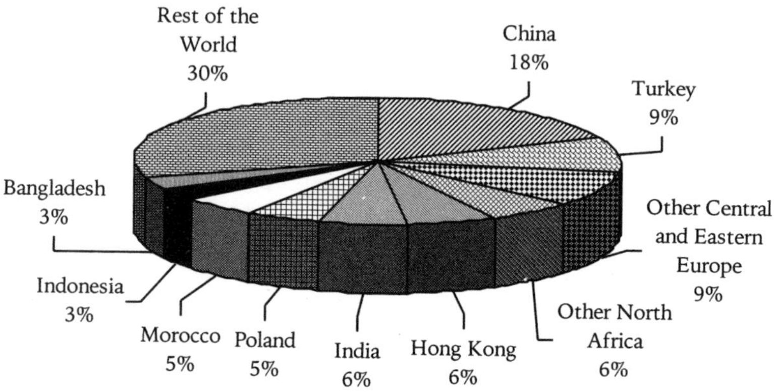

After

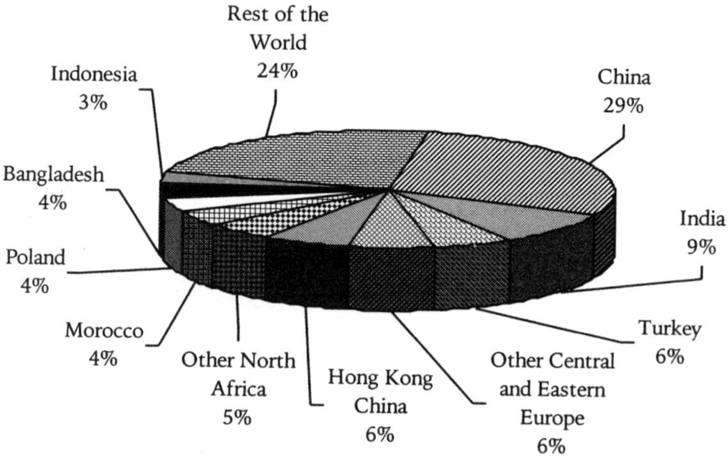

Source: Nordas (2004)

Figure 6.3

Market Shares before and after Quota Elimination (Textile–USA)

Before

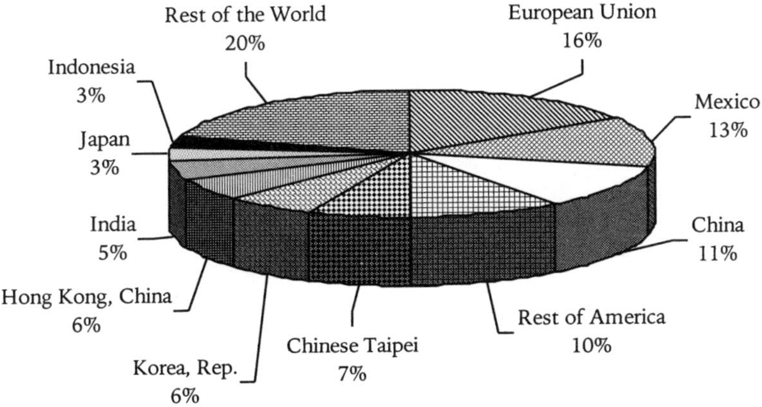

After

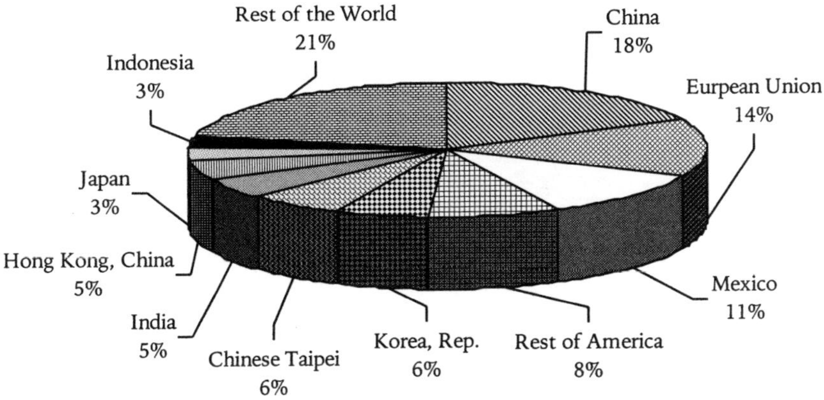

Source: Nordas (2004)

Figure 6.4

Market Shares before and after Quota Elimination (Clothing–USA)

Before

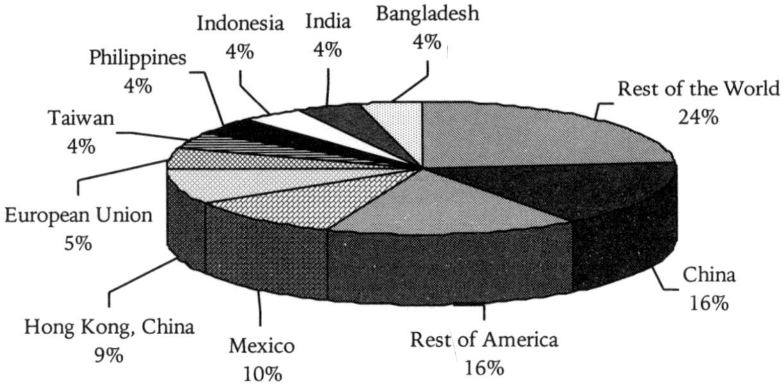

After

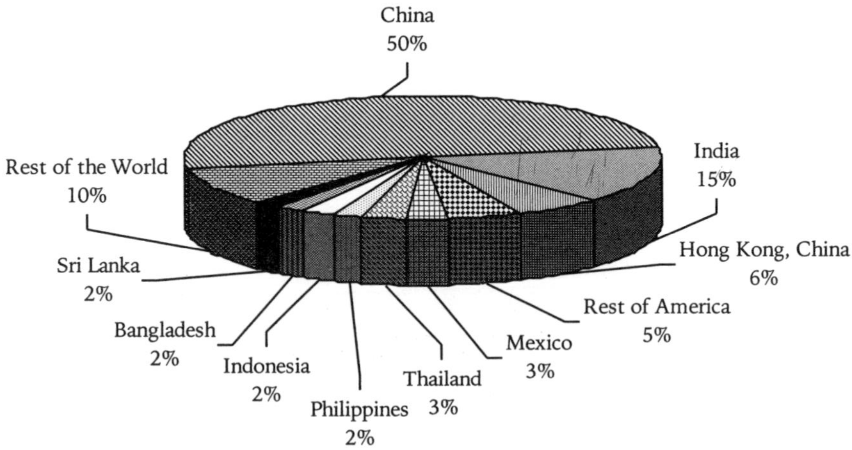

Source: Nordas (2004)

Table 6.2

Analysis of the Indian Textile Industry

(Rs. Crore)

Indicators	*1989*	*1995*	*2001*
Total Sales (Top 50 Firms)	5426.39	16574.77	28249.16
Total Sales (Bottom 50 Firms)	476.47	32.37	49.87
Total Exports (Top 50 Firms)	231.74	2109.23	5154.10
Total Exports (Bottom 50 Firms)	34.75	6.83	6.27
Cash Profit (Top 50 Firms)	30.84	1509.51	282.28
Cash Profit (Bottom 50 Firms)	-27.09	-0.89	-270.73
R&D Expenditure (Top 50 Firms)	0	9.41	7.80
R&D Expenditure (Bottom 50 Firms)	0	0	0.07
Number of Firms Undertaking R&D Expenditure (Top 50 Firms)	0	15	11
Number of Firms Undertaking R&D Expenditure (Bottom 50 Firms)	0	0	1
Total Number of Firms Doing R&D	0	33	27
Number of Firms Earning Negative Profit	24	47	186
Number of Exporting Firms	76	310	310
Number of Exporting Firms Earning Negative Profit	10	26	93
Proportion of Firms in the Industry Earning Profit Lower Than 10 per cent	98.15	62.18	84.25
Proportion of Firms in the Industry Earning Profit Lower Than 5 per cent	87.65	31.49	60.63
Proportion of Firms in the Industry Earning Profit More Than 20 per cent	0.00	13.07	4.72

Source: Chakraborty (2004b).

India Submission to WTO, dated 14 July 2003). Furthermore, since reform is measured in volume terms, developed countries decided to back-load the phase-out schedule by keeping most of high value items of clothing and made-ups out of the integration process till the end of the transition period. Relatively low value items like yarn and fabrics were integrated first. As a result, it has been observed that about 80 per cent of restrained imports were integrated only on the last day of the 10-year phase-out schedule, i.e., on 31 December 2004 (Verma, 2004).

India soon identified the back-loading of the quotas in developed countries as a major source of less than satisfactory expansion of textile and clothing exports, and tried to negotiate along that line in association with other developing countries. The developing country proposal on this aspect highlighted that while the quotas are fully utilised in a number of cases, a number of restraining importing Members maintain that in the post-MFA period there will be no carry forward available (from 2005), thereby significantly hurting their business interest.[3] The developing countries further feared that the denial of carry forward would be reflected in supplies, thereby generating downward pressure on prices in 2004, which is likely to fuel protectionist interest further. Therefore for avoiding any reduction in market access in the context of carry forward in the post-MFA period, the developing countries called for adoption of positive steps.

Increasing initiations of anti-dumping investigations and imposition of duties on the textile and garments imports from the developing countries has also been a major concern area. Often the investigations into the same products were revived back-to-back. For instance, in the case of cotton fabrics these measures continued for almost five years. In the case of bed linen export, these measures were imposed in one form or the other since January 1994.[4] This led the developing countries to suggest, "... Developed members shall implement a grace period of two years during which no investigations in the context of anti-dumping remedies on imports of textile and clothing products from developing countries shall be initiated." However, the developed countries did not accept it. Tariff protection to this sector in the developed countries is another serious issue (Kelegama, 2005).

India has defended its interest at the DSB on textile and clothing related cases quite satisfactorily. Till date it has moved to the DSB

3. "The percentages for advance utilisation (carry forward) of quotas were laid down for each quota product in respective bilateral agreements between the importing and exporting countries concerned. In general, the carry forward rates in US bilateral agreements for a majority of products and exporting countries were 6 per cent-7 per cent. For major exporting Members, however, they were lower, at 1 per cent-3 per cent. In EU bilateral agreements, the general rate was 5 per cent, but for major exporting Members 1 per cent-2.75 per cent. In Canada, the general rates were 5 per cent-6 per cent." Proposal submitted by 15 developing countries (*Document No. WT/GC/W/503*, Dated 14 July 2003).

4. Proposal submitted by 11 developing countries (*Document No. WT/GC/W/502*, Dated 14 July 2003).

seven times as a complainant. On four occasions, it has won the case (DS 32 against US; DS 33 against US; DS 34 against Turkey; DS 141 against EU). DS 141 deserves particular mention, where EU anti-dumping duties on cotton bed linen were found WTO-incompatible and India was forced to move to the compliance panel, as the former did not phase out the alleged provisions even after the completion of the reasonable period. In two cases (DS 140 against EU; DS 229 against Brazil) no cases were formed, as the alleged measures were modified in the following period. However, India was defeated in the last case (DS 243), which concerned the WTO-compatibility of US rules of origin requirements applicable to textiles and apparel imports as set out in Section 334 of the Uruguay Round Agreements Act, Section 405 of the Trade and Development Act of 2000 and the customs regulations implementing these provisions.[5]

However, negotiations at the multilateral level alone cannot safeguard the interest of a sector. The internal response of the government over the last couple of years towards enhancing the competitiveness of the sector is worth mentioning. First, in order to reduce the problem of indebtedness of this sector, the government accepted the N.K. Singh Committee Report, which recommended restructuring of all loans (to the upper limit of nine per cent per year). Second, in order to improve the technological scenario, the government provided a support of five per cent on the loans taken from various bodies like Industrial Development Bank of India (IDBI), etc. under 'Technological Upgradation Fund', used only for new capacity creation, which immensely benefited the sector.[6] Third, the decision to withdraw restriction on import of second hand machinery has been particularly effective for technological upgradation of firms placed in the lower segment of the industry.[7] Among the indirect policies, the steady progress of 'Golden Quadrilateral' project has been a major success in improving the road network and the time cost has

5. On 20 June 2003, the Panel announced that India failed to establish that - (a) section 334 of the Uruguay Round Agreements Act is inconsistent with Articles 2(b) or 2(c) of the *RO Agreement*; (b) section 405 of the Trade and Development Act is inconsistent with Articles 2(b), 2(c) or 2(d) of the *RO Agreement*; and the customs regulations contained in 19 C.F.R. and (c) section 102.21 are inconsistent with Articles 2(b), 2(c) or 2(d) of the *RO Agreement*. WTO, Updates of Disputes, (*Document No. WT/DS/OV/* 22, Dated 14 October 2004).

6. *http://www.eximbankindia.com/techno-up.html*

7. *http://www.thehindubusinessline.com/bline/2003/01/04/stories/2003010401680400.htm*

been substantially lowered. In addition, allowing private investment in ports has been a major step in introducing professionalism in cargo handling, as the loading time in ports like Kandala and Mundra has been drastically reduced. Furthermore, SEBs did not allow the firms earlier to operate own power plants, and the withdrawal of this restriction lowered the per-unit cost of the furnace oil based plant run by textile firms significantly. All these recent policies undid the malice done by the reservation policy to some extent, and allowed a section of the firms to improve their scale of production as well as technological level to face the challenges of the international players.

In the post-MFA period, the textile and clothing export of the Chinese firms increased substantially. It caused EU and US to ask China for adoption of 'corrective' measures. Finally, China announced that it would raise export tariffs on 74 categories of textile products from June 1, 2005. The increment ranged from 1 yuan to 4 yuan per unit from the initial level of 0.2 yuan (*Hindustan Times*, 2005). It is believed that a Sino-US pact on textiles to check the export growth of the former would soon be reached (*Hindustan Times*, 2005).

In the post-MFA period, India has witnessed a mixed success over the first few months. While in the first quarter of 2005, India's textile export fell by 15.4 per cent, in the next quarter it increased by almost 10 per cent (Pal Chaudhuri, 2005). Tewari (2005) notes that for a number of categories in clothing India has experienced indeed a very high export growth rate to the US. Furthermore, in case of textile for a number of categories India has emerged as the market leader, while in some cases it has been second only to China.

While India's export has definitely increased in the post-MFA period, the silence of EU or US on this front is open proof of the fact that its success rate is nowhere near the same achieved by China. Thanks to the recent technology upgradation policies adopted by the government, the industry has been able to set a mark in the international market on textile and clothing. On the whole, it could be concluded that India's negotiation strategy in case of textile has been quite balanced—while on one hand it freed the industry domestically from the hassles of regulations and created a level-playing field to the firms suffering from the impacts of earlier policy regime, it negotiated for better market access at the multilateral level on the other. India's success in the coming years in this front would greatly depend on continuation of this balance.

Table 6.3

Post-MFA Growth of India's Textile Exports to the US (Selected Categories)

SITC No.	Description	2004	2004 YTD (Jan-May)	2005 YTD (Jan-May)	Per Cent Change (2004-05)	The Scenario
		In 1,000 Dollars				
6584	Bedlinen (Bed, Table, Kitchen, Toilet)	554,997	214,546	283,631	32%	India is top supplier; China is 3rd
6585	Curtains and Home Furnishings	151,397	61,576	70,007	14%	India is 2nd after China
6541	Woven Fabric of Silk and Silk Waste	104,061	41,453	41,916	1%	India is top supplier
6589	Made-ups (n.e.s.) of Textile Materials	80,888	32,557	35,695	10%	India ranks 5th
6581	Packaging Materials (Textiles)	26,278	7,996	13,614	70%	India is 3rd largest
6583	Blankets and Travelling Rugs (Not Electric)	20,265	8,057	10,759	34%	India ranks 5th
6539	Woven Pile, Chenile Fabrics of Man-made Fibres	13,686	6,552	8,623	32%	India is top supplier
	Total-(Above 7)	951,572	372,737	464,245	25%	
	Others	691,764	283,591	315,587	11%	
	Total Textiles	**1,643,336**	**656,328**	**779,832**	19%	

Tewari (2005).

Agricultural Negotiations: The Issues and Concerns

The agricultural negotiations since 1995 could be sub-divided in four distinct phases, where the first six years (1995-2000) were the transitory phase. The second phase was initiated in March 2000 and concluded in March 2001, when more than 100 members submitted proposals outlining their future commitments, paving a starting position for negotiations. The third phase began in March 2001 with a stock taking meeting and continued for a year and consequently in Doha the focus was on liberalisation of agricultural trade, WTO-incompatibility of EU policies, etc. The fourth phase of the negotiation was initiated in March 2002 with the Doha Declaration as a reference. The modalities included—setting out scope of the negotiations, the methodology to be followed during actual process; and the discussion was to be concluded over a 12-month period (ending on March 2003).[8] Based on these modalities, members were supposed to submit comprehensive draft schedules by June 2003, which were to be discussed at Cancun (2003) and other WTO forums.[9] However, given the failure at Cancun and the compromise reached at Geneva (2004) later, the negotiations are still going on.

Since Doha Declaration (2001), the long-criticised EU agricultural subsidisation policy has witnessed increasing pressure from global community including India.[10] In response the EU in late 2002 offered tariff cuts on agricultural products by 36 per cent, and assured that these reductions were already incorporated in adjustments made to the CAP along with offering duty-free, quota-free access for primary exports from developing countries.[11] However, the proposal was considered to be grossly inadequate as diary products and sugar industries were kept outside the purview of reforms, despite commitments for reducing export subsidies on wheat, oilseeds, olive oil and tobacco.

Based on the proposals of member countries between March and December 2002, a draft on the modalities of agricultural negotiations was prepared by Stuart Harbinson, the Chairperson of Agricultural Negotiations on 18 December 2002. The "Harbinson Draft" was reviewed at a negotiations session of the Agriculture Committee on 22–24 January 2003, and was circulated to member governments on 12 February 2003, ahead of the negotiations meetings scheduled during 24–28 February. The final version was circulated in March 18, 2003. The draft intended to look for compromises that are necessary to reach a final agreement during the transitory phase.

---

8. While the problems of market access or subsidy issues were addressed during the negotiations, various non-trade concerns including food security, environment, structural adjustment, rural development, poverty alleviation, etc. were also discussed. Naik and Singh (2003), p. 7.

9. The WTO Committee on Agriculture earlier faced a March 2003 deadline for agreeing on modalities for the negotiations to conclude by 2005. "At the November 2001 Doha Ministerial Conference, the agriculture negotiations became part of the single undertaking in which virtually all the linked negotiations are to end by 1 January 2005. *The current negotiations, http://www.wto.org/english/tratop_e/agric_e/negoti_e.htm.*

10. For a detailed account of the impact of subsidisation in EU and US, see Jank *et al.*, (2003), Wickman (2003).

11. However, the move is not an open-ended one. The cuts in subsidies and tariff are conditional on similar cuts from other developed countries, particularly the US. The US, Canada, Japan, Australia and the 15 EU members would also cut export subsidies by 45 per cent and domestic subsidies as part of the deal., *http://news.bbc.co.uk*, 16 December, 2002.

In June 2003, EU came out with a new scheme that proposed to revise the ongoing farm support policy dramatically, by determining subsidy levels on farm existence rather than production by de-linking bulk of direct payments with production.[12] The scheme promoted the possibility of WTO members arriving at a mutual consensus in the due Cancun Ministerial, although the proposal did not necessarily reduce subsidy spending as a whole.[13] Major global players cautiously praised this de-coupling proposal, while countries like Australia were openly sceptical.[14] However, the intra-EU differences on this issue soon became obvious.[15] This led US trade representative Robert Zoellick to comment that the success of Cancun ministerial would be dependent on EU's ability to reform CAP successfully.[16]

Just a month ahead of Cancun, EU and US jointly tabled a proposal to 'liberalise' agricultural trade, which greatly disappointed their developing counterparts. The joint proposal made no definite promise to lower subsidy level within their territories and focused

---

12. The new proposal involved merging of most of the old premiums paid under the CAP into a 'single farm payment' independent from production and linked to compliance with environmental, food safety and animal welfare standards. The single farm payment was supposed to enter into force in 2005, although member states were allowed to apply for a transitional period until 2007. However Naik and Singh (2003) pointed out that "...the changes will allow most subsidies to be shifted to the 'green box' under the Agreement of Agriculture, hence considered to be non-trade distorting or minimally trade-distorting." p. 59.

13. Pascal Lamy commented that the negotiation would be successfully completed only if United States and other trading partners were willing to put their own farm programmes on the negotiating table, referring to the legislation signed last year that boosted U.S. crop and dairy subsidy payments by $57.1 billion US from the previous farm bill. *www.producer.com*, July 8, 2003.

14. In Canberra, Australian Minister for Agriculture, Fisheries and Forestry Mr. Warren Truss said, "After weeks of debate and with a mountain of evidence that the CAP needs to change, EU ministers have adopted what can best be called a marginal and mediocre change. Unfortunately, self-interest has again ruled the day and the addiction to subsidies prevails." *http://www.affa.gov.au/ministers/truss/releases/03/03179wt.html*, 27 June 2003.

15. *http://deltafarmpress.com/ar/farming_eu_subsidy_reform_2/*, Jun 27, 2003. As of now Sweden, U.K., Denmark, Netherlands and Germany are in favour of the reforms while France, Spain and Ireland are maintaining a stance polar opposite.

16. "You probably know our proposal was called a Swiss 25, which means no tariff in agriculture would be higher than 25 per cent and it would take our average tariff down from 12 to 5 per cent. So for developing countries that would like us to cut subsidies there are really two elements for us: one is we've got to bring European and Japanese levels down. The European cap on what's called the amber box domestic subsidies that distort production is, depending on exchange rates, about $65 billion, and ours is $19.1 billion so we've got to bring that down and harmonise it." Press Conference at OECD Meeting, April 30, 2003, Paris.

more on non-agricultural tariff related issues for discussion in the Cancun Ministerial. Several developing countries, led by Brazil, India and China, promptly came out with an alternate proposal (G-20 submission).[17] The proposal called for immediate end to export dumping and production subsidies for improvement of market access in agriculture. At Cancun, EU and US came out with an alternate draft declaration, again with little promise on farm subsidy liberalisation, again rejected by the developing countries. India maintained a strong view that without addressing the question of subsidisation, the distortions already present in agricultural trade cannot be removed, and therefore negotiations on market access would be meaningless.

The Cancun ministerial came out with a Revised Ministerial Draft on 13 September 2003, popularly known as the Derbez Draft (*JOB (03)/156/Rev.* 2). However the Draft, intending to please all members, disappointed everybody. While developing countries felt that Derbez Draft is another version of the EU-US draft, and pressed on taking the G-20 Draft to be the basis of negotiation, the EU and US disapproved the Draft's provisions on domestic support. The International Food and Agricultural Trade Policy Council (2004) pointed out that there exists ample scope to improve the draft for securing the interest of the negotiating partners.[18]

India refused to accept the Derbez Draft mainly on three grounds. First, it felt that the draft is not sympathetic to the developing country perspective on domestic support. Second, while in Doha it was decided that the negotiations on modalities for the Singapore issues would commence only after explicit consensus, the Derbez Draft on its own decided to initiate negotiations on these issues. Finally, while the cotton subsidisation scenario in developed countries and its adverse impact on a number of developing countries was a much-discussed area, the Draft simply promised for technical support and advise to the affected economies for diversification to other crops. In other words, the main concern was bypassed and the responsibility

17. The other members of the group are Argentina, Bolivia, Chile, Colombia, Costa Rica, Guatemala, Mexico, Paraguay, Peru, Thailand and South Africa. The detailed proposal has been outlined in the August 2003 issue of WTO Newsletter of Ministry of Commerce, Government of India.

18. The report actually identified 25 channels to improve the draft, by arguing, ".. if the Derbez text is to be the basis for further negotiations it must be improved considerably to make sure that reforms are real and meaningful for both developed and developing countries." p. 1.

was passed on other bodies, while the ideal move would have been to instruct the developed countries to reduce their subsidy level in the first place. Owing to these dissatisfying features of the draft, India, along with other developing countries turned it down.

The apathy of almost all members to accept Derbez draft as a basis of negotiation stalled agricultural negotiation for almost ten months, as nobody was willing to compromise their interests. However, India as a part of the G-20 initiative remained active in the process of reaching an agreement through informal negotiations during this period.[19] In July 2004, the deadlock in the negotiation process was finally broken as five interested parties (FIPs), namely—Australia, Brazil, EU, India and US, came forward to discuss various issues, which lasted for two weeks. The initial drafts prepared at the meeting failed to include India's concerns on the need for setting disciplines on blue and amber boxes for the developed countries. It also advocated strongly for inclusion of special safeguard mechanisms and special products provisions for developing countries. It was also unhappy with the EU-US proposal of lowering the domestic subsidy limit for developing countries. The negotiating countries finally came out with a draft announcement (henceforth July 2004 Draft), which forms the framework of future negotiations. The Annex A of the Draft text deals with agricultural provisions, proposing formulas for reducing import barriers, export subsidies and domestic support, which would then be turned into complete formulas in the 'modalities'.[20] The new draft is much comprehensive as compared to the Derbez Draft in addressing the developing country concerns, in terms of all three pillars of agricultural trade—market access, domestic support and export subsidy. In addition, the developing country sectoral concerns like that of cotton have been acknowledged in July 2004 text. The parties agreed to resume negotiation on various aspects of freeing agricultural trade. However, the draft is hardly a final (outcome) and various modalities are still subject to future discussions (Chakraborty, 2004a).

---

19. 'On the occasion of the Ministerial Meeting of the G-20 held in Brasilia, on December 11th and 12th, 2003, the Group had the opportunity to meet with Commissioner Lamy to discuss the present status of the Doha Round and how to move forward in the negotiations on agriculture.' *India and the WTO*, Vol. 5, No. 12, December 2003.

20. The text is available at *http://www.wto.org/english/tratop_e/dda_e/draft_text_gc_dg_31july04_e.htm*.

In the recently concluded G-20 meet at New Delhi (18-19th March, 2005), the Ministerial declaration reaffirmed the G-20 position to be adopted at Hong Kong, "the need to observe necessary sequencing of issues identified in the July Framework so as to ensure progress in each of the three pillars."[21] The document also expressed concern over the pace of lowering of subsidies on cotton and elimination of tariff escalation in developed countries and talked about the need for providing S & D treatment to developing countries to fulfill their social concerns.

In October 2005, EU and US came out with another joint proposal which made a conditional offer for reducing farm subsidies in return of greater market access, only to be rejected by India. Also in the FIPS meeting, India rejected two tariff reduction formulae—proposed by US-Australia (Progressivity within a band) and EU (Pivot within a band) respectively, claiming those to be variants of the Swiss formula, already rejected by G-20 (*Hindustan Times*, 2005). G-20 had agreed to the banded formula in the agricultural market access negotiations and proposed a formula with 54 and 36 per cent tariff cuts for developed and developing countries respectively on farm products (*Hindustan Times*, 2005). Recently, EU offered to reduce tariff by 38 per cent, which was rejected by several members including the US (*Hindustan Times*, 2005). The negotiations at Hong Kong ministerial extensively focused on the domestic and export subsidy and market access issues.

India's negotiating strategy in agriculture has been a combination of cautious steps. As a part of the G-20 and G-33 network, it has extensively argued in favour of making Special Products (SP) and Special Safeguard Mechanism (SSM) an integral part of S&D treatment in the agriculture framework.[22] In order to enable developing countries to take full benefit of the proposal, G-33 talked about a stand-alone category for SP, decided exclusively by them, for

---

21. "G-20 Ministerial Declaration", available at *http://www.commerce.nic.in/wto_sub/g20/min_decln.htm*

22. G-33 submission to WTO (*Document No. JOB(04)/65*, Dated 1 June 2004). Earlier India asked that, "A separate safeguard mechanism on the lines of the Special Safeguard provisions (Article 5 of AoA) including a provision for imposition of Quantitative Restrictions under specified circumstances, should be made available to all developing countries irrespective of tariffication in the event of a surge in the imports or decline in prices and to ensure food and livelihood security of their people." Individual submission by India (*Document No. G/AG/NG/W/102*, Dated 15 January 2001).

which there should be no tariff reduction commitment at all.[23] Furthermore, the proposal demanded that products considered as SP must also have access to SSM. As a part of the G-20, it focused on the need to reduce all trade-distorting domestic support measures, elimination of article 6.5 of the Agreement on Agriculture (direct payments under production-limiting programme), capping Green box direct payments for developed countries, maintaining *de minimis* at the existing levels for developing countries, maintaining S & D treatment for developing countries etc.[24] It also criticised the Blended formula approach for tariff reduction proposed by US and EU, which "fails to deliver substantial improvements in market access, especially for products of developing country interests, protected by tariff peaks."[25]

Apart from the submissions made as a part of the developing country coalition, India has also been advocating S & D treatment individually for some time. The submissions defined the goal for a developing country to be, "enhance income levels, reduce vulnerability to market fluctuations and enhance stability of prices of agricultural products, and ensure physical and economic access to sufficient, safe and nutritious food, through governmental support as well as appropriate protection at the border through price-based and quantity-based measures."[26] The document has also been quite vocal about the availability of special safeguard provisions (article 5 of AoA) to all developing countries for all products. Furthermore, obtaining flexibility in domestic policies for agriculture aimed at enhancing food and livelihood security and rural development for developing countries has also been quite important in the submissions.[27] India's negotiating strategy in this field has been motivated from the paragraph 13 of the DDA, which states, "... special and differential

23. The focus on special products has evolved over India's earlier negotiations on 'strategic products' along the same lines with 11 other developing countries earlier (Document No. JOB(03)/59, Dated 20 March 2003). It was proposed that "The total number of self-declared strategic products at any one time are limited to [X] per cent of the total domestically produced agricultural products based on tariff lines in a country's schedule. The notion is well in line with the earlier submissions, .. certain degree of protection in terms of moderately high tariff levels and Special Safeguard clause are a must for sustainable agricultural development in developing countries." Individual submission by India (*Document No. G/AG/NG/W/33*, Dated 13 July 2000).

24. G-20 submission to WTO (*Document No. JOB(03)/162/Rev.1*, Dated 29 August 2003).

25. G-20 submission to WTO (*Document No. TN/AG/GEN/9*, Dated 7 May 2004).

26. Individual submission by India (*Document No. JOB(03)/7*, Dated 22 January 2003).

27. Individual submission by India (*Document No. JOB(02)/175*, Dated 18 November 2002).

treatment for developing countries shall be an integral part of all elements of the negotiations on agriculture and shall be embodied in the Schedules of concessions and commitments and as appropriate in the rules and disciplines to be negotiated, so as to be operationally effective and to enable developing countries to effectively take account of their development needs, including food security and rural development."

As a part of the argument in favour of S & D treatment, India maintained that since the developed countries subsidise their agriculture to an extent unimaginable by developing countries, the latter group has no concessions to make in operational terms with regard to domestic support and export subsidies. This led India to call for reduction of all trade-distorting support, in the Amber Box, the Blue Box and Annex 2 (paragraphs 5, 6, and 7), to *de minimis* level at the end of the implementation period (excluding measures provided under Article 6.2 of the AoA by developing countries)[28] and elimination of export subsidies (except subsidies provided by all developing countries under Articles 9.1(d) and (e) of the AoA).[29] It also focused on the need to assess the causes behind the moderate gains achieved by the developing countries in the post-UR period, despite the reporting of substantial gains in several projections, and urged the necessity of analysing the impacts of the SPS-related barriers on agricultural exports.[30]

It is seen that India's negotiations on market access and tariffication issues are also linked quite closely with S & D treatment. While it has talked about problems associated with tariff peaks, tariff

28. In an earlier submission, India talked about the flexibility requirement of the developing countries—additional flexibility for providing subsidies to key farm inputs for agricultural and rural development; maintenance of appropriate level of tariff bindings on agricultural products, keeping in mind their developmental needs and high distortions prevalent in the international markets; exclusion of product specific support given to low income and resource poor farmers from AMS calculations etc. It furthermore stressed that, "... it would be important to recognise that the 10 per cent *de minimis* level presently provided under the AMS, may not be sufficient for developing countries ... some aspects of the Green Box measures may also need to be reviewed in order to provide a certain degree of flexibility ...". Individual submission by India (Document No. G/AG/NG/S/18 (Dated 16 October 2000). Interestingly, India also talked about accelerated reduction in AMS so as to bring it below *de minimis* by the developed and developing countries in 3 and 5 years respectively. Individual submission by India (*Document No. G/AG/NG/W/114*, Dated 15 February 2001).

29. Individual submission by India (*Document No. JOB(02)/175*, Dated 18 November 2002).

30. Individual submission by India (*Document No. G/AG/NG/W/70*, Dated 18 January 2001).

escalation at times and demanded tariff reduction in developed countries for the benefit of their developing counterparts,[31] the exclusion of developing countries from certain commitments was always a major driving concern.[32] The focus is not new and is in force since the pre-Doha days, when India held the view that developing country members should be exempt from any obligation to provide any minimum market access. Furthermore, it criticised the notion of uniformity in negotiating basis, as suggested by the US between developed and developing countries as well as the concept of Sectoral liberalisation (that is, zero-for-zero initiatives) implied in US and Canadian proposal on market access after Seattle Ministerial.[33] As a part of the agenda, before Doha Ministerial it asked that:

> Even after the abolition of the peace clause (Article 13 of AoA), as a special and differential provision, measures taken by developing countries under Annex 2 (Green Box) and other domestic support measures conforming to Article 6 of AoA shall be exempt for a period of 10 years from imposition of countervailing duties under the Agreement on Subsidies and Countervailing Measures and Article XVI of GATT 1994 and shall also be exempt from actions based on non-violation nullification or impairment of the benefits of tariff concessions under paragraph 1 (b) of Article XXIII of GATT 1994.[34]

While the negotiations in association with other developing countries in contrast to the individual submissions in the pre-Doha days and the isolation in Doha (Singh, 2001) indicate India's growing ability to enter into strategic relationships in the GATT/WTO forums; there is a need to assess whether the negotiating stances are adequately backed with appropriate policy measures followed at home to remove various procedural barrier faced by the players. Stated alternatively, there is a need to focus on the domestic scenario. India has earlier submitted that, "... Developing countries can be expected to reciprocate in market access, subject to their economic and social conditions, development needs, food and livelihood security and rural development requirements, only if they get adequate concessions and

---

31. Submission by 11 countries (*Document No. G/AG/NG/W/37*, Dated 28 September 2000).

32. Special dispensation for developing countries provided under Article 27 read with "... Annex VII of the Agreement on Subsidies and Countervailing Measures should prevail over Article 8 of AoA." Individual submission by India (*Document No. G/AG/NG/W/102*, Dated 15 January 2001).

33. Individual submission by India (*Document No. G/AG/NG/W/33*, Dated 13 July 2000).

34. Individual submission by India (*Document No. G/AG/NG/W/102*, Dated 15 January 2001).

commitments by developed countries in all three pillars."[35] In the recent period, EU is undertaking certain reform measures (Kelch and Normile, 2004), where de-coupled payments would be made to various crops in varying amount with historical payments to be incorporated. The proposed reform includes crops like cotton (de-coupling payment of at least 65 per cent), tobacco (40 per cent), olive oil (60 per cent), hops (75 per cent) etc. US has also initiated reforms, and sooner or later developing countries including India are likely to face the question of freeing farm sector in the negotiating table.

Although the Hong Kong ministerial has provided some respite to the developing countries, the negotiations on various modalities are far from being over. A working hypothesis of three bands for developed countries over AMS has been formulated and it is expected that members in the lower bands with high relative levels of final bound total AMS will undertake higher cuts. Developing country members with no AMS commitments will be exempt from reductions in *de minimis* and the overall cut in trade-distorting domestic support. To ensure market access, tariff cuts under four bands are being discussed. The only gain is that all forms of export subsidies and disciplines on all export measures with equivalent effect are to be eliminated by the end of 2013. It has been further decided that developing country members will have the flexibility to self-designate an appropriate number of tariff lines as special products guided by indicators based on the criteria of food security, livelihood security and rural development. However, regarding designation of special products, there has been a clear divergence between members over the selection criteria to be followed. Similarly, there remains strong divergence on whether, or if so how, a special safeguard should be 'price-based' to deal specifically with price effects. Furthermore, the difference in opinions among the members over coverage of the special safeguard provision also came to forefront at the ministerial.

It is expected that the Government would boost public investment to phase-out procedural hassles for helping the agricultural sector. However, it is observed from Figure 6.5 that since the Uruguay Round the amount of subsidies in India are increasing steadily, while the amount of investment has remained stagnant. It is also noteworthy that the amount of both PSE as well as AMS, the indicators of farm

35. Individual submission by India (*Document No. JOB(02)/175*, Dated 18 November 2002).

support are negative in India. While the product-specific AMS has consistently been negative over 1987-2000, the non product-specific AMS has been positive throughout this period. The negative AMS originates from the lower product prices, which outweighs the input subsidy towards fertiliser, power or irrigation. Given this scenario, India's stance that for developing countries, "Product specific support provided to low-income resource poor farmers should be excluded from the AMS calculations, as is the case for the non-product-specific support as per para. 6.2 of AoA is quite a cautious one.[36] On the other hand, various studies have pointed out that the input subsidies are creating more distortions as compared to the benefits received and sometimes, leading to environmental problems as well.[37] Also the impact of the Minimum Support Price (MSP) system to Indian agriculture on net welfare is subject to questions.[38]

Figure 6.5

Subsidy and Public Investment Trends in Indian Agriculture

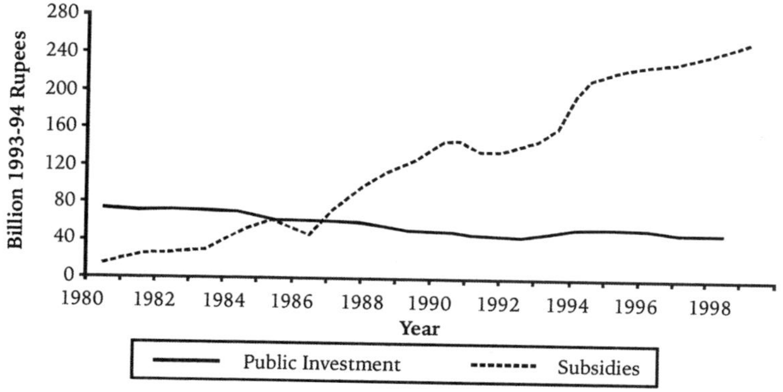

Source: Gulati, Ashok and Sudha, Narayanan (2003).

36. Individual submission by India (*Document No. G/AG/NG/W/102*, Dated 15 January 2001).

37. Sidhu (2002) has shown that in Punjab the excessive use of chemical fertilisers and near monocultural crop pattern has degraded the soil resource alarmingly. Also in the state more than nine lakh tube wells are being supplied electricity free of cost, leading to indiscriminate use, which in turn is causing underground water to deplete at a rate of 23 cm per annum.

38. Parikh, Kumar and Darbha (2003) have shown that the MSP set at a higher than market price has worsened the welfare of 80 per cent of the rural population and all persons in urban areas.

The Indian position at the multilateral negotiations level has often been termed as too protectionist (Draper and Sally, 2004). On the other hand, the negotiations, while denied developed countries a free run, resulted very little in India's favour in practical terms. Although the country has negotiated hard on the flexibility to determine the 'appropriate' number of products as SP for developing countries for some time and the July text has focused on that issue, the draft at the same time has allowed the members to designate the 'appropriate' number of sensitive tariff lines. Clearly the SP benefit for developing countries could be nullified, at least partly, if the developed countries declare a number of these SP as 'sensitive' for them (Chand, 2005). Also the methodology of determining sensitive products ('certain' per cent of tariff lines), negotiations in domestic support ('historical period', 'exceptionally large' percentage of trade-distorting support in the Blue Box etc.) are quite open-ended (Chakraborty, 2004a). On the other side, Mehta *et al.* (2004) have praised the restraint shown by the developing countries on the discussion over tariff reduction formula. However, there exist (areas of) conflicting interest among the developing countries in these coalitions and the real solidarity of the group would be properly tested once the negotiation reaches the next phase (Ranjan, 2005).

There is a need to look into the competitiveness of Indian exports. It is of prime importance because the defensive notion is so strong in India based on the ill-founded conception of lack of competitiveness of the farm sector and motivated India to maintain quantitative restrictions on agricultural imports for some time even in the post-WTO accession period.[39] It has been shown by Gulati *et al.*, (1996) that a number of major Indian products are highly price competitive. The study, concentrating on cereals, fresh fruits and vegetables, and processed fruits and vegetables, came to the conclusion by analysing the Nominal Protection Coefficient (NPC) of these groups. The current analysis focused on the unit price ratio for the primary

39. The US (DS 97) alleged that India's quantitative restrictions on imports of agricultural, textile and industrial products on BoP grounds are inconsistent with Articles XI:1 and XVIII:11 of GATT 1994, Article 4.2 of the Agreement on Agriculture and Article 3 of the Agreement on Import Licensing Procedures. The panel found that India's policies are inconsistent with the first two alleged provisions, which was maintained by the appellate body. Australia (DS 91), Canada (DS 92), New Zealand (DS 93), Switzerland (DS 94) and EU (DS 96) also claimed similar violations, and all these cases were amicably settled. India removed QRs on agricultural imports. However, opening of the market did not prove as harmful as various projections (Sharma, 1995; TWN, *http://www.twnside.org.sg/title/flood-cn.htm*).

product lines at 6-digit level of HS classification. It is observed from the analysis that a number of the Indian primary product groups are fairly price competitive, where HS-5 (Products of animal origin n.e.s. or included), HS–7 (Edible vegetables and certain roots and tubers) and HS–22 (Beverages, spirits and vinegar) are worth mentioning. What needs to be done is to enhance the level of the competitiveness further through allowance of level playing field to the domestic players.

Table 6.4

Domestic Transport Cost of Grains with Oceanic Freight Charges (Rs./Tn.)

Mode (Year)	*From*	*To*	*Rate*
Truck Mid-2000	Punjab	Mumbai	1915
	Punjab	Andhra Pradesh	2610
	Punjab	Tamil Nadu	2750
	Punjab	Kerala	2865
	Punjab	West Bengal	2470
	Delhi	Mumbai	1210
	Delhi	Andhra Pradesh	2278
	Delhi	West Bengal	1611
Ship 2000	Europe	India	1365
	US Ports	India	1886
	Australia	India	1000
	Bangkok	India	534
Railways For FCI-1999	Punjab	Mumbai	800
	Punjab	Andhra Pradesh	878
	Punjab	Tamil Nadu	1014
	Punjab	Kerala	1202
	Punjab	West Bengal	792
	Delhi	Mumbai	684
	Delhi	Andhra Pradesh	814
	Delhi	Tamil Nadu	931
	Delhi	Kerala	1176
	Delhi	West Bengal	675

Source: Chand (2002).

Unfortunately the government policies kept the sector in a disadvantageous position for a long time. For instance, the inter-state barriers to road transport inflated the cost of the exporters to a major extent, and it is often found that the cost of importing grains from abroad (Thailand or even select US ports) is cheaper than transporting the same from one state to another within the country (Chand, 2002). Movement restrictions on primary products by continuations of outdated provisions like Essential Commodities Act also contributed in this process. Jha and Srinivasan (2004) have also noted, "individual states find it attractive to import from abroad than buying locally from other states."[40] Since the transport costs are ultimately reflected in the final price for the consumers, any import restrictions on primary products is actually welfare reducing.

However, the scenario has slightly changed over the last couple of years. In India due to fragmentation of the land-holdings, it is not easy to enjoy economies of scale in input usage in a significant proportion of the agricultural sector. Introduction of cooperative or contract farming would have been one natural outcome in these cases. However, agricultural cooperatives in India suffered from various institutional drawbacks (poor management quality, absence of the right decision-making capability, excessive government control etc.).[41] On the other hand, the Agricultural Produce Marketing Committee (APMC) Act empowered State governments to notify the commodities, and designate markets and market areas where the regulated trade takes place. Once a commodity was notified, the APMC Act made its transaction mandatory in the regulated market where the transactions were taxed. The provision of direct link between private players and farmers or contract farming was not allowed. Such entry barriers created a significant increase in transaction cost apart from lack of accountability, as a result of which important supporting services such as grading, standardisation and market facilities have been neglected. Finally in 2003, the Ministry of Agriculture drafted a Model APMC Act, which the state governments could use as a model for their individual acts. Under the Model Act, private agents can be licensed by the Government (e.g., through State Agricultural Marketing Board) to set up a market or buy produce directly from farmers. The Model Act allows new institutional arrangements, which directly benefits the farmers (contract farming, direct marketing), while allowing for the development of markets in private and cooperative sectors. On the whole, direct marketing under

40. Jha and Srinivasan (2004), p. 90.

41. For a detailed account, see Dutta (2004).

the model act increases productivity and ensures higher income to the farmers (Ramaswamy *et al.*, 2005; Dev and Rao, 2005; and Chadha and Gulati, 2003). Furthermore, the new provision would potentially enhance the competitiveness of the farm sector.

Multiplicity of Acts and involvement of various Government departments for governing processing and marketing of agri-produce, health and hygiene, consumer safety, food testing, packaging is a major problem. While India raised its voice over SPS-TBT concerns at the multilateral level, it is believed that the lack of standardisation is a major impediment to the growth of this sector (Saqib, 2003). There are multiple authorities that approve the trade in agricultural and primary commodities. For instance Fruit Products Order (1955, amended in 1997) is implemented by Ministry of Food Processing Industries, Meat Food Products Order (1973) is implemented by Department of Agriculture and Cooperation, Ministry of Agriculture (earlier done by Ministry of Rural Development), Milk and Milk Products Order (1992) is implemented by the Department of Animal Husbandry and Diary, Ministry of Agriculture etc.[42] Similarly, there exist various regulatory authorities for implementing the orders relating to oils and other foodstuff. The State Governments sometimes apply widely varying commodity-specific standards on various primary and processed products, and while some States are very vigorous in implementing the laws scrupulously, others are not (Debroy and Kaushik, 2001). The recently proposed Food Safety and Standards Bill (2005) is likely to solve a major proportion of the current problems. The Bill covers the entire country and will supersede all State laws as well as the control orders maintained by various departments on food and food processing once it becomes a law ratified by Parliament, thereby creating a streamlined framework. The Bill clearly defines the food items, is in line with the global concerns on food standard and incorporates the provisions of complete traceability on the label of the agriculture produce. Clearly these provisions would enable Indian firms to meet the SPS-TBT challenges in a much better fashion.

Concluding Remarks

It is observed that while concerning trade in textile, India quite actively negotiated for higher market access at the multilateral level, in case of agriculture the stress has been rather on obtaining special

42. For a detailed account, see Vivek (2005).

and differential treatment from the developed countries on various provisions. Furthermore on the domestic front, while in the textile sector the government abandoned most of the restrictive polices and attempted to undo the consequences faced during the earlier regime through appropriate policy measures, a similar process has began only recently in agriculture. One possible reason behind the difference in government actions towards the two sectors might be their proportional shares in India's export basket. While textile and clothing sector accounted for around 30 per cent of India's total exports, the corresponding figures for agriculture has been in the order of 10-14 per cent. The notion of achieving self-sufficiency has been partly responsible for the low share of primary products in the export basket and the resulting mindset.

Now if the trends in post-MFA phase-out on the textile sector are to be taken as any indicator for the same in agriculture, there is an urgent need for boosting the competitiveness of the latter sector in India. Once the developed countries (notably EU and US) introduce reforms in their farm policies, they are bound to link further reform in other interest areas (e.g., Mode 4 in services for India) with opening of agricultural sector in developing countries. Competitiveness cannot be achieved or enhanced through subsidies, which India seems to be learning only in the recent period. In order to help the sector effectively in a WTO-compatible manner, it should try to invest more in agricultural research in connection with environmental programmes, extension and advisory services, marketing and promotion services and infrastuctural services. A vibrant farm sector at home would give India an edge multilaterally so as to pursue the goal of farm sector liberalisation in developed countries with much more vigour.[43]

References

Banik, Nilanjan and Saurabh Bandopadhyay (2000). "Cotton Textile Industry in India, in the Wake of MFA Phase-Out", *RGICS Working Paper* No. 9, New Delhi.

BBC News (2002). "EU offers WTO farm subsidy cuts", *http://news.bbc.co.uk/1/hi/business/2581963.stm*, 16 December.

Carver, Brian, Christy He and Jonah Hister (2004). "India's Textile Industry: What will Happen When the Quotas are Lifted?" paper presented at *GTTL Conference*, June 2, University of Washington.

43. Chakraborty and Singh (2006) give a detailed account of India's negotiating options on agriculture at multilateral level.

Chadha, G.K. and A. Gulati (2003). *Farm-Firm linkages in India: Rationale, Experience and needed Policy Changes*, paper presented at FICCI, New Delhi.

Chakraborty, Debashis (2003). "Corporate Participation in Marketing Activities: Scopes and Challenges to Indian Agriculture," in Bibek Debroy and Amir Ullah Khan (eds.) *Enabling Agricultural Markets for the Small Indian Farmer*, pp. 185-234, Bookwell Publishers, New Delhi,.

———. (2004a) Recent Negotiation Trends on Agriculture under WTO: Mutual Consensus during Transitory Phase?, *RGICS Working Paper* No. 47, September, New Delhi.

———. (2004b) "Challenges and Opportunities for the Indian Textile Industry in the Post-Quota Regime", paper presented at the Workshop by Amity Law School on *The Impact of Removal of MFA Quotas on Indian Textile Industries*, September 4, New Delhi.

———. (2005). "Multi-Fibre Arrangement and Indian Textile Industry: Pre- and Post-Quota Concerns", paper presented at the *Workshop organised by AEDR and T.A. Pai Management Institute*, October 1-2, Bangalore.

———. and Yashika Singh (2006). "Agricultural Subsidy: The Major Hurdle to Free Trade", in Dipankar Sengupta, Debashis Chakraborty and Pritam Banerji (eds.), *Beyond the Transition Phase of WTO: An Indian Perspective on Emerging Issues*, pp. 75-107, Academic Foundation, New Delhi.

Chand, Ramesh (2005). "Post WTO Agriculture Trade and Agenda for Negotiations on Agriculture", *Policy Brief* No. 23, National Centre for Agricultural Economics and Policy Research, September, New Delhi.

———. (2002). *Trade Liberalisation, WTO and Indian Agriculture: Experience and Prospects*, Mittal Publications, New Delhi.

Debroy, Bibek and P. D. Kaushik (2001). "Barriers to Inter-State Trade and Commerce – The Case of Road Transport", background paper provided to *Constitution Review Commission*, Government of India.

Delta Farm Press (2003). "EU subsidy reform on hold again", *http://deltafarmpress.com/ar/farming_eu_subsidy_reform_2/*, Jun 27.

Dev, S. Mahendra and N. Chandrasekhara Rao (2005). "Food Processing and Contract Farming in Andhra Pradesh: A Small Farmer Perspective", *Economic and Political Weekly*, pp. 2705-2713, June 25.

Draper, Peter and Razeen Sally (2004). "Developing-Country Coalitions in Multilateral Trade Negotiations", paper presented in the Seminar entitled *WTO Negotiations: India's Post-Cancun Concerns*, jointly organised by Planning Commission and International Trade and Development Division, JNU, October 18-19.

Dutta, Samar K. (2004). "Co-Operatives in Agriculture', Vol. 24, 'State of Indian Farmer: A Millenium Study", Academic Foundation in association with Ministry of Agriculture, Government of India, New Delhi.

Export-Import Bank of India (1995). "Indian Garment Exports: Implications of the MFA Phase-out", *Occasional paper No. 34*, February, Mumbai.

Government of India, "India and the WTO", the monthly newsletter of Ministry of Commerce (various issues).

———. various submissions to WTO, *www.commerce.nic.in*.

Gulati, Ashok and Sudha Narayanan (2003). "Subsidy Syndrome in Indian Agriculture", New Delhi, Oxford University Press.

———. Anil Sharma, Kailash Sharma, Shipra Das, and Vandana Chhabra (1996). "Export Competitiveness of Selected Agricultural Commodities", Global Business Press in agreement with NCAER, New Delhi.

Hindustan Times (2005). "Progress on Sino-US Pact on Textiles", November 4.

———. (2005). "G-20 to Counter Subsidised Farm Exports from West: Market Access Proposals Filed with WTO", October 14, New Delhi.

———. (2005). "India Rejects US, EU Proposals", October 13.

———. (2005). "No Need to Restore Import Quotas: EU", May 23.

———. (2005). "China ups tax to slow Textile exports", May 21.

International Food & Agricultural Trade Policy Council (2004). "Twenty-Five Ways to Improve the Derbez Draft on Agriculture", February 10, *http://www.agritrade.org/Doha/Derbez/Assessment%20Paper.pdf.*

Jank, Marcos Sawaya, Fuchsloch, Ian and Kutas, Géraldine (2003). "Agricultural Liberalisation In Multilateral And Regional Trade Negotiations", Inter-American Development Bank, Washington, D.C.

Jha, Shikha and P.V. Srinivasan (2004). "Achieving Food Security in a Cost Effective Way: Implications of Domestic Deregulation and Reform Under Liberalised Trade", *MTID discussion paper No. 67*, p. 8, Markets, Trade, and Institutions Division, International Food Policy Research Institute, May, Washington, D.C.

Kelegama, Saman (Ed.), (2005). "South Asia after the Quota System: Impact of the MFA Phase-Out", Institute of Policy Studies of Sri Lanka in association with Friedrich-Ebert-Stiftung, October, Colombo.

Kelch, David and Mary Anne Normile (2004). "CAP Reform of 2003-04", United States Department of Agriculture, *Electronic Outlook Report* from Economic Research Service, August, Washington, D.C.

Mehta, Rajesh, J. George and Pooja Agarwal (2004). "Demystifying Agricultural Market Access Formula: A Developing Country Perspective after Cancun Setback", CUTS Centre for International Trade, *Economics and Environment Research Report*, Jaipur.

Naik, Gopal, and Yashika Singh (2003). "Doha Round Negotiations: Agriculture", *Working paper* No. 217, Indian Institute of Management, November, Bangalore.

Nordas, Hildegunn Kyvik (2004). "The Global Textile and Clothing Industry post the Agreement on Textiles and Clothing", World Trade Organisation *Discussion Paper 5*, Geneva.

Pal Chaudhuri, Pramit (2005). "Textile Export Survives Dragon", *Hindustan Times*, October 3, New Delhi.

Parikh, Kirit S., A. Ganesh-Kumar and Gangadhar Darbha (2003). "Growth and Welfare Consequences of Rise in MSP", *Economic and Political Weekly*, March 1-7, pp. 891-895.

Ramaswamy, Bharat, P.S. Birthal and P.K. Joshi (2005). "Efficiency and Distribution in Contract Farming: The Case of Indian Poultry Growers", *Discussion Paper* 05-01, Indian Statistical Institute, February, New Delhi.

Ranjan, Prabhash (2005). "How Long Can The G-20 Hold Itself Together? A Power Analysis", *Working Paper* No. 1, CENTAD, February, New Delhi.

Saqib, Mohd. (2003). "Setting the House in Order: A Study on Technical Standards that Affect Indian Agricultural Trade", Bazaar Chintan *Working Paper* No. 15, October, New Delhi.

Sharma, Devinder (1995). "GATT-WTO: Seeds of Despair", Konark Publishers Pvt. Ltd., New Delhi.

Sidhu, H.S. (2002). "Crisis in Agrarian Economy in Punjab: Some Urgent Steps", *Economic and Political Weekly*, pp. 3132-38, July 27– August 2.

Singh, Yashika (2001). "India at the Fourth Ministerial Meeting in Doha: Déjà vu – again?" *RGICS Working Paper* No. 32, New Delhi.

Spinanger, D. and Samar Verma (2003), "The Coming Death of the ATC and China's WTO Accession: Will Push come to shove for Indian T & C Exports?" in A.L. Winters and Pradeep S. Mehta (eds.), *Bridging the Differences: Analyses of Five Issues of the WTO Agenda*, pp. 197-245, CUTS Publications, 2003, Jaipur.

Tewari, Meenu (2005). "Post-MFA Adjustments in India's Textile and Apparel Industry: Emerging Issues and Trends", *ICRIER Working Paper* No. 167, July, New Delhi.

The United States Mission to the European Union (2002). "U.S. Cites Support in WTO for Eliminating Agriculture Export Subsidies", *www.useu.be*, June 19, Brusselles.

The Western Producer (2003). "EU Revamps Farm Subsidies", *http://www.producer.com/articles/20030703/market_quotas/20030703mkt05.html*, July 8.

Third World Network, "India: Flood of Food Imports Could Destroy Indian Agriculture", by Binu S. Thomas, August 30, *http://www.twnside.org.sg/title/flood-cn.htm.*

Verma, Samar (2002). "Export Competitiveness of Indian Textile and Garment Industry", *ICRIER Working Paper* No. 94, November, New Delhi.

———. (2004). "How Big is the Bang for India? Market Access in Textiles Post 2004", Outreach Seminar on *WTO and India: Issues and Negotiating Strategies* organised by JNU, ICSSR and Department of Economics, Cotton College, Guwahati, August 11-12.

Vivek, Harsh (2005) "The Food Safety and Standards Bill (2005): Implications for Food Safety", *Bazaar Chintan Working Paper* No. 39, October, New Delhi.

Wickman, Kurt (2003). "Whither the European Agricultural Policy? A Viable Reform of the CAP in the Context of an Enlarged EU and the Doha Development Round", Timbro, *http://www.timbro.se/bokhandel/pdf/000011.pdf.*

World Trade Organisation (2003). "Draft Cancun Ministerial Text: Second Revision", 13th September, Geneva.

———. "WTO Annual Report" (various issues), Geneva.

———. (2001). "Market Access: Unfinished Business - Post-Uruguay Round Inventory and Issues", *Special Studies No.6*, Geneva.

7

TRIPS Compulsions: India's Negotiating Agenda

P.D. KAUSHIK

Intellectual property refers to property that is intangible, conferring a right of ownership to its creator, inventor or originator.[1] Protection of intellectual property rights is a matter of prime importance for developing region in the light of established multilateral trading regime. The Doha Development Agenda (DDA) was instrumental in charting the course of future negotiations under the aegis of the TRIPS Agreement. After rallying for almost a decade, the DDA was drawn to overcome the weaknesses of the Uruguay Round negotiations on trade related aspects of intellectual property. The stalemate of agricultural subsidies, sharpening and broadening the scope of TRIPS remained major issues at the Doha Ministerial and thereafter at Cancun Ministerial. Even at the Hong Kong Ministerial, the negotiating agenda of the developing countries continued to revolve around the same issues.

TRIPS Agreement

The Trade Related Aspects of Intellectual Property Rights (TRIPs) is the sole legally enforceable multilateral agreement on the protection of intellectual property rights, without creating any new substantive IPR legislation. The TRIPs agreement binds its signatory to protect all forms of identified intellectual property within a specified time frame. The TRIPs agreement aims at harmonising the legal and enforcement framework across trading nations under the aegis of the World Trade Organisation (WTO). The protection of IPR is the foremost challenge for the developing region for all forms of intellectual property, including the digital medium. There are essentially seven separate subjects forming part of intellectual property under the multilateral

1. In the IPR context, it means a right to exclusive use of 'applications of ideas and information that are of commercial value'.

framework of TRIPs, namely patents, copyright, trademark, industrial design, geographical indications, layout design of integrated circuits and undisclosed information. Each subject provides a property right, which is the right to prosecute for infringement. It is this entitlement to sue that provides its owner with commercial power and entitles the owner to sell or license that right. The summary of the agreement and legal instrument is provided in Table 7.1.

Table 7.1

Intellectual Property Rights: Legal Instruments and International Agreements

Types of Intellectual Properties Rights	*Instruments*	*Main fields of Application*	*International Agreements*
Industrial Property	Patents	Manufacturing–new and non-obvious industrial inventions.	Paris Convention, Patent Cooperation Treaty, Budapest Treaty.
	Utility Models	Manufacturing–Functional designs.	Paris Convention.
	Industrial Designs	All Industrial Designs –Textile, Ornamental, Automobile and Electronics.	Hague Agreement, Paris Convention, Locarno Agreement.
	Trade Marks	All Industries-Signs and symbols to distinguish the manufacturer's goods and services.	Paris Convention, Madrid Agreement, Nice Agreement, Madrid Protocol, Trade Mark Law Treaty.
	Geographical Indications	Agricultural and Food-Processing Industries, notably for Wines and Spirits.	Lisbon Agreement, Madrid Agreement.
Literary and Artistic Property	Copyrights and Neighboring Rights	Original works of authorship and related contributors (audio, video, movies, software) performers and producers.	Berne Convention, Rome Convention, Geneva Convention, Universal Copyright Convention.
Sui Generis Protection	Breeders' Rights	New, stable, distinctive, homogeneous varieties–Agriculture and Food	Union for the International Protection of New Plant Varieties (UPOV).
	Integrated Circuits	Original layout designs–Microelectronics Industry	IPIC, Washington Treaty.
Trade Secrets	Undisclosed Information	All Industries–Secret business information, such as test reports, etc.	

Source: Carlos Braga, "Trade Related Aspects of Intellectual Property Issues: The Uruguay Agreement and the Economic Implications", *WB Conference Paper* (26-27 January 1995).

The intellectual property rights are the claims entitled to persons over the creations of their mind. These claims give the creator an exclusive right over the use of his creation for a certain period of time. TRIPS or the Agreement ensures that the exclusive rights given to creators for their creation are kept in the balance that has to be found between the legitimate interests of right holders and the users. After the inception of the TRIPS Agreement, all developing countries were required to put their respective IPR regime in line with the provisions of the agreement by 1 January 2000. India was allowed to comply with the provisions by 1 January 2005, because it followed process patent regime. In the past, Indian legal framework on IPR protection revolved around the Indian Patent Act, 1970; Indian Copyright Act, 1957; Indian Design Act, 1911 and Indian Trade & Merchandise Mark Act, 1958. There were no extant laws for other IPRs—like geographical indications, undisclosed information and layout design of integrated circuits. Protection of such rights was not uncommon in the absence of specific statutes as evident in case laws[2]. The Government of India made concerted efforts to put in line its IPR legislation with the provisions of the TRIPS Agreement by introducing the Patents (Amendment) Act, 1999; The Patent (Second Amendment) Bill, 1999; Protection of Plant Varieties & Farmer's Rights Bill, 1999; The Designs Bill, 1999, The Copyright (Amendment) Bill, 1999, The Trade Marks Bill, 1999; The Geographical Indications of Goods (Registration & Protection) Bill, 1999, etc. However, the Indian Patent Regime continued to remain a major impediment in India's effort to put in line its IPR regime with the global regime. In 2005, Government of India introduced the final amendment to the Indian Patent Act, which put Indian IPR regime in line with the TRIPS Agreement. However, scores of gaps and loose ends in the Indian IPR regime makes it vulnerable against stronger IPR regimes. The most vulnerable is the patent and the issue of patentability. Weaker IPR regime against strong ones may result in non-tariff barriers to the free movement of goods and services. Likewise, it can also adversely affect the flow of investment and technology.

2. Case laws under Indian Trade & Merchandise Mark Act show a rich tradition of protecting geographical indication right. Likewise, layout design of IC is protected under the Indian Design Act, etc.

Doha Development Agenda and TRIPs

The TRIPS Agreement essentially covered eight different forms of IPRs—patents, patenting of plant varieties, copyrights and related rights, trademarks, industrial design, geographical indications, layout design of integrated circuits and undisclosed information. The agreement prescribed general rules of protection including enforcement and criminal provisions. But during the transition period, developing countries realised that somewhat TRIPS agreement favoured the developed and technology innovating nations against the interest of developing countries. Major challenge for developing countries at that time was to put their house in order within the specified time frame, especially in terms of appropriate legislation and enforcement procedures. But with changing time and inherent weaknesses of the existing system, many facets of IPRs within and outside the TRIPS framework emerged as new challenges for the developing region. Some of these issues have already been raised at the TRIPS Council review meetings, which resulted in a comprehensive work programme at the Doha Ministerial Conference, broadly known as the DDA, covering comprehensive negotiations in the areas of agriculture, services, subsidies, anti-dumping, regional trading arrangements, dispute settlement, industrial tariffs and some aspects of intellectual property rights.

Developing countries, mainly India, identified a number of deficiencies and imbalances in the TRIPS agreement and suggested specific correctness, usually termed as 'implementation issues'.[3] In the declaration, it was stressed to implement and interpret the Agreement in a way that it supports public health—by promoting both access to existing medicines and the creation of new medicines. It was emphasised that the agreement must not prevent member governments from acting to protect public health. Primarily, this decision clarified certain forms of flexibility in the agreement available in the form of compulsory licensing and parallel imports. The DDA sets two specific task: (1) find a solution to the problems countries may face in making use of compulsory licensing if they have too little or no pharmaceutical manufacturing capacity; and (2) extend the deadline for least-developed countries to apply provisions on pharmaceutical patents until 1 January 2016.

3. See for details on India's communication on IPRs: *WT/GC/W/147*.

Box 7.1

Doha Ministerial Declaration on TRIPS

17. "We stress the importance we attach to implementation and interpretation of the Agreement on Trade-Related Aspects of Intellectual Property Rights (TRIPS Agreement) in a manner supportive of public health, by promoting both access to existing medicines and research and development into new medicines and, in this connection, are adopting a separate declaration.

18. With a view to completing the work started in the Council for Trade-Related Aspects of Intellectual Property Rights (Council for TRIPS) on the implementation of Article 23.4, we agree to negotiate the establishment of a multilateral system of notification and registration of geographical indications for wines and spirits by the Fifth Session of the Ministerial Conference. We note that issues related to the extension of the protection of geographical indications provided for in Article 23 to products other than wines and spirits will be addressed in the Council for TRIPS pursuant to paragraph 12 of this declaration.

19. We instruct the Council for TRIPS, in pursuing its work programme including under the review of Article 27.3(b), the review of the implementation of the TRIPS Agreement under Article 71.1 and the work foreseen pursuant to paragraph 12 of this declaration, to examine, inter alia, the relationship between the TRIPS Agreement and the Convention on Biological Diversity, the protection of traditional knowledge and folklore, and other relevant new developments raised by members pursuant to Article 71.1. In undertaking this work, the TRIPS Council shall be guided by the objectives and principles set out in Articles 7 and 8 of the TRIPS Agreement and shall take fully into account the development dimension."

Another rallying point for the developing countries under the TRIPS agreement was widening the scope and coverage of geographical indications. Geographical indications are associated with the identification of products with a particular characteristic with a name of place, region, area, etc. Under the existing TRIPS provisions, higher level of protection was given to wines and spirits. The long-standing demand of the developing region was to extend the 'higher level of protection' (to protect geographical indication even if there was no risk of misleading consumers or unfair competition from other products) to other products. Some developed nations opposed this demand on the ground of 'whether the relevant provisions of the TRIPS Agreement provide a mandate for extending coverage beyond wines and spirits.'

The Doha Declaration noted that the TRIPS Council would handle this under the declaration's paragraph 12 (which deals with implementation issues). The Declaration offered two tracks: (a) "where we provide a specific negotiating mandate in this Declaration, the relevant implementation issues shall be addressed under that mandate; (b) the other outstanding implementation issues shall be addressed as a matter of priority by the relevant WTO bodies, which shall report to the Trade Negotiations Committee (TNC) by the end of 2002 for appropriate action." Member governments expressed different interpretations of this mandate, for instance Argentina viewed it as "there is no agreement to negotiate the 'other outstanding implementation issues' referred to under (b) and that, by the end of 2002, consensus will be required in order to launch any negotiations on these issues." Bulgaria, the Czech Republic, EU, Hungary, India, Liechtenstein, Kenya, Mauritius, Nigeria, Pakistan, the Slovak Republic, Slovenia, Sri Lanka, Switzerland, Thailand and Turkey argued that there is a clear mandate to negotiate immediately.

Two reviews have taken place in the TRIPS Council, as required by the TRIPS Agreement: (a) review of Article 27.3(b), which deals with patentability or non-patentability of plant and animal inventions, and the protection of plant varieties; and (b) review of the entire TRIPS Agreement (required by Article 71.1). The Doha Declaration charted the work in the TRIPS Council on the implementation issues by specifying that the Council should also look at—the relationship between the TRIPS Agreement and the UN Convention on Biodiversity; the protection of traditional knowledge and folklore; and other relevant new developments that member governments raise in the review of the TRIPS Agreement.

Concerns Raised by India before Hong Kong Ministerial: An Analysis

Since the Millennium Round of negotiations and thereafter DDA and Cancun Ministerial, India's point of view over TRIPS negotiations have remained unchanged. India's concerns revolve around technology transfer, biodiversity and geographical indications. It is evident from the many submissions to the TRIPS Council that developing and least developed countries confront serious impediments in procuring new technologies (Table 7.2). Another area of concern for India is the harmonisation of TRIPS agreement with the UN Convention on Biodiversity. Expanding the coverage of geographical indications to products, other than wines and spirits has been a common concern of many developing countries, including India.

Table 7.2

TRIPS: Indian Stand

Issues	*Key Features*	*Indian Position*
Technology Transfer Article 7, 8, 40, 66.2 and 67	• Contribute to innovation. • Transfer and dissemination of technology. • Prevent abuse of IPRs by right holders. • Licensing in IPRs restrain competition. • Technical and financial cooperation. • DCs to provide incentive to their firms for divesting technology to LDCs.	• LDCs face serious difficulties in procuring new technologies. These could be overcome by suitable safeguards in the domestic IPR laws of LDCs. • Find a commercially viable mechanism for effective implementation of respective provisions.
Bio-diversity Article 27.3	• IPRs are private rights • Patentability of plants and animals. • Benefit sharing in commercial exploitation of *ex situ* materials. • Protection of plant varieties by patents or by an effective *sui generis* system. • CBD reaffirms rights of nations over their own biological resources.	• Harmonisation of TRIPS provisions with the UN Convention on Bio-diversity. • Study the relationship between the provisions of CBD and TRIPS for reconciliation. • Inclusion of a provision in Article 29 requiring a clear mention of the biological source material and the country of origin.
Geographical Indications Article 23	Higher protection of wines and spirits even where the true origin of goods is indicated.	Such protection is not extended to other goods. Extend such protection to goods other than wines and spirits.

Source: Debroy B. (1999), *The WTO Millennium Round Agenda—Towards a Negotiating Agenda for India*. RGICS-CII publication.

Technology has become a major determinant for economic development. Emerging patterns of technology generation and transfer have been researched intensively. A recent analysis of the mode of technology transfers suggests a reversal of the growing popularity of arm's length licensing in the 1970s and mid-1980s to intra-firm transfers since the mid-1980s. For example, 80 per cent of transfers by US corporations and 95 per cent by German corporations in 1995 were made on internal basis compared to 69 per cent and 92 per cent respectively in 1985. This is only one example of the changing pattern of technology transfers, provided here to highlight the need to address in the WTO issues such as transfer, dissemination and innovation. This raises concerns over "implementation issues, especially in terms of ensuring that measures and procedures do not themselves become barriers to legitimate trade. India proposed that Articles 7 and 8.2 are overarching provisions that should qualify other provisions of the Agreement that are meant to protect intellectual property rights."

Transfer of Technology

The TRIPS Agreement recognises that conditions pertaining to IPRs could restrain competition and have adverse effects on trade and may impede the transfer and dissemination of technology. Its provisions grant certain rights to ensure that this does not happen. Article 67 obliges developed country members to provide, on request and on mutually agreed terms and conditions, technical and financial cooperation in their favour. Since developing countries are still struggling to comply with the existing provisions, awareness and capacity to seek such cooperation is lacking. Again, Article 66.2 obliges developed country members to provide incentives to enterprises and institutions in their territories for the purpose of promoting and encouraging technology transfer to least developed countries. There has been little effort to implement this provision, raising doubts about the effectiveness of the Agreement to facilitate technology transfers.

Technology access is the result of licences and technology transfer agreements. Prospective technology seekers in developing countries face serious difficulties in their commercial dealings with technology holders in the developed countries. These difficulties are basically of three kinds, namely:

1) arising from the imperfections of the market for technology;
2) skill of enterprises and institutions in developing countries in concluding adequate legal arrangements for the acquisition of technology; and
3) government practices, both legislative and administrative, in both developed and developing countries, influencing the implementation of national policies and procedures.

These difficulties may have to be addressed specifically in order to fully implement TRIPS provisions relating to transfer and dissemination of technology, particularly in the light of Articles 7, 8,

40, 66.2 and 67. Some difficulties can be overcome by suitable safeguard measures in the domestic IPR laws of developing countries, particularly those arising out of the provisions of Articles 30, 31 and 40. In addition, the transfer and dissemination needs of the developing countries have to be seen from the point of view of the capacity of those in need of accessing technologies, particularly where the cost of technology may be prohibitive due to economies of scale and other reasons. In such cases, in order to implement the related provisions of the TRIPS Agreement, commercially viable mechanisms need to be found.

High cost of technology makes it difficult for the smaller, poorer developing countries to acquire appropriate technology on commercial terms. Such countries can only access and acquire appropriate technologies through government-to-government negotiations and with the financial assistance provided by donor governments and multilateral institutions. For instance, India proposed at the TRIPS Council that owners of environmentally sound technology and products should sell such technologies at fair and favourable terms upon demand to any interested party. Similar concerns regarding the need for the transfer of technology have been expressed with respect to electronics commerce also. Concerns have also been raised on the need for transfer of technology in a commercially viable manner for ensuring positive outcomes for developing countries through the increasing linkage between trade and investment.

Another aspect of technology transfer is the denial of dual-use technologies, even on commercial basis. This unilateral denial widens the technology gap between developed and developing countries. Under this guise a variety of technologies and products are being denied to developing countries that could otherwise have helped to accelerate their growth process. This issue needs to be carefully examined and seriously dealt with as a trade distorting and restrictive measure.

Biodiversity

The preamble of the TRIPS Agreement recognises IPRs to be private rights. Article 27.3 incorporates specific obligations on the issue of patenting life forms to the extent that it obliges members to provide product patents for micro-organisms and for non-biological and microbiological processes. In addition, Article 27.3(b) stipulates that all members shall provide for the protection of plant varieties, either by patents or by an effective *sui generis* system or by a combination thereof. The UN Convention on Biological Diversity stresses that nations have sovereign rights over their own biological resources. It also recognises the desirability of sharing equitably the benefits arising from the use of these resources as well as traditional knowledge, innovations and practices relevant to the conservation of biological diversity and its sustainable use.

Government of India has proposed harmonisation of the approaches to the utilisation of living resources found in the TRIPS Agreement on the one hand and the UN Convention on Biological Diversity (CBD) on the other. These two international agreements are intrinsically linked with one another. India emphasised to study the relationship between the provisions of the CBD and those of the TRIPS Agreement and suggest reconciliation of any contradictions within the overall objective of conservation of biological resources with sustainable development. Sustainable development being an objective of the WTO also, it becomes all the more important for Members to examine ways and means to harmonise the approaches to utilisation of living resources in the CBD and in the TRIPS Agreement.

India strongly sought amendment to the TRIPS Agreement in order to provide that members shall require that an applicant for a patent relating to biological materials or to traditional knowledge shall provide, as a condition to acquiring patent rights:

(i) disclosure of the source and country of origin of the biological resource and of the traditional knowledge used in the invention;

(ii) evidence of prior informed consent through approval of authorities under the relevant national regimes; and

(iii) evidence of fair and equitable benefit sharing under the national regime of the country of origin.

Failure to provide a solution to ensure a mutually supportive relationship between TRIPs and the CBD may turn out to be detrimental to the objectives of both instruments. In implementing their obligations under the CBD, nations would exercise sovereign rights over their biological resources, without impeding innovation, intellectual property rights, etc. At the same time, the right of holders of traditional knowledge to share benefits arising out of such innovation cannot be over emphasised. This is possible only if commercial exploitation of such innovations are encouraged only on the condition that the innovators share the benefits through material transfer agreements/transfer of information agreements. A material transfer agreement would be necessary where the inventor wishes to use the biological material and a transfer of information agreement would be necessary where the inventor bases himself on indigenous or traditional knowledge. Such an obligation could be incorporated through inclusion of provisions in Article 29 of the TRIPS Agreement requiring a clear mention of the biological source material and the country of origin.[4] This part of the patent application should be open to full public scrutiny on filing of the application. A provision like this will permit countries with possible opposition claims to examine the application and state their claims well in time. The entire effort of Indian proposal is to ensure greater transparency in the form of additional information in patent applications, and an approach that allows a harmonious construction of the two international agreements.

Geographical Indications

The Section 3 of Part II of the TRIPS Agreement provides for two different levels of protection for geographical indications. First, the general standards of protection that must be available for all geographical indications against misleading and unfair practices. Second, the additional or 'absolute' protection that must be accorded to geographical indications for wines and spirits. Under the provisions of the latter, there is, among other elements enhancing the protection, no need to prove that the public is misled or that there is unfair competition. This differential treatment of geographical indications can only be explained in the light of the negotiations of the Uruguay Round. The relevant TRIPS provisions are the result of trade-offs, which were specific to the circumstances prevailing at the time of the Uruguay Round negotiations, in particular during the Brussels Ministerial Conference (1990). This was due to the link at that time between the negotiations on geographical indications and the negotiations on agriculture.

There is no systematic or logical explanation for the distinction made in Section 3 of Part II of the TRIPS Agreement. This distinction

---

4. Article 29 deals with conditions on patent applicants.

ignores that geographical indications for categories of goods other than wines and spirits are equally important for trade. The economic and political significance of geographical indications is growing as increasing quality awareness and higher quality requirements promote the demand for products of a specific geographical origin. The added value to exported goods increases the chances for such legitimate goods to reach the market that is part of the global vision for a multilateral trading system. Thus, the awareness of the need for an extension of additional protection to products other than wines and spirits has continuously increased and spread among members. Since not all issues relevant to the protection of geographical indications were settled in the Uruguay Round, the built-in agenda of the TRIPS Agreement provides for the basis for further negotiations on increasing the protection of geographical indications.

This type of additional protection is not available to goods other than wines and spirits. It is an anomaly that the higher level of protection is available only for—wines and spirits. Government of India's submission before the TRIPS Council proposed that such higher level of protection should be available for goods other than wines and spirits also. This would be helpful for products of export interest like *Basmati* rice, Darjeeling tea, alphonso mangoes, *Kohlapuri* slippers in the case of India. Besides India, other members of the WTO also exhibited their interest to extend the coverage of higher level of protection to products of export interest to them like Bulgarian yoghurt, Czech Pilsen beer, many agricultural products of the European Union, Hungarian Szatmar plums and so on. There is a need to expedite work already initiated in the TRIPS Council in this regard, under Article 24, so that benefits arising out of the TRIPS Agreement in this area are spread out wider.

Operationalising Article 7 and 8 of the TRIPS Agreement

The scenes at the negotiation tables at Seattle, Doha and Cancun, both inside and outside, brought out many lessons for the WTO membership. One of the lessons learnt is the urgent need for confidence building measure, especially in terms of clarifications required for legal interpretation of WTO Agreements for long term health of the multilateral trading system. The 'clarificatory' interpretation evolving through the strengthened dispute settlement mechanism is the key to successful implementation of WTO agreements, TRIPS being the most intrusive of all the agreements. Article XVI:4 of the WTO Agreement obliges each member to ensure the conformity of its laws, regulations and administrative procedures with its obligations as provided in the TRIPS Agreement. To determine whether such conformity is being ensured, recourse is available either through discussions in the TRIPS Council or through the Dispute Settlement Understanding (DSU).

The objectives and principles of the TRIPS Agreement demonstrate two things, namely (a) the TRIPS Agreement is a trade agreement with the overarching objective of promoting trade through international transfer of technology, and (b) the Agreement balances the private rights of inventors with the rights of the users of inventions. The Government of India, in order to strengthen the multilateral trading system, proposed before the TRIPS Council some measures for operationalising Articles 7 and 8. These are as follows:

1) A clarification could be made of the language in Articles 7 and 8 for the benefit of national governments pursuing public interest and for the dispute settlement mechanism. For example, it could be clarified that Article 7 contains the objectives of the Agreement and is not circumscribed by any other provisions of the Agreement.
2) The phrase "provided that such measures are consistent with the provisions of this Agreement" in Article 8.1 could be clarified to emphasise that principles of the Agreement contained in this Article cannot be completely negated by this proviso.
3) A number of 'implementation' proposals in paragraphs 21 and 22 of the Draft Ministerial Text (DMT) of the Seattle Ministerial Conference relate to objectives and principles contained in Articles 7 and 8.

Through this proposal, India urged the TRIPS Council to examine the above issues in order to build the confidence of the weaker trading partners or operationalisation of Articles 7 and 8. This would be necessary to preserve the democratic way of functioning of the GATT/WTO. It would also be guidance for the dispute settlement mechanism grappling with the balance between the principles and objectives of the TRIPS Agreement on the one hand and minimum levels of protection required under the Agreement on the other hand.

India and International Support

On number of issues, many member nations have supported India's proposals at the TRIPS Council. Joint *communiqué* on extending the protection of geographical indications from wines and spirits to other products was primarily based on safeguarding common interests and distorting TRIPS provisions. In this *communiqué*, respective members highlighted following concerns:

a) Why the level of protection provided by Article 22 of the TRIPS Agreement for geographical indications for products other than wines and spirits is not sufficient?

b) Why providing two different levels of protection for geographical indications in the TRIPS Agreement (one for wines and spirits and another one for products other than wines and spirits), is not justified? and

c) Why the extension of the protection of geographical indications for wines and spirits to one uniform level of protection for geographical indications is necessary in order to conform Section 3 of Part II to the goals of the TRIPS Agreement and to general WTO principles?

The present differentiation is reminiscent of the perception of geographical indications in the pre-TRIPS era. Respective members conferred that extension of the level of protection for wines and spirits to all other products is in the best interest and benefit of all. It is not a North-South issue, but every country—whether developed, developing or in transition—has products that are the fruits of its culture and know-how, and its unique blend of soil, water or climate, and which, therefore, deserve effective protection. At a time when further trade liberalisation is being striven for, it seems, particularly in relation to the negotiations going on in the field of agriculture, a natural corollary that members should be able to fully reap the advantages of their geographical indications when competing with their products on the liberalised world market. This can only be done effectively by granting them additional protection against erosion of their geographical indications. In conclusion, Bulgaria, Cuba, the Czech Republic, Egypt, Iceland, Jamaica, Kenya, Liechtenstein, Mauritius, Nigeria, Pakistan, Slovenia, Sri Lanka, Switzerland, Turkey and Venezuela proposed that the TRIPS Council continue its negotiations and start without any further delay to work out the legal modalities necessary to eliminate the existing deficiencies in the

TRIPS Agreement in the field of the protection of geographical indications with a view to reaching a mutually agreeable solution.

The most striking point of departure between the CBD and TRIPS in respect of IPRs lies in the objectives that the two treaties have set for themselves. The CBD considers intellectual property protection as a means to achieving the end of sustainable development, but the Agreement on TRIPS, on the other hand, considers strengthening of IPRs as an end in itself. This leads to a very significant difference in that while the former establishes a more inclusive regime where the largest number of stakeholders are brought about in to realise a common good, the latter essentially emphasises the need to protect the sole interests of the owners of intellectual property. On the issue of determining the relationship between TRIPS Agreement and the UN Convention on Biological Diversity, the delegations of Bolivia, Brazil, Cuba, Ecuador, India, Peru, Thailand and Venezuela submitted a Checklist of Issues with the aim of facilitating more focused, structured and result-oriented discussions.[5] The Checklist is as follows:

1. Disclosure of source and country of origin of the biological resource and of the traditional knowledge used in the invention–
    - How would an obligation for disclosure of country and source of origin of biological resource and associated traditional knowledge used in an invention help in better examination of patents and in preventing cases of bad patents?
    - What is the meaning of disclosure of source and country of origin of biological resource and of the traditional knowledge used in the invention?
    - What would be the legal effect of wrongful disclosure or non-disclosure?
    - On whom should the burden of proof lie?
    - In what manner should the proposed obligation of disclosure of source and country of origin and associated traditional knowledge be introduced in the TRIPS Agreement?

5. *IP/C/W/429/Rev.1* and *IP/C/W/438*

2. Disclosure of evidence of prior informed consent under the relevant national regime-
   - How would furnishing the above evidence facilitate achieving the objectives of the CBD of ensuring prior informed consent and harmonious relationship between the CBD and the TRIPS Agreement? Could contractual arrangements for ensuring prior informed consent and benefit-sharing suffice to achieve the objectives of the CBD in this regard?
   - How should the evidence of prior informed consent through approval of authorities under the relevant national regime be provided for?
   - What should be the nature of obligation on the patent applicant that should satisfy the requirement of prior informed consent?
   - What should be the obligation if there is no national regime in the country of origin?
   - What should be the legal effect of not providing evidence of prior informed consent through approval of authorities under the relevant national regime?
3. Disclosure of evidence of benefit sharing under the relevant national regime:
   - What should be the meaning of evidence of benefit sharing under the relevant national regime?
   - When is this evidence to be introduced by the patent applicant?
   - What should be the obligation if there is no relevant national regime in the country of origin?
   - What should be the legal effect of not providing evidence of fair and equitable benefit sharing under the relevant national regime?

The European Commission is now willing to discuss the issue of patent disclosure but emphasises that failure to disclose should lie outside patent law and should be regulated by civil or administrative law. The US has so far strongly opposed the inclusion of disclosure requirements in patent applications, saying it would be incompatible with TRIPs since it would add another substantive condition on patentability beyond those already provided. The patent disclosure route would only be a limited measure to check bio-piracy, but would not go far in mitigating the negative implications of IPRs on developing countries. A group represented by Brazil and India and including Bolivia, Colombia, Cuba, Dominican Republic, Ecuador, Peru, Thailand and some others want to amend the TRIPS Agreement so that patent applicants are required to disclose the country of origin of the biological resources and traditional knowledge used in the inventions, evidence that they received 'prior informed consent' (a term used in the Biological Diversity Convention), and evidence of 'fair and equitable benefit sharing'. They also look at weaknesses of alternative methods such as contracts and databases.

Conclusions

The *Public Citizen*, for example, in an article provocatively titled "WTO—Shrink or Sink!" while demanding the removal of the TRIPS from the WTO, says: "TRIPS agreement promotes monopoly by transnational corporations; prevents access to essential medicines and other goods; leads to private appropriation of knowledge and life forms; undermines biodiversity; and keeps poorer countries from increasing their levels of social and economic welfare and developing their technological capacity." In the light of above, the option of trying to negotiate, loosen and modify TRIPS to suit Indian interests has limited potential. Growing pressures and continued opposition of developed countries on certain issues further complicates the negotiating position of India. India and other developing countries have been trying to ensure that geographical indications are extended to products other than wines and spirits as a means of protecting products such as *Basmati* rice.

A proposal to amend the TRIPS agreement to require patent applications to include a disclosure of the origin of biological materials and traditional knowledge is currently being pushed by Brazil and India, only to be strongly opposed by the United States and Japan. Despite a growing consensus on issues like harmonisation of CBD and TRIPS, issues related to disclosures and patentability remains as the major impediment in striking out a deal with developed countries. Attempts of linking agricultural negotiations with harmonisation of CBD and TRIPS, further makes the negotiating agenda more complicated for India.

Looking at the Hong Kong ministerial declaration, it is observed that the material gains for the developing countries are indeed limited. Referring to all outstanding implementation issues under paragraph 12(b) of the DDA, the Hong Kong ministerial declaration agreed to intensify these negotiations in order to complete them within the overall time frame as foreseen earlier. Given the importance of Paragraph 6 of DDA on the TRIPS Agreement and Public Health, the declaration welcomed the work of the Council for TRIPS and the General Council undertaken earlier (6 December 2005). The ongoing work on extension of the protection of geographical indications (provided for in Article 23 of the TRIPS) to products other than wines and spirits and the relationship between TRIPS and the Convention on Biological Diversity (CBD) were also noted. In addition, the declaration reaffirmed the commitment to "enhance effective trade-related technical assistance and capacity building to LDCs on a priority basis in helping to overcome their limited human and institutional trade-related capacity to enable LDCs to maximise the benefits resulting from the Doha Development Agenda (DDA)."

The 6 December 2005 notification, a major breakthrough, is the approval by General Council to change TRIPS provision relating to patents and public health originally adopted in 2003. It is quite a gain for the developing countries since for the first time a core WTO agreement will be amended. The provision will formally be part of TRIPS Agreement when two thirds of the members would ratify it, the deadline for which is 1 December 2007. The waiver would remain in force until then. In short, this would enable poorer countries to obtain cheaper generic versions of patented medicines, who otherwise lack the capacity to produce them, since it was earlier not easy owing to TRIPS provisions. The WTO declaration notes (*Press/426*, 6 December 2005), "As with the 2003 waiver, the permanent amendment will allow any member country to export pharmaceutical products made under a compulsory licence for this purpose. They may need to change their own laws in order to do so. ... So far, Norway, Canada and India have informed the WTO that their laws are complete, while the Republic of Korea and the EU have said their new laws are on the verge of coming into force." This means increased export potential for India, being a major generic drug producer, apart from increased security for public health concerns. This calls for further negotiations by developing countries on other concern areas of TRIPS agreement.

8

Environmental Service Negotiation and India: Priorities and Concerns

OINDRILA DE and
PAVEL CHAKRABORTY

Background

The environmental issues were mainstreamed in the work programme of the WTO when, at the conclusion of the Uruguay Round in 1994, trade ministers from the member nations launched a focused programme on trade and environment, and created the Committee for Trade and Environment (CTE). The CTE is vested with the broad-based responsibility of issues comprising all the three core areas of multilateral trade—goods, services and intellectual property. In Doha Ministerial Declaration, 2001, the members agreed to launch negotiations on trade and environment with some prioritised objectives under the close supervision of CTE. Paragraph 31 of Doha Ministerial Declaration is a three-point agenda to strengthen the said relationship. Paragraph 31 (iii) calls for liberalisation of trade in environmental goods and services (i.e. the reduction or elimination of tariff and non-tariff barriers with a view to enhance the mutual supportiveness of trade and environment). In the ongoing negotiations in the WTO, environmental goods and environmental services are subject to different legal frameworks and hence are dealt separately. The General Agreement on Tariffs and Trade (GATT) covers all environmental goods and the negotiation takes place in Negotiating Group on Market Access for Non-Agricultural Products (NAMA) whilst the General Agreement on Trade in Services (GATS) covers environmental services and the negotiation is taking place at special Session of the Council for Trade in Services. Environmental services fall within the ambit of GATS in terms of select sectors and sub-sectors included in the WTO Services Sectoral Classification list.[1]

1. WTO, note by secretariat, *MTN.GNS/W/120*, 10 July 1991.

So, before we advance to the environmental service negotiation, let us have a look at the basic framework of GATS commitments and the status of environmental service industry in India.

GATS and Members Commitments

General Agreement on Trade in Services (GATS hereafter) was one of the core agreements of WTO. It intended to establish a multilateral framework of principles and rules for trade in services with an objective to expand such trade under conditions of progressive liberalisation and transparency. Unlike trade in goods, trade in services is not classified under multi-digit Harmonised System of Tariff Classification. During the Uruguay Round in 1991, the service sector was broadly divided into 12 categories[2] on the basis of United Nations Provisional Central Product Classification (CPC). The sectors classified as Business (including professional and computer) Services, Communication Services, Construction and related engineering Services, Distribution Services, Educational Services, Environmental Services, Financial (Insurance and Banking) Services, Health Related and Social Services, Tourism and Travel Related Services, Recreational, Cultural and Sporting Services, Transport Services and other Services not included elsewhere. Article I (2) of the GATS distinguishes between four modes of supplying services such as Cross border supply or mode 1 (mostly through electronic means), Consumption abroad or mode 2 (mostly tourist or restaurant service), Commercial Presence mode 3 (joint ventures/subsidiary/branch offices, etc) and Presence or movement of Natural Persons or mode 4 (independent service suppliers like doctors, engineers, consultants, etc).

The obligations contained in GATS can be categorised into two groups: General Obligations and Specific Commitments. General Obligations apply directly and automatically to all member countries of WTO and includes Most Favoured Nation (MFN) treatment with some special temporary exemptions (no longer than 10 years), transparency and some additional obligations like establishment of administrative review and appeals, procedures and disciplines on the operation of monopolies and exclusive suppliers etc (Article II to XV, GATS). Under specific commitments, a positive list approach is

2. *MTN.GNS/W/120*, 10th July, 1991.

followed where each member identifies the service sectors/ sub sectors and modes of supply where they are willing to make specific commitments through a process called 'scheduling'. It includes Market Access (Article XVI), National Treatment (Article XVII) and Additional Commitments, if any (Article XVIII). The content of schedules of specific commitment is the most crucial aspect of GATS negotiation. The member countries can also schedule horizontal commitments or limitations, which apply to all sectors. The negotiating method under GATS follows request-offer approach between member countries.

Till date India received requests from more than 20 countries, which range over professional, architectural, construction and engineering, legal, health, computer-related, audio-visual, distribution, education, environmental, banking and insurance, telecom, tourism, transport, recreational and sporting services etc. India has also submitted its requests to a number of countries, which cover sectors like architectural, health, computer-related, audio-visual, banking and insurance, maritime transport etc.[3]

Environmental Service: Problems of Definition and Classification

Part IV of GATS agreement aimed at progressive liberalisation of trade in services by the member countries in successive rounds of negotiations, which applies also to environmental service category, initiated at the special session of CTS since 2000. However, one fundamental problem faced by environmental services sector is definition and classification of services that come under this particular category. According to the Service Sectoral Classification List (MTN.GNS/W/120) prepared during Uruguay Round, the environmental services include four broad categories based on United Nations Provisional Central Product Classification (CPC), which are the following:

- Sewage services (CPC 9401),[4]

3. The details of the requests are available in the Ministry of Commerce website, *www.commerce.nic.in.*

4. Sewage services are closely related to waste water treatment services that aim essentially to speed up the natural processes that reduce contaminants to an acceptable level for discharge into the environment.

- Refuse disposal services (CPC 9402),[5]
- Sanitation and similar services (CPC 9403), and
- Other environmental services.[6]

Even though the 'others' category does not explicitly refer to any CPC items, according to WTO,[7] it presumably includes the remaining elements of the CPC environmental services category: cleaning of exhaust gases (CPC 9404),[8] noise abatement services (CPC 9405), nature and landscape protection services (9406), and other environmental protection services not included elsewhere (CPC 9409). But according to WTO, this classification of environmental services is very limited from policy perspective.[9] After the negotiation started at 2000, initially almost all the proposals submitted to WTO addressed the issues of classification. Most of the proposals take the view that W/120 list is insufficient to reflect the present need of the industry. The recent attempts to define environmental services were advanced by the OECD and the Statistical Office of the European Communities (EUROSTAT). The detailed comparable lists under these three arrangements include both environmental goods and services under three broad categories: Pollution management, cleaner technologies and products and resource management, as seen from the following.

---

5. Refuse disposal and sanitation services are virtually synonymous with solid waste management which includes services to collect, transport, treat and dispose waste from homes, municipalities, commercial establishments and manufacturing plants.
6. Although the use of Services Sectoral Classification List is not mandatory, most Members have used it as a basis for scheduling their commitments. Details of the underlying CPC classification are to be found in United Nations (1991). The recently developed CPC Rev. 1 has introduced somewhat greater disaggregation in some of the sub-sectors of environmental services. For instance sewage services have been divided and refuse disposal into non-hazardous and hazardous waste collection, treatment and disposal services.
7. Environmental services background note by secretariat, *S/C/W/46*, 6TH July 1998.
8. Cleaning of exhaust gases closely resembles air quality control services designed to remove pollutants from a gaseous stream or to convert pollutants to a non-polluting or less polluting form prior to discharge into the atmosphere.
9. WTO, Background Note by the Secretariat, *S/C/W/46* (Dated July 6, 1998).

Table 8.1

Classification of Environmental Services

OECD/Eurostat	*CPC Version 1.0*[10]	*GATS*
A. Water and Waste Water Management Sector with Sub-sectors: • Sewage Services • Water for Human Use	941 Sewage Services 94110 Sewage Treatment Services 94120 Tank Emptying and Cleaning Services	1. Sewage Services Excludes Collection, Purification and Distribution Services of Water, and Construction Repair and Alteration of Sewers.
B. Solid and Hazardous Waste Management Sector with Sub-sectors: • Refuse Disposal and Treatment Services • Sanitation Services • Recycling Services	942 Refuse Disposal Services 94211 Non-hazardous Waste Collection Services 94212 Non-hazardous Waste Treatment and Disposal Services 94221 Hazardous Waste Collection Services 94222 Hazardous Waste Treatment and Disposal Services 943 Sanitation and Similar Services 94310 Sweeping and Snow Removal Services 94390 Other Sanitation Service	2. Refuse Disposal Services Excludes Dealing and Wholesale in Waste and Scrap, and R&D Services on Environmental on Environmental Issues. 3. Sanitation and Similar Services
C. Protection of Ambient Air and Climate	94900 Other Environmental Services	4. Other Services
D. Noise and Vibration Abatement	94900 Other Environmental Services	4. Other Services
E. Remediation and Clean-up of Soil, Groundwater.	94900 Other Environmental Services	4. Other Services
F. Protection Surface Water and of Biodiversity and Landscape Services	94900 Other Environmental Protection Services	4. Other Services Excludes Forest and Damage Assessment and Abatement Services
G. Other Environmental/ Ancillary Services: • Design Consulting and Engineering. • Preparation of Sites, Construction, Installation, Assembly, Repair and Maintenance • Environmental Research and Development • Analytical Services, Data Collection, Testing, Analysis, Assessment • Environmental Education, Training and Information	94900 Other Environmental Protection Services	4. Other Services

Source: Compiled from OECD (2000), GATS 2000, EC Submission (*S/CSS/W/38*) and WTO (1998).

10. United Nations Central Product Classification, Version 1.0 covers products that are an output of economic activities including transportable goods, non-transportable goods and services.

Environmental Service and GATS: The Potential Conflicts

The provision of environmental services has an inherent tendency to constitute natural monopoly since high initial investment requirement of this category causes significant barriers to entry. Moreover, some of these services like cleaning of roads, parks and lakes have the characteristics of public goods (i.e. non-exclusive, non-rival nature) and seems to require special interference by Governments. So, most of the environmental services were traditionally considered as public services and until recently the private partnership was not allowed in this sector in fear of consumer exploitation.[11] But the situation has changed considerably in recent years especially in developed countries. Regulated private partnership is preferred over government ownership to achieve the environmental objective in a cost efficient manner. But in the developing countries like India, Government authorities are the sole provider of most of the environmental services and private partnerships are not well established in most of the environmental service sectors. However, GATS does not apply to services supplied under governmental authority (Article I (3)). The governmental authority under clause I (3) (c) is defined as services which are supplied "neither on a commercial basis nor in competition with one or more suppliers." This definition needs further interpretation as it may cause several confusions defining the scope of 'governmental services.' In Indian context, it implies that public sector units undertaking fee-based business/market research service will not be eligible for 'government service' since it would most likely be competing with companies in the private sector offering similar services.[12]

Environmental Service Industry: Global *vis-à-vis* Indian Scenario

As far as size of the industry is concerned, according to a private sector estimate, in 2000 the global environmental market represented around US$ 522 billion in terms of revenue generation, private companies and public sector bodies taken together.[13] Nearly 50 per

11. WTO, Background Note by the Secretariat, *S/C/W/46* (Dated July 6, 1998).
12. *Liberalisation of Environmental Services in India (2005)*, TERI Report, June.
13. Ferrier, G (2003), "The Environmental Industry and prospects for building capacity in developing countries," in *Energy and Environmental Services: Negotiating Objectives and Development Priorities*, UNCTAD, Geneva.

cent of the market is represented by fees generated by services, while the remaining half is almost equally divided between equipment sales and the sale of environmental resources, such as water, energy or reclaimed material.[14] The European Union, United States, and Japan put together control 85 per cent of the global market in these goods and services. In the Indian context, with increasing environmental awareness and improved regulations, the demand for pollution control equipments and related services is growing at a faster pace than ever before. This sector, which was virtually non-existent in India until recently, has subsequently caught up fast, especially in the 1990s. Since the onset of economic liberalisation in 1991, the environmental market has grown at an average rate of 12 per cent per annum to reach to the estimated size of US $3.0 billion. These estimates, prepared by United States-Asia Environment partnership (2005), also include market for basic water and sanitation projects.[15] A separate study conducted by private sector[16], estimates that the total size of environmental market in 1997, in India was at around $2.05 billion, which has increased to $2.85 billion in 2002. Another study by the Indo German Chambers of Commerce (Market Estimates) (2001) have revealed that during the last decade demand for pollution control equipment, particularly equipment for industrial wastewater treatment, monitoring equipment for industrial air pollution control, and hazardous waste management has significantly increased.[17] Though there are many domestic players in the country, and many joint ventures with Western companies have been set up to cater to the demand, a large number of environmental goods are still required to be imported in the country. The breakdown of Indian environmental products market is provided in Figure 8.1 in the following:

14. The WTO *Document WT/CTE/W/96*(1998), discussed in *UNCTAD Expert Meeting on Strengthening Capacities in Developing Countries to Develop their Environmental Services Sector.*

15. *US-AEP India: FY 2005 Work Plan*, available at *http://www.usaep.org/downloads/2005%20-%20India.pdf*.

16. Environment Business International (EBI), San Diego, USA (2003).

17. *Study on the Indian Environmental Scenario and Market*, Indo German Chamber of Commerce, New Delhi (February 2001).

Figure 8.1

Indian Environmental Market Breakdown

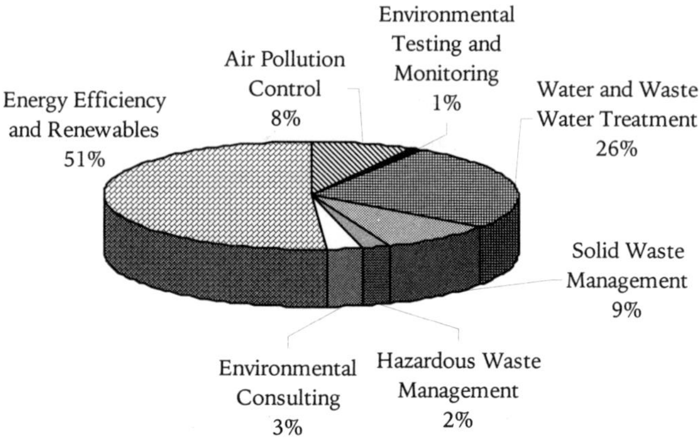

Source: EQMS India Ltd., as quoted in Singh, 2004.[18]

However the domestic environmental industry in India is still highly disorganised and is dominated by Small Scale Industry (SSI) units, which lack resources to invest in Research & Development as well as towards creation of marketing and servicing infrastructure. Off late many Indian companies have also entered into joint ventures with western companies, and some western companies have also started setting up wholly owned subsidiaries after the government permitted 100 per cent FDI for equipment manufacturing and for consulting/ management services in the sector.[19] On the other hand there are many smaller companies specialising in environmental consulting services, i.e., the companies offering services related to environmental management systems facilitation, environmental audits, environmental impact assessment and development of environmental standards. Indian environmental industry over the years has developed capabilities in diverse range of equipments and services, but their expertise is limited in developing advanced technologies, such as

18. Singh, S. (20004) "Trade Preference and Growth of Environmental Industry: Issues and implications for India", *Indian Journal of Economics and Business*, Vol. III, issue III (New Delhi)
19. For instance, the wholly owned subsidiaries like Pentair Water India Ltd, ERM (India) Pvt. Ltd could be mentioned in this regard.

those required for dealing with special gaseous pollutants, coal beneficiation, hospital waste management and manufacturing high precision monitoring and analytical equipments. The high-end technology products are usually imported from other countries. The Environmental Service Providers' survey conducted by TERI[20] indicates no major export potential for India even if the commitments are made in WTO. With most Indian respondents in that survey complaining of inadequate funds, R&D and data unavailability, little hope is left for expansion in foreign markets through exports in coming future.

Environmental Service Negotiation and India

As mentioned earlier, the negotiation on environmental services has started at the special session of Council for Trade in Services (CTS) since 2000 following the request-offer approach under GATS rule. It was supposed to be finished by January 2005, but the deadline has been missed. Total 38 countries have made commitments in at least one sub sector of environmental services so far. Except mode 2, there are very few full commitments in mode 1, 3 and 4 (5 per cent in mode 1, very few in mode 3 and nil in mode 4).[21] The major players like US, EC, Canada and Australia have made full commitments under mode 2 and 3. However for mode 4, they kept it unbound except for those referred to horizontal section. India has revised its offer for service sector in August 2005 to include environmental services with some other new sectors/sub sectors[22]. India has offered no limitation on market access for mode 1 and mode 2 and no limitations on national treatment on mode 1, 2 and 3 for two environmental sub-sectors of W/120 list, namely, Refuse disposal services (9402) and sanitation and similar services (9403). Mode 4 is kept unbound except as in the horizontal section (for example Access to Scheduled areas and Tribal areas covered under the V and VI Schedule of the Constitution of India may be denied)[23]. For Mode 3, market access is not restricted subject to incorporation and the condition that foreign investors having prior collaboration in specific service sector in India would require FIPB approval.

20. "Liberalisation of Environmental Services in India", *TERI Report*, June 2005.
21. For details see the Services and Environment section under *www.wto.org*.
22. *TN/S/O/IND/Rev.1* (2005).
23. *TN/S/O/IND* (2004).

India has proposed a new approach bringing environmental goods and services together for negotiation under paragraph 31 (iii) of Doha Development Agenda (DDA) in April 2005. According to India's submission in WTO, "this approach would address diversity in environmental standards with common but differentiated responsibilities and would bring in trade liberalisation to meet the environmental as well as development goals of both the Doha Development Agenda and Agenda 21."[24] Under the proposed approach, a Designated National Authority (DNA) will consider a project that meets certain criteria as *Environmental Project*. The goods and services included in that project will qualify for specified concessions for the duration of the projects. The projects will be decided keeping in mind national requirements as well as the objectives of any bilateral and multilateral environmental agreements. It can include air pollution control, water and waste management, remediation and clean up, renewable energy facilities etc. The commitments that the members may include are: (a) reduction or elimination of tariffs on import of all project related goods; (b) reduction, elimination or appropriate treatment of standards, licensing restrictions, non-tariff barriers and other related issues, and (c) specific commitments required in all modes of service delivery.

This approach is strikingly different from what was being suggested previously. First of all, "While the aim of the proponents of environmental goods and services (EGS) liberalisation, such as the EU and the US, is a permanent elimination of tariffs on EGS on a most-favoured-nation basis, India's new proposal suggests a different approach: temporary market opening for goods and services deemed necessary for achieving specific environmental goals[25]." Secondly, this approach recognised the linkages between environmental goods and services and synergy between the two is an important element of this approach.[26] According to the India's negotiating stance, environmental products and related technological services are frequently provided on an integrated basis. Firms bring together the range of materials and expertise to undertake an environmental project and under the said approach; firms can procure these goods and services on the basis of

24. *TN/TE/W/51* (2005).

25. "Environmental Goods: A Hong Kong Deliverable", *Bridges News Weekly*; Year 9, No. 6-7, June/July 2005.

26. *TN/TE/W/60*, 19th September, 2005.

their comparative advantage. So, arguably the broader objective of environmental benefit is addressed in a focused and integrated way in the proposed approach.

Several developed countries have questioned whether India's proposed modality would have as widespread effects as envisaged under Paragraph 31 (iii) mandate, since it is based on case-by-case and temporary basis. But India is quite optimistic about the new approach as it believes that this method is likely to solve the problem of dual use of environmental goods, integrate the two interdependent segments of environmental industry and also will leave sufficient policy space for developing countries to address their other development concerns.

Conclusion

Since the inception of WTO, India along with other developing countries opposed inclusion of environmental agenda in the WTO regime in the fear of increased protectionism coming in the form of environmental standards. After TRIPS and Public Health was compromised by developed countries in the favour of developing world in Doha Round and possibility of continuing domestic support in agriculture started fading away, EU tried to push the Environment agenda as a whole with a vigorous support from Switzerland and some other developed countries with a twin objective of protecting their agriculture and enjoying greater market access in Non-agricultural product categories and service sectors of their interest. For instance, the developed countries have put forward nearly 400 non-agricultural products for consideration as environmental goods and demanded tariff concessions on those products.[27] Such a move can jeopardize NAMA negotiation in general since it goes against the interests of developing countries.

India has so far negotiated quite cautiously in the multilateral forum on this issue, given the lack of competitiveness of the domestic players as discussed in the analysis earlier. Moreover, since till date the definition or classification of environmental goods and services is in a fluid stage, India has a reason to be a little careful before committing fully before WTO. In the famous gambling dispute

27. WTO, Submissions by member countries under TN/TE/W so far.

between US and Antigua and Barbuda[28], the later country complained against certain US measures restricting the cross boarder supply of gambling and betting services from foreign operators. The panel ruled in favour of Antigua. US argued they should be allowed to restrict Internet gambling since it was not the part of GATS commitments. The appellate body, though upheld the panel judgments, made few changes over public moral concerns, which said that US can address the public moral concern engaging in bilateral or multilateral consultations. According to acting US trade representative; US can maintain restrictions on Internet gambling subject to certain clarifications.[29] This case reveals the difficulties in realising the potential implication of sector specific commitments in the coming future. Therefore India should be very careful in scheduling commitments under environmental service sector. The omission of environmental services from the Hong Kong ministerial declaration is indeed welcome in this light.

---

28. DS 285 (Starting on June 2003).
29. *Bridges Weekly Trade News Digest*, Vol. 9, No. 12, 13th April, 2005.

9

Deconstructing France at the WTO

JEAN-PIERRE LEHMANN

Perhaps the main impression from the WTO ministerial meeting held in Hong Kong last December was that it was all so predictable. The scripts were prepared well in advance, there had been plenty of rehearsals, and the *dramatis personae* were well known. Prominent among them, France did not disappoint. Anyone harbouring any illusion that the WTO process was about boosting international trade, increasing global welfare, reducing poverty and constructing a dynamic global market, would very quickly have been disillusioned by spending not more than just a few minutes with the French delegation. What we were served instead was mercantilism in a very raw form.

The French delegation was jointly led by the Trade Minister, Christine Lagarde, and the Agriculture Minister, Dominique Bussereau. Though this is the Doha 'Development' Round of the World 'Trade' Organisation and not the World Agriculture Organisation, the absence of the Minister for Overseas Development in contrast with the omnipresence of the Agriculture Minister is more than just revealing. This particular ministerial duo was not limited to France and true of many delegations, including that of the EU, which included both Trade Commissioner Peter Mandelson and European Agriculture Minister Mariann Fischer Boel. The EU Commissioner for Development and Humanitarian Aid, Louis Michel, may have been in Hong Kong for the Doha Development Agenda Ministerial Conference, but he was emphatically not conspicuously present. The ministerial trade-agriculture pattern represents one of the (many) fundamental flaws of both the Hong Kong and Cancun WTO ministerial meetings.

So far as the French Trade-Agriculture seemingly inseparable duo was concerned, they came across as a Gallic version of Cervantes' famous classic, *Don Quixote*. Trade Minister Christine Lagarde, the elegant, tall, thin aristocratic, fluent English speaker was the feminine reincarnation of Don Quixote, while her short, earthy, non-English speaking (and proud of it!), roly-poly colleague, Agriculture Minister Dominique Bussereau, was the perfect Sancho Panza. The windmills they were battling? Global trade liberalisation and its threats to France!

The atmosphere among the French delegation was that of a bunker. Though comments were made to the effect that France and the EU were seeking 'concessions' from the large developing countries in services, not once was any mention made of the benefits France gains from international trade. Not once was reference made to the important role in the French economy of France's many successful multinational companies. And perhaps most surprising of all, there was hardly any discussion at all about Greater China. The fact the meeting was being held in Hong Kong, that icon of free trade situated in currently the world's most dynamic trading region, from all the discussions would seem to have been irrelevant.

At one meeting, after assuring agricultural lobbies that the French government would not budge on tariffs and subsidies, Agriculture Minister Bussereau added: "We are of course defending a lifestyle, we did not invent McDonald's even though there are many on our territory." The clear implication is that the McDonalds on French territory are part of the American globalisation invasion, and not due to the fact that millions of French consumers-regrettably or otherwise-love the golden arches. The facile populist dig at McDonald's also masks the fact that not only does the chain procure primarily French produce in France, but also that it is a significant employer, especially of young people—something for which a French minister could show some recognition, when noting that the French youth unemployment rate is 24 per cent.

French Tactics at Hong Kong

France's tactics at Hong Kong consisted of a number of different prongs.

- One constant theme was the solidarity of France with the European Commission and the other 24 member states. In almost the same breath, however, it was made clear that solidarity would not be at the price of vigilance. France was with the European Union, so long as the European Union was clearly behind France. The clear implication in respect to agriculture was that there would be no compromise on the position that had been tabled in July.

- European Trade Commissioner Mandelson's position was consequently in part hostage to France and also to the acrimonious budget deliberations that were taking place simultaneously in Brussels. The fact that in essence the 'success' of Hong Kong was to obtain a date by which the European Union would end agricultural export subsidies, 2013, was in turn due to the very watered-down compromise settlement reached on the EU budget just-in-time! Global trade talks, the future of the 21st century world economy and global welfare are all determined by the interests of French agriculture. This may be a bit of a caricature, but a reflection of reality nevertheless.
- From the amount of time devoted to the subject, it was also clear that the French delegation was greatly concerned about cotton. France, of course, does not produce any cotton. There were no French interests at stake, no 'sacrifices' to be made. On the other hand, former French African colonies, notably Benin, Mali, Niger and Chad, do produce cotton. They are the four countries that confronted the United States for its massive domestic cotton subsidies at the WTO Cancun Ministerial Meeting in 2003, providing one of the primary reasons for Cancun's collapse. (The other was the insistence on the part of the EU Trade Commissioner Pascal Lamy that the so-called Singapore issues—investment, government procurement, trade facilitation and competition policy—should be accepted unbundled in the proposed package.) This allowed the French delegation to position itself as a champion of those poor countries exploited by that global trade ogre, the United States. The point of course is that the United States' position on cotton is totally unacceptable, but that it is a bit rich that France of all countries should position itself as chief accuser: the pot calling the kettle black!
- France (and the European Union) sought to distinguish between different types and levels of developing countries. Developing countries are not a homogeneous group of nations; participants at French delegation debriefings and press conferences were regularly reminded. The biggest rogue among developing countries from the perspective of the French delegation was Brazil. In order to be able to play the potential

victim, the picture generally presented was that the main gainers from any agricultural trade liberalisation would be the very rich, very large landowners (*latifundistas*) in Brazil at the expense of the small French family farms and the poor developing countries.

- The proposal to extend duty-free market access to 97 per cent of the exports of the poorest developing countries (the so-called Least Developed Countries), which the EU trumpeted, is insignificant in terms of trade, but also disingenuous. The poorest countries are poor for many reasons, but one of them that almost invariably stand out is poor governance. Countries like Chile, Brazil, China, Thailand, Malaysia, India, South Africa and others, that have succeeded in generating sustained growth and competitive export sectors, whether in agriculture, manufacturing or services, have done so in good part thanks to better economic governance. In effect, the proposal favours the failures at the expense of the successful. It also is quite hypocritical in that it is the more dynamic and successful developing countries that pose a challenge to the rich countries, not the poorest of the poor that generally have very little to export in any case.
- It is of course true that there are vast differences in many respects between developing countries; the impact of global agricultural trade liberalisation would differ considerably among developing countries. None of these factors, however, had any effect on the formation of alliances. France and the European Union were not able to forge any special relationship with developing countries, including with those it was allegedly defending in their battle against the United States on cotton. The position of the rich countries, including prominently France, is clearly seen to be too self-serving for any developing countries to break ranks even for the purpose of a purely tactical alliance. The French ministers were clearly surprised and discomfited when informed on the third day of the Ministerial Conference that a joint statement had been issued by 110 developing countries, composed of the G-20 and the G-90, criticising the North. The attempted policy of divide and rule was obviously not working.

Although tensions and divisions between the EU and the US over trade in general and the Doha Agenda in particular are arguably more acute than at any time since the launching of the Round, from the perspective of the South, the WTO is still very much an 'us *versus* them', i.e., a South *versus* North, arena.

Trade and French Economic Policy and Philosophy

One of the eerie elements in the French ministerial debriefings was that there was no dissent among the French participants. Although a seminal paper ("The Common Agricultural Policy: Moment of Truth in France?") had just recently been published by the very high calibre French institute Groupe d'Economie Mondiale, under the direction of one of France's most eminent and internationally respected economists, Patrick Messerlin, which, among other things, shows how inequitable the agricultural subsidies are—one per cent of the richest farmers get more subsidies than 40 per cent of the poorer! — and the negative impact that the agricultural policy generally has on the French economy, not once was this publication referred to. French agricultural policy was taken as dogma. The French delegation included all the usual suspects representing agricultural associations and lobbies, trade unions and diverse anti-globalisation movements, such as ATTAC, and of course that icon of the French peasant struggle against globalisation, Americanisation and GMOs, José Bové. Although presumably there must have been representatives from French industrial and business associations in Hong Kong, they were conspicuously silent. The bunker mentality was buttressed by a trench 'we're all in this together' attitude. Don Quixote and Sancho Panza were leading a strongly supported charge.

In fact, the position of the Trade Minister Christine Lagarde is strange. Her extremely fluent English comes from the fact that she lived many years in the United States, including in Chicago. She became French Trade Minister in June 2005, in the cabinet reshuffle carried out by Jacques Chirac following the disastrous results of the French referendum on the European Constitutional Treaty. For the previous quarter-of-a-century (she is 49), she was with the prominent international American law firm Baker & McKenzie, rising to become Chair of its Global Policy Committee and the only woman on its executive committee. Forbes ranked her as 76th among the world's 100 most powerful women and the *Wall Street Journal* placed her 5th among influential European businesswomen. She also played various important roles in the leading US Republican think-tank CSIS (Centre for Strategic and International Studies) of which former USTR Robert Zoellick was previously director. Among her many other positions, she was also member of the international business advisory committee of the Mayor of Beijing.

Given her rich professional experience, she would seem an ideal person to lead the French government to adopt a far more global, visionary and liberal foreign economic policy. However, her CV notwithstanding and in spite of the many years she spent in Chicago, judging from her words and acts as French Trade Minister in Hong Kong, the Chicago school of economics does not seem to have had much impact on her. Her tone throughout the Hong Kong ministerial was definantly mercantilist. Furthermore, she is a member of a government whose President, Jacques Chirac, publicly declared that liberalism is as dangerous as communism. This is also the same government that pre-emptively pulled up the drawbridge to prevent a rumoured possible takeover bid of the large French dairy and agri-business conglomerate Danone by Pepsi, which Patrick Messerlin described as the French government's "strategic yogurt industry" policy! It is also the same government that upbraided the European Commission President José Barroso for "failing to prevent" the loss of 6,000 jobs following the closure of a Hewlett Packard plant in France. As noted earlier in Minister Bussereau's remarks regarding McDonald's, French policy insinuates hostility to both foreign trade and foreign investment.

France's economic nationalism, interventionism and protectionism had also been stridently expressed by the Chirac government in the furore in 2004 over the proposed liberalisation of services in the European Union, the so-called 'Bolkestein directive', after Frits Bolkestein, former EU Commissioner for the Internal Market, whom the French delighted in calling "Frankenstein." The directive was blocked. This has not prevented the European Union, including France, to insist that developing countries such as Brazil should open their services markets on the grounds that it will be good for them!

The great paradox is that while this government charges against the windmills of global trade and investment, France counts among some of the world's most successful global firms—Axa, L'Oreal, Renault, Alsthom, etc.—and sectors, notably in tourism, fashion, food, wines and spirits, transport equipments, nuclear power stations, etc.

France both significantly contributes to and benefits from globalisation—e.g., in terms of trade as share of GDP, inflows and outflows of foreign direct investment, trade, investment and tourism generated employment, etc. Yet this reality is totally absent whether in the forays against windmills or in the French Hong Kong WTO ministerial delegation bunker.

The idea behind the Doha Development Agenda when it was launched in 2001 was that the outcome should favour low and middle-income countries, which, by any objective criteria, have suffered unfair discrimination in a tilted global trade playing field for decades. This is true not only of agriculture, but of most labour-intensive industries, such as textiles and footwear, in which developing countries have a comparative advantage. So far as agriculture is concerned, the French position has been that it is committed to protecting its small family based farming community. That is one of the myths that been totally exploded by the Groupe d'Economie Mondiale study mentioned above, which in fact shows that the whole system of subsidies is formidably skewed to favour the rich agricultural landlords and agri-based companies.

In putting a brake on global trade, France is responsible for lower growth, less welfare, less poverty reduction and less employment generation, not only across the planet, but also at home. The recent riots in the deprived suburbs are one of many illustrations that the French 'social model' is not working. The French, especially French youth, would be the first beneficiaries of an open, dynamic liberal, globalisation embracing economic policy. In the meantime, if the French government is asked about the consequences of its agricultural policy on the poor, presumably the answer will be: "let them eat cake!"

Prospects for Going Forward in 2006?

Following the baby footstep taken in Hong Kong, the pressure is on to try to complete the Doha Agenda by the end of 2006. This, it is argued, is essential in order for the Doha deal to be presented to Congress prior to the expiry of trade promotion authority, which occurs in the spring of 2007. There is, however, another event scheduled in spring 2007 and that is the French presidential election. Although Jacques Chirac has occasionally hinted that he may stand for a third term, in reality he is already seen as history and an increasingly lame duck. Hence, the election is already well under way. The two most likely candidates of the Right, Nicols Sarkozy and Dominique de Villepin, the current Interior Minister and Prime Minister respectively, are both economic nationalists and populists. They are likely to campaign on a protectionist platform, hence will be more likely to urge more rigidity than flexibility in the French government position. It must also be recalled that in the previous presidential election in 2002 the extreme Right candidate, Jean-Marie le Pen, gained more than 20 per cent of the vote, a 20 per cent that all parties will seek to enlist. Thus, candidates of the Left will also take a protectionist stand on the fallacious, but nevertheless quite widely believed, grounds that protectionism protects jobs. One of the possible socialist candidates, Dominique Strauss-Kahn, is the only one that could be described as a liberal, but, partly for that reason, he is unlikely to be even a remote front-runner.

Thus, while the impending expiry of trade promotion authority may be an incentive to try to accelerate the Doha Agenda, the French presidential elections will act as a break. France, of course, is only one of the 25 member states of the EU. Regrettably, however, France's position has the support of the majority of the EU member states, including some of the bigger countries such as Spain, Italy and Poland. In EU, the relatively free traders tend to be smaller and less influential countries such as Sweden, Denmark, Finland and the Netherlands. Ireland, sadly, in spite of the huge gains it has obtained from global trade, is an arch protectionist on agricultural matters. The UK is also among the EU free traders, but London has comparatively little influence in Brussels.

In previous decades and trade rounds, ultimately Europe adopted a liberalising trade policy in great part due to the influence and leadership of Germany. Both the governments of Helmut Schmidt from the Social Democratic Party (1974-1982) and Helmut Kohl of the Christian Democratic Union (1982-1998) were free-trade oriented and, thus, able to counter French protectionism. Under the chancellorship of Gerhard Schröder (1998-2005), however, German foreign economic policy began adopting a protectionist position. Though German economic nationalism has never been as strident as that of France or Italy, nevertheless under Schröder Germany has lost its position of economic leadership and consequently the EU has lost the German liberal influence it had had in the past. Whether Angela

Merkel, the new German Chancellor, takes up the liberal mantle that Schröder had discarded remains to be seen.

The Doha Agenda is in fact, potentially highly beneficial to Europe, including France, and Europe would be one of the largest net gainers from its successful conclusion. The rather sclerotic European economies, especially those of the Euro-zone, are in desperate need of some strong Schumpeterian creative destruction. This dynamics is supposedly what lay behind the ambitious Lisbon Strategy set out by the European Council in 2000 to make Europe 'the world's most dynamic and competitive economy'. To achieve this Europe needs to discard old industries and emphasise innovation and high technology. The Doha Agenda could provide a good fillip to that end.

However, in contrast to the ambitiousness of the Lisbon Agenda, never has the European Union actually been more adrift. The pattern of successive weak and vacillating presidents of the Commission following the tenure of Jacques Delors (1985-1995) has not, alas, been broken with the current incumbent, José Manuel Barroso. Europe is like an orchestra of 25 players who simply ignore the conductor. In the ensuing cacophony, the music that does emerge tends to be set by the loudest player. At present, this position is undoubtedly held by France.

The problems of the Commission in the area of trade are compounded by the fact that appointing Peter Mandelson as Trade Commissioner was clearly a mistake. He is a pure product of parochial British politics and is very obviously out of place in a broader European, let alone, global setting. Known for his mastery of spin in the British political domain, this has little relevance or application to international trade. Though Pascal Lamy, then European Trade Commissioner, promoted policies that were unacceptable to many of Europe's trading partners, he did manage to retain good relations with all or most of his ministerial counterparts. Mandelson, in contrast, seems to have irritated most of his counterparts and to be on bad terms with them. He also lacks the professionalism of previous European trade commissioners. The ridicule he earned in the ignominious European policy *vis-à-vis* China in the so-called 'bra wars' of the summer of 2005 should in fact have resulted in his resignation. He has not since been able to regain credibility or respect.

In the *Financial Times* predictions for 2006 (30 December 2005), in respect to the Doha Agenda Martin Wolf wrote: "It appears that an ambitious package is impossible but necessary, while a modest package is feasible but unacceptable." Wolf adds that while trade negotiators may ultimately muddle through, "maybe they will just postpone reaching a conclusion indefinitely instead."

The French position, which, unless Angela Merkel wakes up, is likely to be the European position, will favour a very modest package or an indefinite postponement. 2006 *a priori* does not seem very promising.

Index

A

B

C

E

N

S

T

U

V

W